100 BEST STOCKS

TO OWN IN AMERICA

SIXTH EDITION

Gene Walden

DEARBORN™

A **Kaplan Professional** Company

Y, AND RYAN

This publication is designed to provide accurate and authoritative information in regard to the subject matter covered. It is sold with the understanding that the publisher is not engaged in rendering legal, accounting, or other professional service. If legal advice or other expert assistance is required, the services of a competent professional person should be sought.

Associate Publisher: Cynthia A. Zigmund
Managing Editor: Jack Kiburz
Interior Design: Elizandro Carrington
Cover Design: Jody Billert, Billert Communications
Typesetting: Elizabeth Pitts

Library of Congress Cataloging-in-Publication Data

Walden, Gene.
    The 100 best stocks to own in America / Gene Walden. — 6th ed.
        p.   cm.
    Includes index.
    ISBN 0-7931-3169-3
        1. Stocks—United States.   I. Title   II. Title: One hundred best
stocks to own in America.
    HG4963.W35   1999   99-43476
    332.63′22′0973—dc21   CIP

Dearborn books are available at special quantity discounts to use as premiums and sales promotions, or for use in corporate training programs. For more information, please call the Special Sales Manager at 800-621-9621, ext. 4514, or write to Dearborn Financial Publishing, Inc., 155 North Wacker Drive, Chicago, IL 60606-1719.

Contents

Alphabetical Listing of the Best 100 Stocks

Abbott Laboratories (34)

AFLAC, Inc. (32)

Albertson's, Inc. (31)

Alliance Capital Management, LP (4)

American International Group, Inc. (71)

American Home Products Corp. (33)

Anheuser-Busch Cos. (93)

Automatic Data Processing, Inc. (53)

Bank One Corp. (97)

Becton Dickinson and Co. (36)

Bemis Co., Inc. (66)

Bestfoods (89)

Biomet, Inc. (86)

Bristol-Myers Squibb (94)

C&K Witco Corp. (100)

Campbell Soup Co. (83)

Cardinal Health, Inc. (44)

Carlisle Cos., Inc. (58)

Carnival Corp. (18)

Cintas Corp. (52)

Cisco Systems, Inc. (42)

Clorox Co. (56)

Coca-Cola Co. (59)

Colgate-Palmolive Co. (72)

Computer Associates International, Inc. (55)

Computer Sciences Corp. (74)

ConAgra, Inc. (65)

Danaher Corp. (85)

Dell Computer Corp. (67)

Dionex Corp. (73)

Walt Disney Co. (99)

Dollar General Corp. (26)

Donaldson Co., Inc. (24)

Ecolab, Inc. (60)

Emerson Electric Co. (78)

Equifax, Inc. (90)

Fannie Mae (11)

Fastenal Co. (49)

Fifth Third Bancorp (7)

Firstar Corp. (2)

Fiserv, Inc. (47)

Franklin Resources, Inc. (13)

Freddie Mac (30)

G&K Services, Inc. (87)

The Gap, Inc. (69)

General Electric Co. (8)

Genuine Parts Co. (96)

Gillette Co. (20)

Harley-Davidson, Inc. (16)

H. J. Heinz Co. (88)

Hershey Foods Corp. (82)

The Home Depot, Inc. (3)

Hubbell Inc. (63)

Illinois Tool Works, Inc. (25)

Intel Corp. (48)

Interpublic Group of Cos., Inc. (23)

Jefferson Pilot Corp. (38)

Johnson & Johnson (14)

Kohl's Corp. (68)

M&T Bank Corp. (22)

Maxim Integrated Products (45)

May Department Stores Co. (80)

McDonald's Corp. (76)

MCI WorldCom, Inc. (92)

Medtronic, Inc. (1)

Acknowledgments

Composed as it is of some 17,000 facts, figures, calculations, and computations, and spun together under a tight deadline, this is a book that would have been impossible to complete if not for the tremendous contributions of others. As he has for most of the six editions of this book, Larry Nelson did much of the fact-gathering and organizing for the project, collecting financial reports, contacting companies, crunching numbers, compiling tables and graphs, and keeping the project organized and under control.

I also want to thank my editors, Cynthia Zigmund and Jack Kiburz, who helped shape the book into a concise, attractive, and professional format.

Introduction

It has been a full decade since I wrote the very first edition of *The 100 Best Stocks to Own in America.* A lot has changed since then. Revolutionary advances in computers, telecommunications, and medical technology have dramatically altered the landscape of American industry. Technology innovators, service providers, and financial institutions have raced to head the pack in the new economic order as we enter the 21st century.

Those changes are reflected in the vivid contrast between the stocks and industries represented in the first edition a decade ago and those in this current edition. For instance, among the 100 stocks in the 1989 edition, there were three printers, five publishers, and four paper producers; there are none in this edition. The "paperless society" may still be far from reality, but the Internet has certainly begun to take its toll.

The first edition also featured five aerospace and defense contractors, four tobacco companies, three waste handlers, two automotive manufacturers, and one petroleum company; none remain in this edition. In their place is a new breed of technology-driven operations that were little-known start-ups a decade ago, including Microsoft, Cisco Systems, Oracle, Tellabs, Dell, Biomet, Maxim, Fiserv, and Paychex.

There are, however, a few holdovers from the original list, including two that are still ranked in the top ten of this edition—First Third Bancorp (7) and Merck (9).

In all, only 25 of the original 100 stocks are still on the list, and several of them are fading fast. Six of the originals are rated among the bottom ten stocks of this edition (Anheuser-Busch, Bristol-Myers Squibb, Genuine Parts, Bank One, PepsiCo, and Disney).

It's hard to beef about the returns those stocks have provided over the past ten years. If you had been fortunate enough to invest $1,000 in each of those original 25 stocks when the first edition was published in 1989, your $25,000 investment would have grown to about $160,000. That's an average annual return of just over 20 percent. (If you had invested $1,000 in all 100 stocks in the first book, that $100,000 investment would now be worth about $450,000.)

If there is a lesson in all this for investors, it is to be persistent but flexible. Continue to invest in the best companies available but be willing to shift your portfolio weighting from time to time in favor of the faster growing sectors.

The stock market is constantly evolving and investors must be willing to change with it in order to keep their portfolios growing. That's not to say that you should sell off all your old favorites and start fresh. But from time to time it's good to weed out the slower-moving stocks and add some young emerging picks to the mix to tilt the balance to the faster-growing sectors.

WELCOME TO THE SIXTH EDITION

For the first time ever, the defending number-one stock has claimed the top spot again. Medtronic, the world's leading heart pacemaker manufacturer, is number one in this edition just as it was in the fifth edition. Medtronic sells its implantable devices worldwide for patients whose heartbeats are irregular, too slow, or too rapid. The company also makes a variety of related devices, such as blood pumps, catheters, and heart valves. Over the past ten years, Medtronic's shareholders have earned an average annual return of about 37 percent. That outstanding return, along with a steadily increasing dividend and 14 consecutive years of record sales and earnings, helped make Medtronic America's number one stock again.

Rounding out the top ten are Firstar, a Milwaukee-based bank holding company; Home Depot, the fast-growing retailer; Alliance Capital, an investment firm; Paychex, a payroll outsourcing operation; Schering-Plough, a leading pharmaceuticals manufacturer; Fifth Third Bancorp, a Cincinnati-based bank; General Electric, one of the nation's largest diversified operations; Merck, one of the world's leading pharmaceuticals manufacturers; and Procter & Gamble, a leading maker of household cleaning products and related consumer goods.

This edition features 78 stocks that were also in the fifth edition and 22 that are new to the Best 100 list.

Here are the 25 companies that have made the *Best 100* list in all six editions:

Abbott Laboratories	Sherwin-Williams
PepsiCo	Fifth Third Bancorp
Albertson's	Genuine Parts
American Home Products	H.J. Heinz
Pitney Bowes	Valspar
Anheuser-Busch	Hershey Foods
RPM	Wal-Mart
Automatic Data Processing	Walgreen
Bank One	McDonald's
Sara Lee	Walt Disney
Bemis	Merck
Bristol-Myers Squibb	William Wrigley
ConAgra	

Four stocks that had appeared in each of the previous five editions were dropped from this edition—Kellogg, Tyson Foods, Torchmark, and Pall Corp. They were eliminated because of subpar financial performance.

FUTURE PROSPECTS

This book makes no pretense of projecting the future performance of any stock. The rankings are based strictly on the past performance of the companies. I looked at several factors:

- Has the company had consistent earnings growth and consistent stock growth for the past ten years (or longer)?
- Is the company well-diversified?
- Is it a leader in its market sector?

Out of more than 2,000 stocks I evaluated for this book, the companies listed here have all passed with flying colors. They are the 100 major U.S. corporations that have fared the best over the past decade and given their shareholders the most.

While there is no assurance that any of these companies will outperform the market in the years to come, they do have a couple of strong points in their favor. For one, each company featured here has proven its ability to compete as a market leader in one or more areas. Their concepts are working; their lines of products or services have made an impact in the marketplace; and they have been highly profitable over the past 10 to 15 years. Each of these companies has a management team that also has proven capable of turning a buck on a consistent basis. They've ridden the ups and downs of the economy over the past decade, survived the rash of mergers and acquisitions (and probably made a few of their own), weathered the downtimes, and have still come away with an outstanding record of earnings and stock price growth. Presumably, most of these companies will continue their success throughout this decade.

While it is certainly possible that companies like Abbott Laboratories (28 consecutive years of record earnings), Automatic Data Processing (49 consecutive years of double-digit growth in both earnings and revenues), and RPM (51 consecutive years of record sales and earnings) could slip into a sudden free fall after decades of uninterrupted growth, the odds would seem to bode otherwise.

Traditionally, the type of top-quality stocks selected for this book tend to do very well compared with the overall market. For instance, a portfolio of the top 40 ranked stocks of the first edition of this book would have grown 102 percent over the following five years—a record good enough to outperform 89 percent of all mutual funds for that period! The top ten picks of the fifth edition were up 44 percent in the first 18 months after publication—a performance record that surpassed well over 90 percent of all mutual funds for the same period.

THE CASE FOR STOCKS

While an individual's first investment priority should be money in the bank—everyone needs a cash cushion to fall back on—stocks should be a key component of any well-balanced portfolio. Why buy stocks rather than collecting that safe, consistent flow of interest earnings a bank account would offer? Here are some numbers to reflect on.

On average, over the 70 years for which records are available—which includes both the stock market crash of 1929 and the crash of 1987—stocks have provided an average annual return of about 11 percent, roughly double the return of bonds and three times the return of money market funds. The difference is even more dramatic when put in real dollar terms. A dollar invested in U.S. government bonds in 1925 would have grown to about $36 by 1999. That same dollar invested in the broad stock market would have grown to nearly $1,800 during the same period. While stocks may have their ups and downs, if you can live with the volatility, you would be a far richer investor by keeping your money in the stock market.

Sometimes stock market investing requires great patience. Stock performance can vary dramatically from one ten-year period to another. An investor entering the market in 1965, for instance, would have experienced an agonizing 1.2 percent average annual return over the next ten years. But an investor in the market from 1949 to 1958 would have reaped a 20 percent average annual return. And, as you well know, the stock market in the decade of the 1990s has been as profitable as any decade of this century.

STOCKS OR STOCK MUTUAL FUNDS?

The other issue for many investors is whether to buy individual stocks or stock mutual funds. The fact is, mutual funds probably should be the investment of choice for many investors—particularly those who haven't the time, the expertise, or the resources to invest in a well-diversified selection of stocks.

But if you have an interest in the market, the time to spend researching it, and the money to diversify your portfolio, individual stocks can offer several advantages over mutual funds.

For one thing, stocks are just more fun than funds. Investing in the market can be challenging, stimulating, sometimes nerve-racking, and ultimately very fulfilling. You pit your wits against the market and against the millions of other unseen investors who also are scouring the market for a bargain. It is a test of your insight, your shrewdness. At times, it also can be a test both of your endurance during downturns in the market and of your courage as you hold fast to your position in anticipation of that next market rally.

When you pick a winner, the results can be exhilarating. You watch the price move up. You see the stock split two-for-one. Suddenly, your 500 shares become 1,000. Your investment grows to a multiple of your initial outlay. You've won at the age-old game of picking stocks. And the victory is a boon not only to your pocketbook but also to your ego. It's that psychological reward of picking a winner that motivates so many investors to set aside mutual funds and test their hand in the stock market.

There's another important, though less publicized, reason to choose stocks over mutual funds. As they say, money is power. But it's only power if you control it yourself and decide exactly where each dollar is put to work. Socially conscious individuals who wouldn't dream of investing in companies that pollute the environment, produce tobacco products, or build weapons of mass destruction can unwittingly invest in those types of companies when they invest in stock mutual funds. Most mutual funds pay little heed to social concerns.

There are, of course, mutual funds that take an ethical approach and avoid investing in companies with questionable ethical connections. The problem is, when you invest in those funds you're still letting someone else decide the fate of your money. After all, you may not necessarily agree with all the fund's ideals. You might, for instance, enjoy a beer on a hot afternoon and see no reason to avoid investing in alcoholic beverage producers. You may prefer not to invest in a weapons manufacturing company, but you may think nuclear power is the best thing since windmills. So, a mutual fund that invests according to all the popular ethical issues of our time may not be exactly the investment for you. Stocks give you the freedom to make those choices for yourself.

RATING THE COMPANIES

In selecting the 100 companies for this book, I looked at several key financial factors, the most important of which was earnings performance. I wanted companies with a long history of annual increases in earnings per share, because if a company is able to raise its earnings year after year, the stock price will ultimately follow.

Other factors such as revenue growth, stock price performance, and dividend yield also played into the screening process, but none carried the same weight as earnings growth. I made my selections after reviewing the financial histories of more than 2,000 major U.S. companies.

After narrowing the list to the final 100, the next step was to rank them 1 to 100 based on a five-part rating system. Each category is worth up to four points—except shareholder perks, which is worth a maximum of two points—for a maximum of 18 points. The categories are *earnings per share growth, stock growth, dividend, consistency,* and *shareholder perks.*

I've also tried to bridge the long-term performance with the short-term performance. Stock growth was judged on ten-year performance, while earnings growth and dividend growth were rated based on the most recent five-year period. And finally, the consistency category rated stocks based on year-to-year earnings gains over a ten-year period. That gives the rating system a blend of the long term and the short term. Accompanying each company profile, you will see a ratings chart similar to this:

Earnings Growth	★ ★ ★ ★
Stock Growth	★ ★ ★
Dividend	★ ★ ★
Consistency	★ ★ ★
Shareholder Perks	★ ★
NYSE: ABC	**15 points**

Each star represents one ratings point. This company scored the maximum four points for stock growth and somewhat less for the other categories. The lower left indicates both where the stock is traded (e.g., NYSE, or New York Stock Exchange) and the stock's ticker symbol (ABC). The lower right gives the total score.

The following charts offer an exact breakdown of the point system for the earnings and stock growth categories:

Earnings Per Share Growth

5-Year Growth Rate	Average Annual Rate	Points Awarded
50%–79%	9%–12%	★ (1 point)
80%–114%	13%–16%	★ ★
115%–139%	17%–19%	★ ★ ★
140% and above	20% and above	★ ★ ★ ★

Stock Growth

10-Year Growth Rate	Average Annual Rate	Points Awarded
155%–249%	10%–13%	★ (1 point)
250%–399%	14%–17%	★ ★
400%–599%	18%–21%	★ ★ ★
600% and above	22% and above	★ ★ ★ ★

Dividends

In previous editions of the book, I had two categories for dividends—yield and growth—but that put companies that paid no dividends at a great disadvantage. Not only did they lose all eight points for the two dividend categories, they also struck out on the two points under shareholder perks awarded for companies that offer a dividend reinvestment and stock purchase plan.

To attempt to even the playing field somewhat, I combined the two dividend categories into one. The scoring was a little more complicated, but here is how it worked: A company with a dividend yield of at least 2.5 percent, at least nine consecutive years of increased dividends, and at least 75 percent growth in the dividend payout over the past five years would receive a perfect four points. One point is subtracted for growth of under 75 percent, and one point is deducted for fewer than nine consecutive years of dividend increases. One point is also deducted for stocks with a dividend yield of under 2.5 percent; two points are deducted for a yield of under 1 percent; three points are deducted for a yield of 0.5 percent; and all four points are deducted for a yield of under 0.3 percent.

Consistency

A company that has had a flawless run of increases in earnings per share over the past ten years would score four points. The consistency of the stock price growth is not taken into account here, because the volatility in a stock price often can be dictated by market factors beyond the control of the company. But if the company is strong and growing steadily, the stock price over time should reflect that.

★★★★   Score four points for a company that has posted increased earnings at least ten consecutive years.

★★★   Score three points for a company that has had a nearly flawless run of earnings increases, with gains nine of the past ten years.

★★   Score two points for a company that has had a fairly consistent growth record, with earnings increases eight of the past ten years.

★   Score one point for a company that has been somewhat inconsistent, with earnings increases seven of the past ten years.

Score zero points for a company with a very volatile growth record, although no company can make the top 100 list if it has had fewer than seven years of increased earnings out of the past ten.

Shareholder Perks

This category carries a maximum score of two points. The grading in the perks category is very simple. If a company has a dividend reinvestment and stock purchase plan, it receives two points in this category. If not, it receives no points. In pasts editions of this book, I also added a point or two for other perks, such as discounts on products or services for shareholders or free welcome kits with product samples for new shareholders. Other companies pass out product samples and coupons at the annual meetings. I try to mention those perks for each company, but I don't award them extra points, in part because companies have become much stingier with their handouts in recent years and because even the better perks have no real bearing on the shareholders' return on investment.

There is certainly some investment value in the dividend reinvestment plans offered by about 80 of the companies in this book. These programs enable shareholders not only to reinvest their dividends in additional shares automatically but also to buy more stock in the company either commission-free or for a nominal fee (usually under $5).

For example, Coca-Cola shareholders may buy up to $125,000 a year in additional shares through the company plan, and McDonald's shareholders may make up to $250,000 a year in commission-free stock purchases. May Department Stores puts no upper limit on its program.

The only drawback to such plans is that the shareholder has no control over when the stocks are purchased. Most companies have a date set each month or each quarter (depending on how the plan is set up) to make all shareholder stock purchases. You should also note that shareholders must pay income taxes on their dividends, even though the dividends are automatically reinvested in additional stock. These programs are perfect for investors who want to build a position in three or four companies at a time with relatively small monthly contributions (minimum contribution limits range from $10 to $100 per payment). The savings can be immense. For instance, commission costs even through a discount broker would run on average at least $40 per stock purchase per month—a total of $160 per month for four stocks. That adds up to $1,920 per year. With the free reinvestment plans, you can either put that $1,920 into your pocket or invest it in additional stock. Either way, the commission-free programs are a great perk and well worth the two points my system awards to each company that offers such a program.

Dividend reinvestment plans are generally reserved for existing shareholders, but a number of companies have begun to offer a direct stock purchase plan that allows investors to buy their initial shares directly through the company. In this book, if a company offers such a plan, we mention it in the company profile under shareholder perks.

Breaking Ties

The 100 companies are ranked in order by points. The company with the most points is ranked first, and the company with the fewest points is ranked 100. To break ties between companies with identical point scores, I looked at several factors, including ten-year total return, earnings growth momentum, and earnings growth consistency over the past 10 to 20 years.

Performance Graphs

At the end of each profile, you will see a five-year financial At a Glance summary of the company's performance, including revenue, net income, earnings per share, dividend, dividend yield, and price-earnings ratio (PE).

Also included is a "high-low-close" stock growth chart similar to the one below.

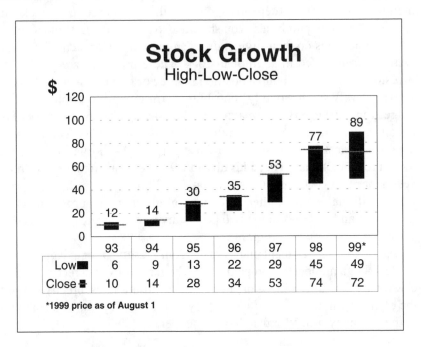

This stock growth graph shows:

- The yearly stock price range (all figures are adjusted for stock splits), including high price for the year, low price for the year, and closing price for the year
- The price range for 1993 through August 1, 1999. The price range indicated is for the 52-week period from August 1, 1998, to August 1, 1999.

Now you're ready to begin making this book work profitably for you!

How to Use This Book Profitably

Think of this book as a sales catalog for investment shoppers. You can page through it, look over the merchandise, and make your selections.

Let's assume that you have $20,000 to invest in stocks. Here is the process I recommend you use to select the best stocks for you based on the entries in this book:

1. Begin by reading through the 100 profiles and narrowing your choices to 10 to 12 stocks by asking these questions:
   * Are they companies you like?
   * Are they involved in business activities that you think have a strong future?
   * Are they located in your part of the country? This is not essential, but it is easier to follow companies based close to home because the local press tends to give those companies better coverage and you can stay better informed on your investment.
   * Do they represent a diverse cross-section of industries? Spread your choices around. You might select a financial institution, a computer maker, a medical products firm, a retailer, a food company, a consumer products maker, or a telecommunications operation. Choose no more than two or three companies from the same industrial segment. By selecting a broad portfolio, you can minimize your losses if one sector goes sour.
2. The next step is to narrow that list of 10 or 12 favorites to the four to six companies that you will ultimately invest in.
3. If you wish to use a stockbroker or financial adviser, call your adviser, read your list of choices, and ask if he or she has any current research on those stocks. If so, find out which ones the broker recommends and buy the stocks through your broker.
4. If you are interested in enrolling in the dividend reinvestment plan or in receiving the special perks your chosen companies might offer, instruct your broker to put your stocks in your name rather than holding them at the brokerage office in "street name." Most dividend reinvestment plans and perks programs are available only to shareholders of record.

GOING IT ALONE

If you have no broker or wish to go it alone through a discount broker, here are some steps you can use to narrow your list to the four to six companies you will ultimately invest in:

1. Write or call those 10 to 12 companies to request their annual report and their 10-K report (which is a supplement to the annual report), then skim through the reports. (The phone numbers and addresses of each of the 100 companies are listed in this book along with their corporate profiles.) You also can go online and visit their Web sites. Web sites for all 100 companies are listed along with their addresses.
2. Look up recent articles on those stocks on the Web or at the library. If it's a local company, there's a good chance your library will have an entire file on the firm. Make sure the company hasn't become involved in any major scandals or business problems. The library also may have two or three investment research books you can use to check up on your stock selections. *Value Line Investment Survey* and *Standard & Poor's Report* both offer up-to-date information and recommendations on hundreds of companies.
3. Keep an eye on the stock prices of the companies you are interested in. Find out what range each stock has been trading over the past few months. Then select the four or five stocks that appear at present to be the best values.

Timing can be very important to your overall success. All stocks fluctuate greatly in price, tugged along by the current of the overall market. Some stocks vacillate more than others. For instance, you could have bought Walt Disney stock in 1973 for $27 a share and sold it for a mere $4 a share a year later. You could have reinvested in the stock in 1976 at $15 a share and sold out in disgust in 1984 at $11.50 a share. Or, on the other hand, you might have bought the stock for that same $11.50 a share in 1984 and sold out with a grin for more than ten times that price ($136 a share) in 1990. Even with stocks like Disney that qualify as a Best 100 entry, timing can make a significant difference.

WHEN TO BUY

Volumes have been written on this topic. But the best advice may have come from Baron von Rothschild in the mid-1800s. He said, "Buy when the enemy is at the gate and sell when you hear your cavalry's bugle sounding charge."

Wall Street has a popular adage that reinforces that concept: "Pessimism is always most rampant just before the market hits bottom."

Two extraordinary buying opportunities have arisen in the past several years. The first came in 1987 following the October "Black Monday" crash. The crash frightened many investors out of the market, but those who bought when everyone else was selling got in on the bottom of a market that grew more than 50 percent over the next 18 months.

The second great opportunity came during Iraq's occupation of Kuwait, when oil prices were rising, and the world was transfixed by the Middle East crisis. The market dropped about 15 percent in the months after Iraq invaded Kuwait, then roared back more than 20 percent in a three-month span that began the day the Allies started bombing.

Barring war or disaster, the best strategy for most investors is a steady, persistent, long-term investment program.

Though investors may strive to buy stocks while they are well below their peak prices, market experts advise against buying a stock on its way down. Or, as they say in the brokerage business, "Don't fight the tape." Wait until a falling stock has bottomed out and shown some upward momentum before buying.

BENEFITS OF DOLLAR COST AVERAGING

One of the easiest and most effective investment strategies is called dollar cost averaging, and it's as simple as this: Pick a number, any number—$100 for instance—and invest that amount every month (or every quarter or every year) in the same stock. Period. It's that simple. Elementary as it sounds, however, the dollar cost averaging method is also a very effective technique for beating the market. The reason? By sticking to a set sum each time you invest, you automatically buy fewer shares when the stock price is high and more shares when the price is low.

The following table illustrates the advantages of dollar cost averaging. The table assumes that the stock price fluctuates somewhat each month (and lists the monthly price of the stock). The table compares the number of shares purchased through a dollar cost averaging strategy with the number of shares purchased through a method in which the investor buys a set number of shares each month.

Example of Dollar Cost Averaging

(Investing a set dollar amount each month versus buying a set number of shares each month.)

	Jan	Feb	Mar	Apr	May	June	July	Aug	Sept	Oct	Nov	Dec	Totals
Stock Price[1]	$ 10	9	12	13	9	10	8	7	9	12	10	11	
Investor A Dollar Cost Averaging[2] Investment:	$100	100	100	100	100	100	100	100	100	100	100	100	$1,200
Shares	10	11.1	8.3	7.7	11	10	12.5	14.3	11	8.3	10	9.1	123.5
Investor B Set Quantity[3] Investment:	$100	90	120	130	90	100	80	70	90	120	100	110	$1,200
Shares	10	10	10	10	10	10	10	10	10	10	10	10	120

1. Indicates average stock price each month.
2. Assumes investor invests $100 a month in the stock.
3. Assumes investor buys 10 shares of the stock per month.

As the table indicates, using the dollar cost averaging method investor A would have purchased 3½ more shares than investor B, who bought a set amount of shares each month, even though both spent a total of $1,200 during the year.

Tip: The dollar cost averaging method is most effective when you make your purchases at no commission (or minimal commission) through a company's dividend reinvestment and voluntary stock purchase plan. Such plans are ideal for dollar cost averaging, because they enable you to buy fractional shares and to make regular contributions (some companies offer stock purchase options once per month, others once per quarter). However, if the company you're interested in has no stock purchase plan, the brokerage commission you would have to pay to make regular investments in the company's stock would greatly diminish the advantages of a dollar cost averaging plan. Most of the 100 top performers in this book offer a dividend reinvestment and voluntary stock purchase plan.

PICKING WINNERS

There is no infallible system for predicting tomorrow's market winners—only ratios and theories and computer-generated formulas that seem fool-proof, but aren't. For investors who trade actively in stocks, the key to beating the market is not so much which stocks to buy, but when to buy them and when to sell them. And that's about as easy to predict as next month's weather.

Even Wall Street's finest can't consistently outfox the market. Stock mutual funds offer an interesting example. Despite being actively managed by some of the sharpest, most well-supported analysts in the investment industry, the average rate of return of stock mutual funds traditionally trails the overall market averages. Generally speaking, history has shown that you can do better just buying and holding a representative sample of stocks—without ever making a single trade—than most mutual fund managers do with their wealth of investment research, their finely honed trading strategies, and all their carefully calculated market maneuvers.

Nor do investment newsletters, on average, fare any better than the mutual fund managers at timing their trade recommendations, according to Mark Hulbert, publisher of the *Hulbert Financial Digest* newsletter. "Most newsletters have not kept up with the Standard & Poor's 500," says Hulbert. In fact, in tracking the seven-year performance of a sampling of investment newsletters, Hulbert found that the ones that recommended the greatest number of buys and sells (switches) were the ones that did the worst.

"We've also conducted some studies that show that in the case of most newsletters, if you had bought and held the stocks they recommended at the first of the year, you would have done better than if you had followed all of their trading recommendations throughout the year," Hulbert adds.

The moral? For sustained, long-term growth, it's hard to beat a buy-and-hold strategy. Buy good companies with the intention of holding onto them for many years. But if the company shows little progress during a period when most of the rest of the market is moving up, it may be time to look for some more promising stocks.

The Strategy of Benign Neglect

Most of us know someone who bought a few shares of a stock many years ago, stashed the certificates in a drawer, and then discovered years later that the stock had grown to a multiple of the original cost. Benign neglect is often the smartest policy for stock market investors. Besides avoiding the difficulties of making timely buying and selling decisions, the buy-and-hold approach offers some other excellent advantages.

No commission costs.   Let's assume you turn over your stock portfolio just once a year. You sell out all the stocks you own and buy new stocks that you think have greater short-term potential. Typically, you would incur about a 2 percent commission to sell the old stocks and a 2 percent commission to buy new ones—a total of 4 percent in roundtrip commissions. That means, for instance, that a respectable 12 percent gain on your investments would suddenly shrink to 8 percent after paying off your broker. That commission may not seem like much at the time, but over the long term, it can add up to a significant amount. See the chart on the hidden costs of a buy-and-sell approach. (Online brokers have cut those costs considerably. Ameritrade, for instance, offers trades for $8, regardless of how many shares you buy or sell.)

Tax-sheltered earnings.   A buy-and-hold strategy is one of the best tax-advantaged investments available today. You pay no taxes on the price appreciation of your stocks until you sell them—no matter how long you keep them. (However, you are taxed on any stock dividend income.) Every time you sell a stock, the federal government taxes you up to 33 percent on your gains (for most working professionals). State taxes would very likely nibble away another 3 to 5 percent. That means each year Uncle Sam bites off more than a third of your investment profits. So, you're looking at losing 36 percent of your gains, plus the brokerage house commission, every time you sell a stock at a profit. How does that translate into real dollars?

Let's assume that (1) you start with an investment of $10,000; (2) your stock portfolio appreciates at a rate of 12 percent per year; and (3) you sell your stocks, take the profit, and buy new stocks once a year. The following chart compares your performance with that of a buy-and-hold investor with an identical 12 percent compounded average annual appreciation rate.

As you can see, over a 20-year period the buy-and-hold portfolio could earn five times the profit of a buy-and-sell approach—even though both portfolios earn an average annual return of 12 percent.

Less emotional wear and tear.   By adhering to a buy-and-hold strategy, you also avoid the high anxiety of trying to buy and sell stocks actively—watching the financial pages each day to see how your stocks have fared

The Hidden Costs of a Buy-and-Sell Approach

$10,000 investment @ 12% annual growth	Buy-and-hold (No commission and no taxes)	Buy-and-sell results[1] With commission[2]	And with taxes[3]
After 1 year	$11,200	$10,800	$10,512
After 5 years	17,600	14,700	12,850
After 10 years	31,000	21,600	16,400
After 20 years	96,500	46,600	27,200
Total 20-year profit (minus initial $10,000)	$86,500	$36,600	$17,200

1. Assumes investor sells all stocks in portfolio one time per year (and reinvests in new stocks).
2. Assumes commission of 2% to buy and 2% to sell (an annual total of 4% of total portfolio price).
3. Assumes 32% federal and 4% state tax (an annual total of 36% of profits).

and the inevitable disappointment of watching them rise and fall, then rise and fall again. Every stock goes through many ups and downs each year. There are no exceptions. The market moves like the tide of the ocean, and every time it ebbs and flows it carries with it the broad market of individual stocks. Typically, about 70 percent of a stock's movement is attributable to the stock market itself. If the broad market is moving up, almost any stock you pick will also rise. If the market is in a tailspin, almost any stock you pick—even those with record earnings—will fall with it. The remaining 30 percent of the movement of a stock is attributable to its industry group and the performance of the company that issued the stock.

You skirt much of the emotional pressure the market inflicts if you invest with a buy-and-hold approach. You don't have to concern yourself with the inevitable daily ups and downs—or even the yearly ups and downs—of the market. Over the long term, if you've bought stocks of good, solid, growing companies, the value of your portfolio will eventually reflect the strong performance of those companies. That's why it's crucial to select your stocks carefully—that one decision takes on much greater importance.

When Not to Buy

Assuming that you've selected 10 to 12 prospective stocks, that you've researched the companies, and that you're ready to buy, what financial factors should you look at to decide which four to six of those prospective stocks represent the best value at the time?

The easiest way to select your finalists might be through the process of elimination: Weed out the stocks that appear to be overvalued and invest in the others.

To assist you with your elimination process, here are two of the most common "don'ts."

Don't buy when a stock is at an all-time high.   Stocks constantly rise and fall. A noteworthy adage in the securities industry goes like this: "The market always gives you a second chance." In almost every case, when a stock reaches an all-time high, it will eventually drop back in price, bounce back up, and then drop again. Nothing goes in a straight line. If you see that a stock is at its all-time high, it's probably not a very good value at that time. Prior to the October 1987 crash, many stocks were at or near their all-time highs, which is one reason why many investment experts claimed— correctly—that there were few good values in the market.

Don't buy when the price-earnings ratio (PE) is unusually high.   It sounds complicated, but the PE is actually a very simple formula that offers yet another barometer of a stock's relative value. And best of all, the PE is listed along with the company's stock price in the financial section of most newspapers, so you don't have to calculate it yourself. Specifically, the ratio is the current price of the stock divided by the company's earnings per share.

Example:

ABC Corporation's stock price is $30.
Its earnings per share is $3.

$$\text{Stock price} \div \text{Earnings per share} = \text{PE}$$
$$\$30 \div \$3 = 10$$

PEs are like golf scores—the lower the better. Generally, the PEs of most established companies are in the 10 to 20 range (although a handful of the stocks listed in this book have PEs over 20 and a few have PEs under 10). The real key is not how the PE of one company compares to the PE of another, but how a company's current PE compares to its own previous PEs.

In this book, at the end of each company profile, you will see a financial At a Glance table that shows the PE for the past six years. (The PEs in this book were calculated based on the earnings of the company's most recent four quarters, just as they are in the daily newspaper.) You might use that PE as a guidepost to provide a relative point of comparison.

If you find on comparing the company's current PE (as listed in your morning newspaper) with its past PE range (as listed in this book) that the PE is near or above the high end of its past range, that could be an indication the stock is relatively overvalued.

WHEN TO SELL

The decision of when to sell is best made before you ever buy. Decide then how low you're willing to go before you sell, how long you'll wait for the stock to move, or how high you hope to ride the stock before you sell it out.

The most common mistake investors make in selling their stocks is to sell their winners to take a (fully taxable) profit and hold onto their losers in hopes that those stocks will someday rebound. That's an excellent way to assemble a portfolio of losers. Prevailing wisdom in the investment business calls for just the opposite approach: "Cut your losses and let your profits run."

With that in mind, you might consider following a couple of basic strategies for selling stocks.

Sell when the news is grim.   If you own stock in a company that comes under legal siege or becomes involved in some type of disaster or health controversy, take your lumps and get out as fast as you can dial up your broker.

Sell when the stock price drops relative to the market.   Barring disaster, you also might want to set up some other type of safety valve for your stocks. For instance, if the stock drops 10 to 20 percent while the market in general is moving up, it might be time to move on to something more promising. Some investors use a 10 percent/10 percent rule in which they sell a stock when it (1) drops 10 percent from its recent high, and (2) drops 10 percent relative to the market. For example, if your stock drops 10 percent from $100 to $90, it meets the first criterion. But if the market has also gone down with it, then the stock still hasn't met the second criterion. If, on the other hand, the broad market has stayed the same or moved up while your stock dropped 10 percent, then it's time to sell—based on the 10 percent/10 percent rule.

Patient investors might lean toward a modified version of this rule: call it the 20 percent/20 percent rule. If your stock drops 20 percent and drops 20 percent relative to the market, sell it and move on to something more promising.

Sell when earnings drop.   Investment professionals sometimes call it the "cockroach theory." When you see one disappointing earnings report, that may mean more bad periods loom around the corner—just as the sight of a single cockroach usually means that others are hiding under the sink or behind the cupboard. Money managers who follow the cockroach theory get out of a stock at the first sign of trouble—even if it means taking a small loss to avoid taking a bigger loss later should the bad news continue.

Sell when the company no longer meets your investment objectives. If you bought a stock because the company had enjoyed 40 consecutive years of record earnings, you should continue to hold the stock as long as the company continues to pile up record earnings. But if it hits a slump and earnings stop growing, that company no longer meets your objectives. That's a time to sell. Weeding out your portfolio every two or three years can help make you a more successful investor.

But timing can be a tricky business. As Mark Hulbert puts it: "You need to approach those decisions realizing that more than half the time you're inclined to sell you would be better off holding than selling. So you'd better make sure there's a preponderance of evidence in your favor before you sell."

That's why your buying decision is so important. This guide can help steer you to 100 of the best stocks of the past ten years.

I hope you can cull from this collection some of the all-star stocks of the next millennium.

Medtronic, Inc.

7000 Central Avenue, NE
Minneapolis, MN 55432
612-514-4000
www.medtronic.com

Chairman and CEO: William W. George
President: Arthur D. Collins Jr.

Earnings Growth	★ ★ ★ ★
Stock Growth	★ ★ ★ ★
Dividend	★ ★
Consistency	★ ★ ★ ★
Shareholder Perks	★ ★
NYSE: MDT	**16 points**

Medtronic keeps hearts ticking around the world. The leading manufacturer of heart pacemakers and other implantable biomedical devices,
Medtronic markets its products in more than 120 countries. About 39 percent of its sales come from outside the United States. The company has
grown rapidly, with 14 consecutive years of record sales, earnings, and
book value per share.

The Minneapolis-based operation designs and manufactures pacing
devices for patients whose heartbeats are irregular or too slow, as well as
for patients whose hearts beat too rapidly. Medtronic's pacing devices can
adjust electrical pulse intensity, duration, rate, and other characteristics.

Medtronic's pacemakers are small, coin-sized, implantable pulse generators with extended battery life. The implantable pacemaker is among a growing line of biomedical devices that Medtronic manufactures as part of its mission to "alleviate pain, restore health, and extend life."

The company's pacing business—its cardiac rhythm management division—accounts for about 64 percent of its $4.1 billion in annual sales.

Cardiovascular products, such as blood pumps, heart valves, oxygenators, catheters, and other blood management systems, contribute about 21 percent of the company's sales. In addition to its line of cardiovascular products, Medtronic provides such value-added services as physician education programs.

The company also makes neurological devices used for treating pain and controlling movement disorders. The company makes implantable neurostimulation devices used for spinal cord and brain stimulation to treat pain and tremors. It also makes drug delivery systems, neurosurgery products, and diagnostic systems. Neurological devices account for about 15 percent of total sales.

Medtronic pioneered the pacemaker 41 years ago when Dr. C. Walton Lillehei of the University of Minnesota Medical School identified a medical need for young heart block patients. Working with Earl Bakken, an electrical engineer, Dr. Lillehei developed the first wearable, external, battery-generated pulse generator.

Founded in 1949 and incorporated in 1957, Medtronic has about 14,000 employees and 33,000 shareholders. The company has a market capitalization of about $44 billion.

EARNINGS PER SHARE GROWTH ★ ★ ★ ★

Past five years: 200 percent (25 percent per year)
Past ten years: 595 percent (21 percent per year)

STOCK GROWTH ★ ★ ★ ★

Past ten years: 2,100 percent (36 percent per year)
Dollar growth: $10,000 over ten years (including reinvested dividends) would have grown to $240,000.
Average annual compounded rate of return (including reinvested dividends): 37 percent

DIVIDEND

Dividend yield: 0.5 percent
Increased dividend: 12 consecutive years
Past five-year increase: 178 percent (23 percent per year)

CONSISTENCY ★ ★ ★ ★

Increased earnings per share: 14 consecutive years
Increased sales: 14 consecutive years

SHAREHOLDER PERKS ★ ★

Good dividend reinvestment and stock purchase plan; voluntary stock purchase plan allows contributions of $25 to $4,000 per month.

MEDTRONIC AT A GLANCE

Fiscal year ended: April 30
Revenue and net income in $ millions

	1994	1995	1996	1997	1998	1999	5-Year Growth Avg. Annual (%)	Total (%)
Revenue ($)	1,391	1,742	2,169	2,438	2,605	4,130	24	197
Net income ($)	232	294	438	530	725	905	31	290
Earnings/share ($)	0.51	0.64	0.94	1.11	1.25	1.53	25	200
Dividends/share ($)	0.09	0.10	0.13	0.19	0.22	0.25	23	178
Dividend yield (%)	0.9	0.8	0.5	0.6	0.5	0.4	—	—
PE ratio range	13–24	14–22	15–33	20–31	30–54	49–84	—	—

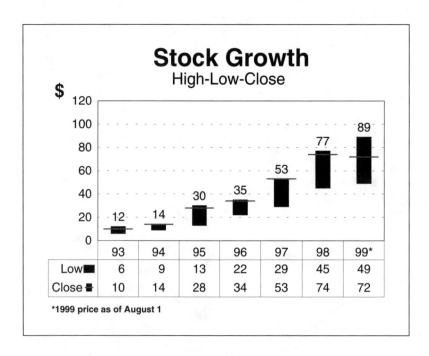

Stock Growth
High-Low-Close

$	93	94	95	96	97	98	99*
Low	6	9	13	22	29	45	49
Close	10	14	28	34	53	74	72

*1999 price as of August 1

Firstar Corporation

777 East Wisconsin Avenue
Milwaukee, WI 53202
414-765-4321
www.firstar.com

Chairman: Thomas A. Jacobsen
President and CEO: Jerry A. Grundhofer

Earnings Growth	★ ★ ★ ★
Stock Growth	★ ★ ★ ★
Dividend	★ ★ ★
Consistency	★ ★ ★
Shareholder Perks	★ ★
NYSE: FSR	**16 points**

On the heels of its huge 1998 merger with Star Banc, Firstar Corporation stopped just long enough to catch its breath before setting its sights on an even bigger game. In 1999, the company acquired Mercantile Bancorporation in an exchange-of-shares deal valued at about $10.6 billion.

Prior to the acquisition, Firstar was a $38 billion bank holding company with 720 banking offices in Ohio, Wisconsin, Kentucky, Illinois, Indiana, Iowa, Minnesota, Tennessee, and Arizona.

Mercantile was a $36 billion bank holding company with 500 locations in Missouri, Iowa, Kansas, Illinois, Arkansas, and Kentucky.

The combined company is the second largest banking organization in the Midwest and the 13th largest in the nation—although its network of about 1,200 branch offices in 12 states ranks seventh among all U.S. banks. Its system of more than 2,000 automated teller machines ranks as the tenth largest nationally.

The company will continue to have its corporate headquarters in Milwaukee, while corporate banking operations will be conducted out of Mercantile's former headquarters in St. Louis.

Firstar has traditionally offered a full range of banking services as well as insurance products and trust, investment, brokerage, and other financial services. Its two leading subsidiaries are Firstar Finance, a consumer finance company, and Firstar Investment Research & Management Company, an investment advisory firm.

Mercantile also has offered a broad range of banking services, and through its subsidiaries has provided brokerage services, asset-based lending, factoring, investment advisory services, leasing services, and credit life and other insurance products.

Through the merger, the new Firstar expects to cut administrative costs by about $169 million by centralizing corporate activities, consolidating data processing and operations, and streamlining other phases of the business.

The combined operation also is expected to push more aggressively into key banking areas, including consumer loans, commercial and small business lending, asset management, mortgage banking, correspondent banking, and cash management.

Founded in 1853, Firstar has well over 20,000 shareholders. Prior to the Mercantile merger, the company had a market capitalization of about $20 billion.

EARNINGS PER SHARE GROWTH   ★ ★ ★ ★

Past five years: 146 percent (20 percent per year)
Past ten years: 333 percent (16 percent per year)

STOCK GROWTH

Past ten years: 1,116 percent (28.5 percent per year)
Dollar growth: $10,000 over ten years (including reinvested dividends) would have grown to $155,000.
Average annual compounded rate of return (including reinvested dividends): 32 percent

DIVIDEND

Dividend yield: 1.4 percent
Increased dividend: 27 consecutive years
Past five-year increase: 154 percent (21 percent per year)

CONSISTENCY

Increased earnings per share: nine of the past ten years

SHAREHOLDER PERKS

Good dividend reinvestment and stock purchase plan; voluntary stock purchase plan allows contributions of $50 to $10,000 per quarter.

FIRSTAR AT A GLANCE

Fiscal year ended: Dec. 31
Total assets and net income in $ millions

	1993	1994	1995	1996	1997	1998	5-Year Growth Avg. Annual (%)	Total (%)
Total assets ($)	7,637	9,391	9,573	10,094	10,959	38,476	39	404
Net income ($)	100	117	137	158	195	605	43	505
Earnings/share ($)	0.37	0.43	0.50	0.60	0.73	0.91	20	146
Dividends/share ($)	0.13	0.16	0.18	0.21	0.27	0.33	21	154
Dividend yield (%)	3.2	3.7	3.3	2.6	1.8	1.5	—	—
PE ratio range	10–12	9–11	8–14	10–16	12–24	27–47	—	—

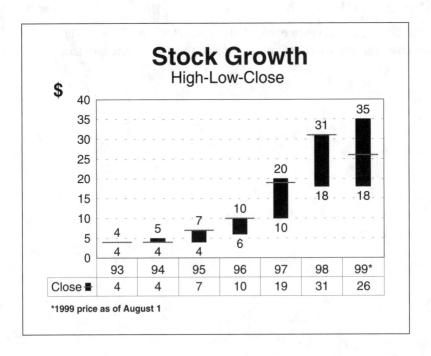

Stock Growth
High-Low-Close

	93	94	95	96	97	98	99*
Close ■	4	4	7	10	19	31	26

*1999 price as of August 1

The Home Depot, Inc.

2455 Paces Ferry Road, NW
Atlanta, GA 30339
770-433-8211
www.homedepot.com

Chairman: Bernard Marcus
President and CEO: Arthur Blank

Earnings Growth	★ ★ ★ ★
Stock Growth	★ ★ ★ ★
Dividend	★
Consistency	★ ★ ★ ★
Shareholder Perks	★ ★
NYSE: HD	**15 points**

Home Depot is as close as it comes to handyman heaven. With its long aisles of tools, hardware, and building supplies, the Atlanta-based operation has become the world's largest home improvement retailer. It has about 800 stores in 44 states and five Canadian provinces. The company plans to double its store count by 2002.

Each of the company's cavernous warehouse-style outlets, which average about 100,000 square feet, stock 40,000 to 50,000 different items, including nuts, bolts, brushes, boards, carpet, screens, saws, spades, power tools, appliances, and lawn and garden supplies. The newer stores also include garden centers ranging in size from 16,000 to 25,000 square feet.

The company also offers installation services of select products such as carpeting and kitchen cabinets. In select test markets, it also offers roofing, siding, and window installation services.

Home Depot has built its business by offering a vast selection of merchandise at low prices. The company avoids special sales, but routinely offers wholesale-type prices on all of its merchandise. In addition to the aisles and aisles of hardware, most stores also feature a small stage and bleachers for how-to clinics.

One of the secrets to Home Depot's success is its well-trained sales force. Store employees are cross-trained in all departments, and many have a background in the building industry. Customers with questions about home projects usually can learn all they need to know by talking with sales clerks. About 95 percent of the company's employees are full-time, and the company offers above-average salary and benefits to keep its employees in the fold.

The Home Depot's primary customers are do-it-yourself homeowners, although many remodeling contractors and building maintenance professionals also buy supplies at Home Depot stores.

Of the company's $30.2 billion in annual revenue, 34 percent comes from building materials, lumber, and floor and wall coverings; 27 percent from plumbing, heating, lighting, and electrical supplies; 14 percent from hardware and tools; 15 percent from seasonal and specialty items; and 10 percent from paint and other products.

The company also operates eight EXPO Design Centers that focus on interior design and renovation projects.

The Home Deport was founded in 1978 by Bernard Marcus (who still serves as the company's chairman), Arthur Blank (Home Depot president and CEO), and Kenneth G. Langone (a company board of directors member). For six consecutive years, the company has been ranked by *Fortune* magazine as America's most admired specialty retailer.

The company has 125,000 employees and 61,000 shareholders. It has a market capitalization of about $86 billion.

EARNINGS PER SHARE GROWTH   ★ ★ ★ ★

Past five years: 212 percent (26 percent per year)
Past ten years: 1,414 percent (31 percent per year)

STOCK GROWTH

Past ten years: 3,042 percent (41 percent per year)
Dollar growth: $10,000 over ten years (including reinvested dividends) would have grown to $320,000.
Average annual compounded rate of return (including reinvested dividends): 41.5 percent

DIVIDEND

Dividend yield: 0.3 percent
Increased dividend: 11 consecutive years
Past five-year increase: 200 percent (25 percent per year)

CONSISTENCY ★ ★ ★ ★

Increased earnings per share: 12 consecutive years
Increased sales: 18 consecutive years

SHAREHOLDER PERKS

The company offers a direct stock purchase program. To buy stock directly from the company, investors must invest an initial minimum of $250. The dividend reinvestment and stock purchase plan allows shareholders to invest as little as $25 per payment or as much as $100,000 a year.

HOME DEPOT AT A GLANCE

Fiscal year ended: Jan. 31
Revenue and net income in $ millions

	1994	1995	1996	1997	1998	1999	5-Year Growth Avg. Annual (%)	5-Year Growth Total (%)
Revenue ($)	9,239	12,477	15,470	19,536	24,156	30,219	27	227
Net income ($)	457	605	732	938	1,160	1,614	29	253
Earnings/share ($)	0.34	0.44	0.51	0.65	0.78	1.06	26	212
Dividends/share ($)	0.04	0.05	0.06	0.08	0.10	0.12	25	200
Dividend yield (%)	0.3	0.3	0.4	0.4	0.4	0.3	—	—
PE ratio range	31–50	27–36	24–32	21–30	20–38	25–57	—	—

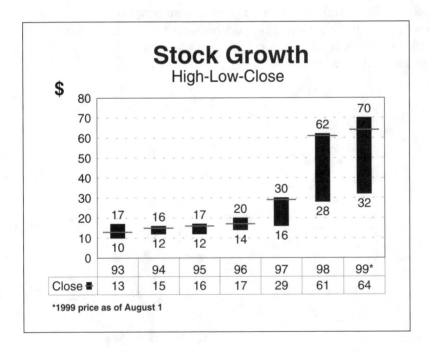

Stock Growth
High-Low-Close

	93	94	95	96	97	98	99*
Close	13	15	16	17	29	61	64

*1999 price as of August 1

Alliance Capital Management, LP

AllianceCapital ®

1345 Avenue of the Americas
New York, NY 10105
212-969-1000
www.alliancecapital.com

Chairman: Bruce Calvert
President: John Carifa

Earnings Growth	★ ★ ★
Stock Growth	★ ★ ★ ★
Dividend	★ ★ ★ ★
Consistency	★ ★ ★ ★
Shareholder Perks	
NYSE: AC	**15 points**

With about $300 billion in assets under management, Alliance Capital is the nation's largest publicly traded asset management investment firm. The company manages 118 mutual funds and provides investment management services to employee benefit plans for about a third of the Fortune 100 companies.

The New York operation also manages public retirement funds in 34 states, plus accounts for hundreds of other corporations, unions, foundations, endowments, and financial institutions in the United States and overseas.

Alliance Capital markets its line of mutual funds through brokers, financial advisers, banks, and insurance agents. Its family of 118 mutual funds includes a wide range of stock and bond funds, 24 cash management funds, 14 closed-end funds traded on the New York Stock Exchange, a group of funds for foreign investors, and a variety of variable annuity policies.

Mutual funds and related products account for about 41 percent of the company's $287 billion in assets under management and for about 72 percent of its total revenue. The company's leading mutual fund segment is its equity and balanced funds, followed by taxable fixed-income funds, tax-exempt fixed-income funds, and closed-end funds.

The other 59 percent of assets under management ($168 billion) is in managed accounts for institutional investors (employee benefit plans, public employee retirement systems, endowments, foundations, and other institutions) and high-net-worth individuals. The fees earned from the management of those accounts generate about 28 percent of the company's total revenue. In all, the company has about 2,000 managed account clients.

Alliance was founded in 1962 as the investment management department of Donaldson, Lufkin & Jenrette to specialize in pension fund management. In 1985, it was acquired by The Equitable Life Assurance Society, which took Alliance public with an initial stock offering in 1988. The Equitable still holds about 57 percent of Alliance stock.

The company, which is technically a limited partnership, has about 2,000 employees and 1,700 shareholders (technically they are considered "unit" holders). Alliance has a market capitalization of about $5 billion.

EARNINGS PER SHARE GROWTH   ★ ★ ★

Past five years: 124 percent (17 percent per year)
Past ten years: 1,409 percent (31 percent per year)

STOCK GROWTH   ★ ★ ★ ★

Past ten years: 1,092 percent (28 percent per year)
Dollar growth: $10,000 over ten years (including reinvested dividends) would have grown to $208,000.
Average annual compounded rate of return (including reinvested dividends): 37 percent

DIVIDEND ★ ★ ★ ★

Dividend yield: 6.8 percent
Increased dividend: ten consecutive years
Past five-year increase: 113 percent (16 percent per year)

CONSISTENCY ★ ★ ★ ★

Increased earnings per share: ten consecutive years
Increased sales: ten consecutive years.

SHAREHOLDER PERKS

Alliance does not offer a dividend reinvestment and stock purchase plan,
nor does it provide other shareholder perks.

ALLIANCE CAPITAL AT A GLANCE

Fiscal year ended: Dec. 31
Revenue and net income in $ millions

	1993	1994	1995	1996	1997	1998	5-Year Growth Avg. Annual (%)	5-Year Growth Total (%)
Revenue ($)	500	601	639	789	975	1,324	21	165
Net income ($)	108	134	155	193	250	293	22	171
Earnings/share ($)	0.74	0.85	0.95	1.14	1.44	1.66	17	124
Dividends/share ($)	0.75	0.82	0.91	1.10	1.40	1.60	16	113
Dividend yield (%)	6.8	7.7	9.5	8.9	9.0	6.5	—	—
PE ratio range	18–29	10–16	8–12	9–13	16–26	11–17	—	—

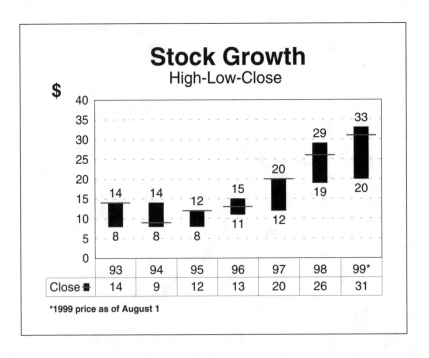

Stock Growth
High-Low-Close

	93	94	95	96	97	98	99*
Close ■	14	9	12	13	20	26	31

*1999 price as of August 1

Paychex, Inc.

PAYCHEX®

911 Panorama Trail South
Rochester, NY 14625
716-385-6666
www.paychex.com

Chairman, President, and CEO:
B. Thomas Golisano

Earnings Growth	★ ★ ★ ★
Stock Growth	★ ★ ★ ★
Dividend	★ ★
Consistency	★ ★ ★
Shareholder Perks	★ ★
Nasdaq: PAYX	**15 points**

Every day is payday for Paychex. The company cuts the checks for about 300,000 companies nationwide. In all, it issues checks for about four million workers—133 million paychecks a year. Paychex also delivers about seven million W-2 forms. It's the nation's second leading payroll processing service.

The Rochester, New York operation works primarily with small to midsize companies. On average, client companies have about 14 employees. Paychex has 110 offices in 35 states and the District of Columbia.

In addition to paycheck production, Paychex also offers a variety of other related services for employers, including:

- **Taxpay.** The firm offers an automatic tax filing and payment service, including preparation and submission of federal, state, and local payroll tax returns and the deposit of funds with tax authorities. About 75 percent of its payroll clients also use the Taxpay service.
- **Direct deposit.** Paychex makes direct bank deposits of wages for the employees of about 100,000 companies.
- **Check signing and inserting.** About 34,000 firms use Paychex to apply authorized signatures to checks and insert them in envelopes for distribution.
- **Human resources services.** The company offers a wide range of services designed to assist companies in providing additional products and services for employees, including employee handbooks, personnel forms, compliance kits, insurance plans, and 401(k) plan recordkeeping.
- **Professional employer organization services.** Paychex offers a new service in which the company becomes a coemployer of the client company's workers, handling employment regulatory compliance, workers' compensation coverage, health care benefits, and other programs related to human resources management.

Paychex was founded in 1971 but took its present form in 1979 through the consolidation of 17 small companies in the payroll services business.

The company has about 5,000 employees and 4,000 shareholders. Paychex has a market capitalization of about $7 billion.

EARNINGS PER SHARE GROWTH ★ ★ ★ ★

Past five years: 377 percent (37 percent per year)
Past ten years: 1,450 percent (31 percent per year)

STOCK GROWTH ★ ★ ★ ★

Past ten years: 2,130 percent (36 percent per year)
Dollar growth: $10,000 over ten years (including reinvested dividends) would have grown to about $235,000.
Average annual compounded rate of return (including reinvested dividends): 37 percent

DIVIDEND

Dividend yield: 0.8 percent
Increased dividend: eight consecutive years
Past five-year increase: 633 percent (48 percent per year)

CONSISTENCY

Increased earnings per share: nine consecutive years (through fiscal 1999)
Increased sales: nine consecutive years

SHAREHOLDER PERKS ★ ★

Good dividend reinvestment and stock purchase plan; voluntary stock purchase plan allows contributions of $100 to $10,000 per quarter.

PAYCHEX AT A GLANCE

Fiscal year ended: May 31
Revenue and net income in $ millions

	1993	1994	1995	1996	1997	1998	5-Year Growth Avg. Annual (%)	Total (%)
Revenue ($)	190	224	267	325	400	494	21	160
Net income ($)	20	28	39	52	75	102	38	410
Earnings/share ($)	0.13	0.18	0.26	0.34	0.47	0.62	37	377
Dividends/share ($)	0.03	0.04	0.07	0.10	0.15	0.22	48	633
Dividend yield (%)	0.7	0.7	0.9	0.7	0.7	0.7	—	—
PE ratio range	24–40	22–32	22–43	29–61	27–55	28–65	—	—

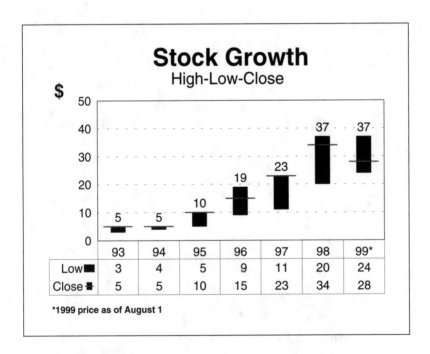

Stock Growth
High-Low-Close

	93	94	95	96	97	98	99*
Low	3	4	5	9	11	20	24
Close	5	5	10	15	23	34	28

*1999 price as of August 1

Schering-Plough Corp.

One Giralda Farms
Madison, NJ 07940
973-822-7000
www.schering-plough.com

Chairman and CEO: Richard Jay Kogan
President: Raul E. Cesan

Earnings Growth	★ ★ ★
Stock Growth	★ ★ ★ ★
Dividend	★ ★
Consistency	★ ★ ★ ★
Shareholder Perks	★ ★
NYSE: SGP	**15 points**

Schering-Plough produces a broad line of prescription and over-the-counter remedies that focus on allergic and inflammatory disorders, infectious diseases, oncology, cardiovascular diseases, central nervous system disorders—and tender feet.

The Madison, New Jersey operation is the parent company of Dr. Scholl's footcare products, including shoe cushions, Cushlin Gel Corn Wraps, Bunion Guard, and Pedicure Essential foot grooming products. It also makes Lotrimin AF, which is the nation's leading athlete's foot medication, and "fast-actin" Tinactin antifungal medication.

Schering-Plough's leading product segment is allergy and respiratory medications, which account for about 41 percent of the company's $8.1 billion in annual sales. Its Claritin antihistamine, now sold in more than

90 countries, is the world's best-selling antihistamine brand with worldwide sales of $2.3 billion a year.

With its Coppertone, Solarcaine, and Tropical Blend lotions, Schering-Plough also leads in every segment of the U.S. sun care industry. And the company continues to introduce new sunscreen products as medical evidence mounts over the dangers of exposure to the sun.

Its other leading over-the-counter products include Afrin and Duration nasal decongestants, Chlor-Trimeton antihistamine, Coricidin and Drixoral cold and decongestant products, Correctol laxative, and Di-Gel antacid.

While its over-the-counter products are most familiar to consumers, Schering-Plough's line of pharmaceuticals is what powers the company's balance sheet. In addition to its respiratory medications, the company makes drugs for cancer and infectious diseases, skin disorders, and cardiovascular disorders.

The company also operates an animal health business focusing on medications for dogs, cats, cattle, and other farm animals. It is the world's fifth largest animal health care business.

The company's second leading segment is anti-infective and anticancer medications, which account for about 15 percent of total revenue. Other segments include dermatologicals, 7 percent; cardiovasculars, 9 percent; other pharmaceuticals, 8 percent; over-the-counter medications, 2 percent; foot care, 4 percent; animal care, 8 percent; and sun care, 2 percent.

Schering-Plough generates about 37 percent of its revenue in foreign markets. Europe is its leading overseas market, although the company also has substantial sales in Latin America, Canada, Asia, and Africa.

The company has about 25,000 employees and 35,000 shareholders. It has a market capitalization of $79 billion.

EARNINGS PER SHARE GROWTH   ★ ★ ★

Past five years: 125 percent (18 percent per year)
Past ten years: 436 percent (18 percent per year)

STOCK GROWTH

Past ten years: 1,122 percent (28.5 percent per year)
Dollar growth: $10,000 over ten years (including reinvested dividends) would have grown to about $150,000.
Average annual compounded rate of return (including reinvested dividends): 31 percent

DIVIDEND

Dividend yield: 0.9 percent
Increased dividend: 12 consecutive years
Past five-year increase: 95 percent (14 percent per year)

CONSISTENCY

Increased earnings per share: 17 consecutive years
Increased sales: 19 consecutive years

SHAREHOLDER PERKS

Good dividend reinvestment and stock purchase plan; voluntary stock purchase plan allows contributions of $25 to $4,000 per month.

Schering-Plough sometimes hands out a sample packet of newer products to shareholders at its annual meeting. It recently handed out foot care and sun care products.

SCHERING-PLOUGH AT A GLANCE

Fiscal year ended: Dec. 31
Revenue and net income in $ millions

	1993	1994	1995	1996	1997	1998	5-Year Growth Avg. Annual (%)	5-Year Growth Total (%)
Revenue ($)	4,341	4,657	5,104	5,656	6,778	8,077	13	86
Net income ($)	825	922	1,053	1,213	1,444	1,756	16	113
Earnings/share ($)	0.53	0.60	0.71	0.83	0.99	1.19	18	125
Dividends/share ($)	0.22	0.25	0.28	0.32	0.37	0.43	14	95
Dividend yield (%)	2.7	3.0	2.5	2.1	1.5	0.9	—	—
PE ratio range	12–17	11–16	12–21	15–22	16–32	25–48	—	—

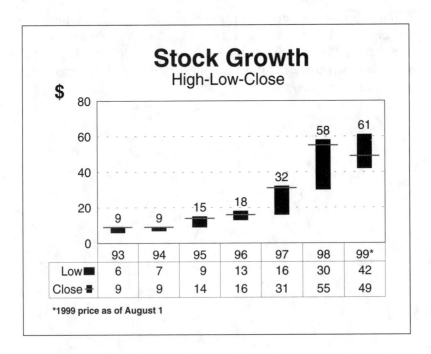

Stock Growth
High-Low-Close

	93	94	95	96	97	98	99*
Low	6	7	9	13	16	30	42
Close	9	9	14	16	31	55	49

*1999 price as of August 1

Fifth Third Bancorp

Fifth Third Center
38 Fountain Square Plaza
Cincinnati, OH 45263
513-579-5300
www.53.com

President and CEO: George A. Schaefer, Jr.

Earnings Growth	★ ★
Stock Growth	★ ★ ★ ★
Dividend	★ ★ ★
Consistency	★ ★ ★ ★
Shareholder Perks	★ ★
Nasdaq: FITB	**15 points**

Over the past quarter-century, the banking business has gone through some major ups and downs, punctuated by the savings and loan crisis, a recession, the stock market crash of 1987, and some volatile swings in interest rates. Yet through it all, Fifth Third Bancorp has posted an amazing run of 25 consecutive years of record earnings. It has been the most consistent banking organization in America.

The 141-year-old Cincinnati institution has thrived under strong management and steady, sustained growth of its branch network.

Fifth Third has about 470 branches throughout Ohio, Kentucky, Indiana, Florida, and Arizona, including about 110 seven-days-a-week offices in supermarkets.

The company has grown rapidly the past few years through a series of acquisitions, including more than 40 acquisitions of other financial institutions and related companies.

The Cincinnati-based institution has consistently ranked in the top 1 percent of all publicly traded companies based on dividend growth. Its growth has come through aggressive new product development, increasing market share in existing markets, and geographic expansion into new markets.

Fifth Third acquired its improbable-sounding name in the early part of the century through the merger of the Fifth National and Third National Banks of Ohio. Fifth Third has a reputation for quick response to credit problems, high credit standards, a strong sales culture, and strict cost control measures. The bank also is noted for eagerness to extend loans to businesses and consumers in the local markets it serves.

The company has won customers over the years through its mix of convenience and personal service delivered along with a comprehensive package of banking services. The bank helped pioneer the use of automatic teller machines (ATMs) more than 20 years ago and continues to operate the Jeanie System (with more than 1,000 ATMs). The company is also part of the Money Station network of more than 5,000 ATMs operated by several Ohio bank holding companies, and the PLUS System, which is a nationwide network of more than 170,000 ATMs.

Fifth Third's loan portfolio breaks down this way: commercial loans, 26 percent; consumer loans, 19 percent; residential mortgages, 26 percent; commercial mortgages, 6 percent; commercial leases, 8 percent; consumer leases, 12 percent; and construction loans, 3 percent.

Fifth Third's Midwest Payment Systems subsidiary is the nation's largest third-party provider of electronic funds transfer services. The subsidiary processes Visa and MasterCard transactions for more than 20,000 retail outlets throughout the country. In all, it handles more than 220 million transactions per month.

Fifth Third has about 8,300 employees and 19,000 shareholders. The company has a market capitalization of $18.8 billion.

EARNINGS PER SHARE GROWTH   ★ ★

Past five years: 110 percent (16 percent per year)
Past ten years: 292 percent (15 percent per year)

STOCK GROWTH ★ ★ ★ ★

Past ten years: 958 percent (26.5 percent per year)
Dollar growth: $10,000 over ten years (including reinvested dividends) would have grown to $128,000.
Average annual compounded rate of return (including reinvested dividends): 29 percent

DIVIDEND ★ ★ ★

Dividend yield: 1.2 percent .
Increased dividend: 25 consecutive years
Past five-year increase: 137 percent (19 percent per year)

CONSISTENCY ★ ★ ★ ★

Increased earnings per share: 25 consecutive years

SHAREHOLDER PERKS ★ ★

Good dividend reinvestment and stock purchase plan; voluntary stock purchase plan allows contributions of $25 to $2,500 per month.

FIFTH THIRD BANCORP AT A GLANCE

Fiscal year ended: Dec. 31
Total assets and net income in $ millions

	1993	1994	1995	1996	1997	1998	5-Year Growth Avg. Annual (%)	5-Year Growth Total (%)
Total assets ($)	11,966	14,957	17,053	20,549	21,375	28,922	19	142
Net income ($)	196	245	289	335	401	552	22	166
Earnings/share ($)	0.97	1.13	1.29	1.41	1.69	2.04	16	110
Dividends/share ($)	0.30	0.36	0.43	0.49	0.57	0.71	19	137
Dividend yield (%)	1.9	2.4	2.5	2.0	1.4	1.2	—	—
PE ratio range	15–18	12–14	11–18	13–23	15–32	26–41	—	—

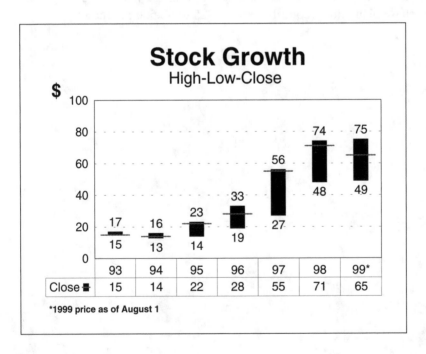

Stock Growth
High-Low-Close

	93	94	95	96	97	98	99*
Close	15	14	22	28	55	71	65

*1999 price as of August 1

General Electric Company

3135 Easton Turnpike
Fairfield, CT 06431
203-373-2211
www.ge.com

Chairman and CEO: John F. Welch

Earnings Growth	★ ★
Stock Growth	★ ★ ★ ★
Dividend	★ ★ ★
Consistency	★ ★ ★ ★
Shareholder Perks	★ ★
NYSE: GE	**15 points**

Things are going about as well as possible for General Electric (GE), a company that traces its roots to the Edison Electric Company, founded in 1878 by the great Thomas A. Edison.

With a market capitalization of about $375 billion, GE is one of the world's largest and most successful companies. It has posted record earnings for 23 consecutive years, including double-digit earnings growth the past six years—a rare feat for a company the size of GE. Little wonder it was recently rated "the world's most respected company" by readers of the *Financial Times,* and "the most admired company in America" by *Fortune* magazine.

The Fairfield, Connecticut operation breaks its business into several key segments. Its largest manufacturing segment is its industrial products and systems division, which accounts for about 11 percent of the company's $51.5 billion in annual revenue. The company manufactures factory automation products, motors, electrical equipment, transportation systems (including locomotives and transit propulsion equipment), light bulbs, and other types of lighting products.

GE's other leading divisions include:

- **Power systems** (8 percent of total revenue). The company builds power generators (primarily steam-turbine generators) and transmitters for worldwide utility, industrial, and government customers.
- **Aircraft engines** (10 percent of revenue). It is a leading manufacturer of jet engines and engine parts for short-, medium-, intermediate-, and long-range commercial aircraft and military aircraft and helicopters.
- **NBC** (5 percent of revenue). GE owns the National Broadcasting Company (NBC), which serves more than 200 affiliated stations throughout the United States. NBC also owns the cable channel CNBC and television stations in Chicago, Philadelphia, Los Angeles, Miami, New York, and Washington, D.C.
- **Appliances** (5 percent of revenue). The company is known for its GE, Hotpoint, and Monogram appliances, including refrigerators, ranges, microwaves, freezers, dishwashers, clothes washers and dryers, and room air conditioners.
- **Plastics** (7 percent of revenue). GE makes high-performance plastics for such uses as automobile bumpers, computer casings, and other office equipment. It also produces silicones, superabrasives, and laminates.
- **Technical products and services** (5 percent of revenue). The company manufactures a variety of medical instruments, including scanners, X-ray, nuclear imaging, ultrasound, and other diagnostic equipment. It also manufactures communications systems.
- **GECS (formerly GE Capital Services)** (49 percent of revenue). GE operates a number of financial, leasing, and insurance subsidiaries. Its largest division is GE Capital, a financing institution that specializes in revolving credit, credit cards, and inventory financing for retail merchants.

GE has about 290,000 employees and 530,000 shareholders. It has a market capitalization of about $350 billion.

EARNINGS PER SHARE GROWTH

Past five years: 84 percent (13 percent per year)
Past ten years: 198 percent (11.5 percent per year)

STOCK GROWTH

Past ten years: 741 percent (24 percent per year)
Dollar growth: $10,000 over ten years (including reinvested dividends) would have grown to $105,000.
Average annual compounded rate of return (including reinvested dividends): 26.5 percent

DIVIDEND

Dividend yield: 1.5 percent
Increased dividend: 23 consecutive years
Past five-year increase: 92 percent (14 percent per year)

CONSISTENCY

Increased earnings per share: 23 consecutive years
Increased sales: eight of the past ten years

SHAREHOLDER PERKS ★ ★

Direct purchase plan allows new investors to buy GE shares with a minimum $250 investment. Excellent dividend reinvestment and stock purchase plan allows voluntary contributions of $10 to $10,000 per week.

GENERAL ELECTRIC AT A GLANCE

Fiscal year ended: Dec. 31
Revenue and net income in $ millions

	1993	1994	1995	1996	1997	1998	5-Year Growth Avg. Annual (%)	5-Year Growth Total (%)
Revenue ($)	37,822	39,630	43,013	46,119	48,952	51,546	6	36
Net income ($)	5,102	5,915	6,573	7,280	8,203	9,296	13	82
Earnings/share ($)	1.52	1.73	1.95	2.20	2.50	2.80	13	84
Dividends/share ($)	0.65	0.75	0.85	0.95	1.08	1.25	14	92
Dividend yield (%)	2.8	3.0	2.9	2.2	1.7	1.5	—	—
PE ratio range	17–22	13–16	13–19	13–19	19–31	24–37	—	—

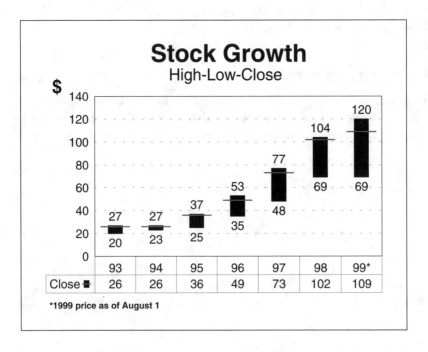

Stock Growth
High-Low-Close

	93	94	95	96	97	98	99*
Close	26	26	36	49	73	102	109

*1999 price as of August 1

9

Merck and Company, Inc.

One Merck Drive
Whitehouse Station, NJ 08889
908-423-1000
www.merck.com

Chairman, President, and CEO:
Raymond Gilmartin

Earnings Growth	★ ★
Stock Growth	★ ★ ★
Dividend	★ ★ ★ ★
Consistency	★ ★ ★ ★
Shareholder Perks	★ ★
NYSE: MRK	**15 points**

Founded in 1881, Merck is the world's leading maker of pharmaceuticals, with a pipeline that just keeps turning out winners.

Some of its biggest recent hits include:

- The hair growth medication Propecia, which became the first tablet approved by the U.S. Food and Drug Administration for the treatment of male pattern hair loss. About 400,000 American men began using the medicine its first year on the market.
- Zocor, a cholesterol medication, is the world's second largest selling medication. Mevacor, another Merck cholesterol medication, is also among the leaders, with gross sales of more than $1 billion a year.
- Cozaar, an antihypertensive medication, reached annual sales of $1 billion a year in its fourth year on the market.

- Maxalt became the fastest growing oral migraine medicine within weeks of its introduction in the U.S. market.
- Singulair has become the top-selling asthma medicine in every country where it is sold.

Merck's biggest selling segment is its cholesterol treatments, which account for about 17 percent of the company's $26.9 billion in annual sales. Cardiovascular medications, which are used to treat heart problems and hypertension, account for 16 percent.

Other leading segments include antiulcerants, 4 percent; vaccines and biologicals, 3 percent; osteoporosis, 3 percent; antibiotics, 3 percent; HIV medications, 3 percent; ophthalmologicals, 3 percent; and other products, 6 percent.

The company's other leading division is its Merck-Medco operation, which provides managed prescription drug services and managed patient health services. Its sales account for about 42 percent of Merck's total revenue.

Merck has operations in about 20 countries, with sales in more than 100 countries. Sales outside of North America account for about 25 percent of total revenue.

The Whitehouse Station, New Jersey manufacturer spends about 12 percent of its annual revenue on research and development.

The company has about 58,000 employees and 270,000 shareholders. It has a market capitalization of about $179 billion.

EARNINGS PER SHARE GROWTH ★ ★

Past five years: 84 percent (13 percent per year)
Past ten years: 322 percent (15.5 percent per year)

STOCK GROWTH

Past ten years: 564 percent (21 percent per year)
Dollar growth: $10,000 over ten years (including reinvested dividends) would have grown to $80,000.
Average annual compounded rate of return (including reinvested dividends): 23 percent

DIVIDEND

Dividend yield: 1.6 percent
Increased dividend: 15 consecutive years
Past five-year increase: 83 percent (13 percent per year)

CONSISTENCY

Increased earnings per share: 17 consecutive years
Increased sales: 18 consecutive years

SHAREHOLDER PERKS ★ ★

Merck offers a direct purchase plan with a minimum initial investment of $350, or $50 a month for a minimum of seven months. The company's dividend reinvestment and stock purchase plan allows contributions of $50 to $50,000 per year.

MERCK AT A GLANCE

Fiscal year ended: Dec. 31
Revenue and net income in $ millions

	1993	1994	1995	1996	1997	1998	5-Year Growth Avg. Annual (%)	Total (%)
Revenue ($)	10,498	14,970	16,681	19,828	23,636	26,898	20	156
Net income ($)	2,687	2,997	3,335	3,881	4,614	5,248	14	95
Earnings/share ($)	1.17	1.19	1.35	1.60	1.92	2.15	13	84
Dividends/share ($)	0.52	0.57	0.62	0.71	0.85	0.95	13	83
Dividend yield (%)	2.9	3.4	2.5	2.1	1.8	1.5	—	—
PE ratio range	15–24	12–17	13–25	18–26	20–28	23–37	—	—

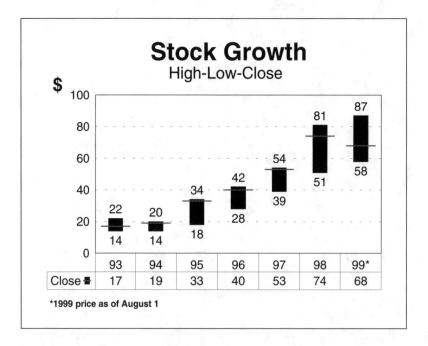

Stock Growth
High-Low-Close

	93	94	95	96	97	98	99*
Close	17	19	33	40	53	74	68

*1999 price as of August 1

Procter & Gamble Company

Procter&Gamble

One Procter & Gamble Plaza
Cincinnati, OH 45202
513-983-1100
www.pg.com

Chairman and CEO: John Pepper
President: Durk Jager

Earnings Growth	★★
Stock Growth	★★★★
Dividend	★★★
Consistency	★★★★
Shareholder Perks	★★
NYSE: PG	**15 points**

Since its founding more than 160 years ago, Procter & Gamble (P&G) has been working its way into homes all over America—and the world.

From dish soaps and laundry detergent to coffee and cosmetics, the Cincinnati operation puts more than 300 product brands on the market in more than 140 countries. About 48 percent of its $37.2 billion in annual revenue comes from sales outside of North America.

P&G's best-selling product is Tide laundry detergent. Introduced in 1946, Tide is the nation's number-one detergent. The company also makes Cheer, Downy, Joy, Ace Bleach, Ariel, Bounce, Dawn, and Mr.

Clean. Laundry and cleaning products account for about 30 percent of total revenue.

In addition to cleaning products, the company produces leading products in several key categories, including:

- **Paper products** (29 percent of revenue). Leading brands include Bounty, Pampers, Puffs, Luvs, Tampax, Always, Charmin, Whisper, and Attends.
- **Beauty care** (20 percent of revenue). The company makes a wide range of beauty care products, including Cover Girl, Vidal Sassoon, Secret, Clearasil, Noxzema, Coast, Lava, Oil of Olay, Safeguard, Zest, Max Factor, Sure, Head & Shoulders, and Old Spice.
- **Food and beverages** (12 percent of revenue). Leading products include Crisco, Folgers, Hawaiian Punch, Jif, Olean, Pringles, and Sunny Delight Florida Citrus Punch.
- **Health care** (9 percent of revenue). The company makes Crest, Gleem, Scope, Metamucil, Vicks, Pepto Bismol, Nyquil, and a number of prescription and over-the-counter medications.

In 1999, the company announced a six-year global restructuring plan designed to cut costs. The plan calls for the closing of ten plants and layoffs of about 15,000 employees over the next six years.

Founded in 1837 by William Procter and James Gamble, the company is the world's leading producer of soaps and cosmetics. P&G has managed to maintain its strong market position through a relentless advertising approach. For many years, the company has been TV's biggest advertiser.

P&G has 110,000 employees and about 275,000 shareholders. It has a market capitalization of about $120 billion.

EARNINGS PER SHARE GROWTH   ★ ★

Past five years: 82 percent (16 percent per year)
Past ten years: 241 percent (13 percent per year)

STOCK GROWTH ★ ★ ★ ★

Past ten years: 650 percent (22 percent per year)
Dollar growth: $10,000 over ten years (including reinvested dividends) would have grown to $86,000.
Average annual compounded rate of return (including reinvested dividends): 24 percent

DIVIDEND ★ ★ ★

Dividend yield: 1.1 percent
Increased dividend: 42 consecutive years
Past five-year increase: 96 percent (18 percent per year)

CONSISTENCY ★ ★ ★ ★

Increased earnings per share: 13 consecutive years
Increased sales: nine of the past ten years

SHAREHOLDER PERKS ★ ★

Good dividend reinvestment and stock purchase plan; investors may contribute a minimum of $100 per payment to a maximum of $120,000 annually.

PROCTER & GAMBLE AT A GLANCE

Fiscal year ended: June 30
Revenue and net income in $ millions

	1993	1994	1995	1996	1997	1998	5-Year Growth Avg. Annual (%)	Total (%)
Revenue ($)	30,433	30,296	33,434	35,284	35,764	37,154	3	22
Net income ($)	2,015	2,211	2,645	3,046	3,415	3,780	17	88
Earnings/share ($)	1.41	1.55	1.86	2.15	2.28	2.56	16	82
Dividends/share ($)	0.55	0.62	0.70	0.80	0.90	1.08	18	96
Dividend yield (%)	2.2	2.3	2.2	2.0	1.6	1.3	—	—
PE ratio range	15–20	17–21	16–24	19–26	21–34	24–35	—	—

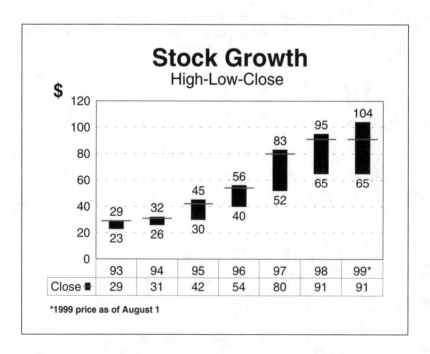

Stock Growth
High-Low-Close

Close ■	93	94	95	96	97	98	99*
	29	31	42	54	80	91	91

*1999 price as of August 1

Fannie Mae

3900 Wisconsin Avenue, NW
Washington, DC 20016
202-752-7115
www.fanniemae.com

Chairman and CEO: James A. Johnson
President: Lawrence M. Small

Earnings Growth	★ ★
Stock Growth	★ ★ ★ ★
Dividend	★ ★ ★
Consistency	★ ★ ★ ★
Shareholder Perks	★ ★
NYSE: FNM	**15 points**

For young families looking for a permanent roof over their heads, the Federal National Mortgage Association (Fannie Mae) has been a beacon of hope in a sea of miserly bankers.

The Washington, D.C.–based operation is the nation's largest provider of residential mortgage funding.

Fannie Mae was created by Congress in 1938 as a U.S. government agency to supplement the mortgage market in order to help low-, moderate-, and middle-income American families buy new homes. It also lends stability to the market by buying, selling, and guaranteeing mortgages.

Since its founding, Fannie Mae has issued more than $2.5 trillion in mortgage financing, which has helped about 30 million families afford homes.

The company buys mortgages from lenders, such as banks, mortgage banks, and savings and loan associations, thereby replenishing their funds for additional lending. That leaves more money available for institutions to lend to other homebuyers.

Fannie Mae's primary business is buying mortgages that they fund by issuing debt securities on the global capital markets. Their profit comes on the spread between the yield on the mortgages and the cost of the debt. The company holds a mortgage portfolio of about $450 billion—and growing.

The company also is active in the mortgage-backed securities business. It guarantees the timely payment of principal and interest on securities backed by pools of mortgages, earning a guaranty fee on the amount of mortgage-backed securities outstanding.

Fannie Mae also offers a variety of services to lenders and related operations for a fee. Services include issuing certain types of mortgage-backed securities and providing technology services in support of originating and underwriting mortgage loans.

Fannie Mae became a shareholder-owned company in 1968 but is still subject to explicit federal regulation. In fact, 5 members of its 18-member board are appointed by the President. In terms of total assets, Fannie Mae is the nation's largest company with assets of about $500 billion. It is also the largest investor in home mortgage loans in the United States. The company has posted 12 consecutive years of record earnings.

Fannie Mae has about 3,200 employees and 239,000 shareholders. It has a market capitalization of about $75 billion.

EARNINGS PER SHARE GROWTH ★ ★

Past five years: 89 percent (14 percent per year)
Past ten years: 509 percent (20 percent per year)

STOCK GROWTH ★ ★ ★ ★

Past ten years: 813 percent (25 percent per year)
Dollar growth: $10,000 over ten years (including reinvested dividends) would have grown to $109,000.
Average annual compounded rate of return (including reinvested dividends): 27 percent

DIVIDEND

Dividend yield: 1.5 percent
Increased dividend: 13 consecutive years
Past five-year increase: 109 percent (15.5 percent per year)

CONSISTENCY

Increased earnings per share: 12 consecutive years

SHAREHOLDER PERKS ★ ★

Direct stock purchase plan for new investors requires a minimum initial investment of $250. Dividend reinvestment and stock purchase plan allows contributions of $25 to $5,000 per month.

FANNIE MAE AT A GLANCE

Fiscal year ended: Dec. 31
Mortgage loans and net income in $ millions

	1993	1994	1995	1996	1997	1998	5-Year Growth Avg. Annual (%)	Total (%)
Mortgage loans ($)	190,861	222,057	253,511	287,052	316,678	415,223	17	118
Net income ($)	1,873	2,132	2,144	2,725	3,068	3,418	13	82
Earnings/share ($)	1.71	1.94	1.95	2.48	2.84	3.23	14	89
Dividends/share ($)	0.46	0.60	0.68	0.76	0.84	0.96	16	109
Dividend yield (%)	2.3	2.9	2.9	2.3	1.9	1.7	—	—
PE ratio range	10–12	9–12	9–16	11–16	13–20	15–23	—	—

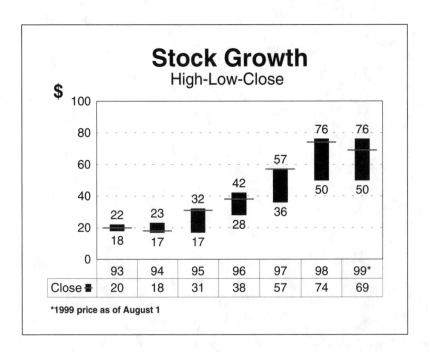

Stock Growth
High-Low-Close

	93	94	95	96	97	98	99*
Close	20	18	31	38	57	74	69

*1999 price as of August 1

State Street Corporation

225 Franklin Street
Boston, MA 02110
617-786-3000
www.statestreet.com

Chairman and CEO: Marshall N. Carter
President: David A. Spina

Earnings Growth	★ ★ ★
Stock Growth	★ ★ ★ ★
Dividend	★ ★
Consistency	★ ★ ★ ★
Shareholder Perks	★ ★
NYSE: STT	**15 points**

State Street is a banking organization that places very little emphasis on the traditional banking business. The bulk of its revenue comes from servicing the institutional investment industry.

Its customers include investment companies, mutual funds, corporate pension plans, corporations, investment managers, nonprofit organizations, endowments, foundations, unions, and other financial companies. State Street offers its institutional investors a wide range of services, including accounting, custody, daily pricing, and information services for investment portfolios.

State Street also offers its customers foreign exchange services, cash management, securities lending, fund administration, recordkeeping, banking services, and deposit and short-term investment facilities.

The company is the nation's largest mutual fund custodian and accounting agent, with assets under custody of $2.1 trillion. Its mutual fund custodial services include safekeeping portfolio assets, settling trades, collecting and accounting for income, monitoring corporate actions, and reporting investable cash.

In addition to fund custody services, State Street also assists mutual fund companies by offering accounting and administration, daily pricing, accounting for multiple classes of shares, and services for offshore funds and local funds in locations outside the United States.

State Street has focused much of its marketing emphasis recently on foreign financial companies. About 24 percent of the company's revenue comes from the foreign market. It has offices in 24 countries and does business in 85 markets.

The company also offers a broad range of investment management services for corporations, public funds, and other institutional investors. State Street was a pioneer in the development of domestic and international index funds.

The company also provides traditional commercial lending services such as corporate banking, specialized lending, and international banking for businesses and financial institutions, although that is a small part of its business.

State Street traces its roots back two centuries to the Union Bank, which opened shortly after the American Revolution in 1792. The company has 17,000 employees and 6,500 shareholders. State Street has a market capitalization of about $13 billion.

EARNINGS PER SHARE GROWTH   ★ ★ ★

Past five years: 127 percent (18 percent per year)
Past ten years: 343 percent (13 percent per year)

STOCK GROWTH ★ ★ ★ ★

Past ten years: 838 percent (25 percent per year)
Dollar growth: $10,000 over ten years (including reinvested dividends) would have grown to $105,000.
Average annual compounded rate of return (including reinvested dividends): 26.5 percent

DIVIDEND ★ ★

Dividend yield: 0.8 percent
Increased dividend: 20 consecutive years
Past five-year increase: 92 percent (14 percent per year)

CONSISTENCY ★ ★ ★ ★

Increased earnings per share: 22 consecutive years

SHAREHOLDER PERKS ★ ★

Dividend reinvestment and stock purchase plan; voluntary stock purchase plan allows contributions of $100 to $1,000 per quarter.

STATE STREET AT A GLANCE

Fiscal year ended: Dec. 31
Total assets and net income in $ millions

	1993	1994	1995	1996	1997	1998	5-Year Growth Avg. Annual (%)	5-Year Growth Total (%)
Total assets ($)	18,720	21,730	25,785	31,524	37,975	47,082	20	152
Net income ($)	180	207	247	294	380	436	19	142
Earnings/share ($)	1.17	1.34	1.49	1.78	2.32	2.66	18	127
Dividends/share ($)	0.26	0.30	0.34	0.38	0.44	0.50	14	92
Dividend yield (%)	1.4	1.6	1.9	1.4	0.9	0.8	—	—
PE ratio range	13–21	10–16	9–15	12–19	13–27	18–27	—	—

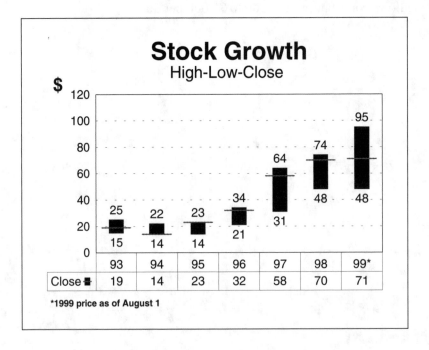

Stock Growth
High-Low-Close

	93	94	95	96	97	98	99*
Close	19	14	23	32	58	70	71

*1999 price as of August 1

13

Franklin Resources, Inc.

777 Mariners Island Boulevard
San Mateo, CA 94404
650-312-2000
www.frk.com

President and CEO: Charles B. Johnson

Earnings Growth	★ ★ ★ ★
Stock Growth	★ ★ ★ ★
Dividend	★
Consistency	★ ★ ★ ★
Shareholder Perks	★ ★
NYSE: BEN	**15 points**

With a financial management business that has been in operation more than 50 years, and a product offering of more than 200 mutual funds, it's little wonder Franklin Resources has enjoyed exceptional growth during the bull market run of the 1990s. But trouble in the Asian markets slowed the company's growth recently and prompted management to restructure the company with layoffs, office closings, and product discontinuations.

With the restructuring, management hopes to regain the company's status as one of the nation's top-performing investment firms.

The San Mateo, California operation has long been known for its line of Franklin mutual funds. Traditionally, its specialty has been tax-exempt bond funds. In recent years, Franklin has bolstered its offerings through a couple of major acquisitions. In 1992, it acquired the Templeton Funds, which were founded by investment legend John Templeton. With its line of international funds and foreign investment offices, Templeton gave Franklin a major stake in the global market.

The other key acquisition was the 1996 buyout of the Mutual Series family of five mutual funds founded by Michael F. Price.

Franklin now has offices in more than 20 countries, with a total of about 9 million shareholder accounts. The company offers about 235 mutual funds, including 165 based in the United States and 70 that are sold outside the U.S. The Franklin funds are marketed nationwide through a network of brokers, financial planners, and investment advisers.

Including its mutual funds and institutional investment accounts, Franklin has about $210 billion in assets under management.

In addition to its investment management operations, the company owns the Franklin Bank (formerly the Pacific Union Bank & Trust Company), which has about $105 million in assets. It also operates real estate and insurance divisions and a capital corporation that specializes in auto loans. However, those services account for less than 1 percent of the company's $1.8 billion in annual revenue.

Franklin, which was founded in New York City in 1947, has about 8,600 employees and 3,900 shareholders. It has a market capitalization of $11 billion.

EARNINGS PER SHARE GROWTH ★ ★ ★ ★

Past five years: 179 percent (22 percent per year)
Past ten years: 607 percent (21.5 percent per year)

STOCK GROWTH ★ ★ ★ ★

Past ten years: 993 percent (27 percent per year)
Dollar growth: $10,000 over ten years (including reinvested dividends) would have grown to $118,000.
Average annual compounded rate of return (including reinvested dividends): 28 percent

DIVIDEND ★

Dividend yield: 0.4 percent
Increased dividend: 12 consecutive years
Past five-year increase: 122 percent (17 percent per year)

CONSISTENCY   ★ ★ ★ ★

Increased earnings per share: 15 consecutive years
Increased sales: ten consecutive years

SHAREHOLDER PERKS   ★ ★

Good dividend reinvestment and stock purchase plan; voluntary stock purchase plan requires an initial minimum investment of $1,000, with subsequent contributions of not less than $50.

FRANKLIN RESOURCES AT A GLANCE

Fiscal year ended: Sept. 30
Revenue and net income in $ millions

	1993	1994	1995	1996	1997	1998	5-Year Growth Avg. Annual (%)	Total (%)
Revenue ($)	656	850	876	1,031	1,501	1,792	22	173
Net income ($)	176	251	269	314	434	500	23	185
Earnings/share ($)	0.71	1.00	1.08	1.26	1.72	1.98	22	179
Dividends/share ($)	0.09	0.11	0.13	0.15	0.17	0.20	17	122
Dividend yield (%)	0.7	0.8	1.0	0.8	0.6	0.4	—	—
PE ratio range	15–24	11–17	10–18	12–19	13–30	13–29	—	—

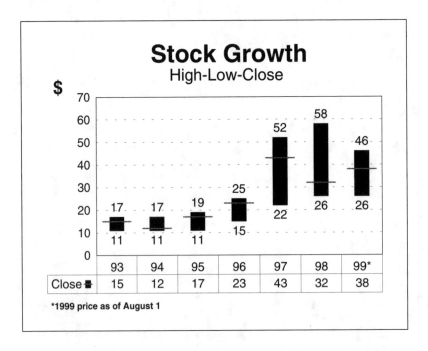

Stock Growth
High-Low-Close

	93	94	95	96	97	98	99*
Close	15	12	17	23	43	32	38

*1999 price as of August 1

Johnson & Johnson

Johnson&Johnson

One Johnson & Johnson Plaza
New Brunswick, NJ 08933
732-524-0400
www.jnj.com

Chairman and CEO: Ralph Larsen

Earnings Growth	★ ★
Stock Growth	★ ★ ★ ★
Dividend	★ ★ ★
Consistency	★ ★ ★ ★
Shareholder Perks	★ ★
NYSE: JNJ	**15 points**

For more than 110 years, Johnson & Johnson has specialized in finding solutions to the cuts, bumps, bruises, and other problems of consumers of all ages. Among its leading products are Band-Aids, Tylenol, Imodium A-D, and Mylanta antacid. And, of course, Johnson & Johnson is known worldwide for its long line of baby products, including soaps, shampoo, powders, and lotions.

Consumer products account for about 28 percent of the company's $23.7 billion in annual revenue. Other leading consumer products from Johnson & Johnson include Nicotrol smoking cessation products, Carefree Panty Shields, Clean & Clear skin care products, Monistat, Pepcid AC, Neutrogena skin and hair products, Sundown and Piz Buin sun care products, Reach toothbrushes, Act Floride Rinse, and Stayfree and Sure & Natural sanitary protection products.

The New Brunswick, New Jersey operation has manufacturing plants in 35 foreign countries, with sales in 175 countries. International sales make up about 47 percent of total revenue.

In addition to its consumer products, the company turns out a wide range of pharmaceuticals, including contraceptives, antifungals, central nervous system medications, allergy and asthma medications, gastrointestinal treatments, and skin care formulas. Pharmaceutical products account for about 36 percent of total revenue.

Its other primary segment is professional medical products, which account for about 36 percent of total revenue. The company produces sutures, mechanical wound closure products, endoscopic products, dental products, diagnostic products, medical equipment and devices, ophthalmic products, surgical instruments, and medical supplies used by physicians, dentists, therapists, hospitals, and clinics.

Some of the company's latest innovations include Band-Aid Brand Cushions for Feet, Neutrogena Extra Gentle Cleanser and Extra Gentle Cleansing Bar for very sensitive skin, the Mitek Meniscal Repair System used by sports medicine arthroscopists to repair torn knee cartilage, Tylenol Arthritis caplets, and Pepcid AC Chewables for heartburn and indigestion.

Johnson & Johnson spends about $2.1 billion a year on product research and development. The company has research facilities in the United States and seven other countries.

Founded in 1887, Johnson & Johnson has 93,000 employees and 166,000 shareholders. The company has a market capitalization of about $125 billion.

EARNINGS PER SHARE GROWTH   ★ ★

Past five years: 95 percent (14 percent per year)
Past ten years: 271 percent (14 percent per year)

STOCK GROWTH

Past ten years: 627 percent (22 percent per year)
Dollar growth: $10,000 over ten years (including reinvested dividends) would have grown to $86,000.
Average annual compounded rate of return (including reinvested dividends): 24 percent

DIVIDEND

Dividend yield: 1.2 percent
Increased dividend: 33 consecutive years
Past five-year increase: 90 percent (14 percent per year)

CONSISTENCY ★ ★ ★ ★

Increased earnings per share: 12 consecutive years
Increased sales: 23 consecutive years

SHAREHOLDER PERKS ★ ★

Good dividend reinvestment and stock purchase plan; voluntary stock purchase plan allows contributions of up to $50,000 per year.

JOHNSON & JOHNSON AT A GLANCE

Fiscal year ended: Dec. 31
Revenue and net income in $ millions

	1993	1994	1995	1996	1997	1998	5-Year Growth Avg. Annual (%)	5-Year Growth Total (%)
Revenue ($)	14,138	15,734	18,842	21,620	22,629	23,657	11	67
Net income ($)	1,787	2,006	2,403	2,887	3,303	3,669	15	105
Earnings/share ($)	1.37	1.56	1.86	2.17	2.41	2.67	14	95
Dividends/share ($)	0.51	0.57	0.64	0.74	0.85	0.97	14	90
Dividend yield (%)	2.4	2.4	1.9	1.5	1.4	1.3	—	—
PE ratio range	13–18	12–18	14–25	19–25	20–27	28–39	—	—

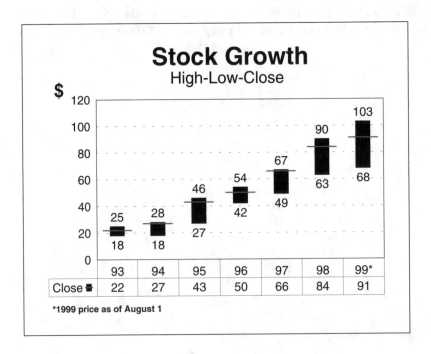

Stock Growth
High-Low-Close

	93	94	95	96	97	98	99*
Close	22	27	43	50	66	84	91

*1999 price as of August 1

15

Synovus Financial Corp.

P.O. Box 120
Columbus, GA 31902-0120
706-649-2387
www.synovus.com

Chairman and CEO: James H. Blanchard
President: James D. Yancy

Earnings Growth	★ ★
Stock Growth	★ ★ ★ ★
Dividend	★ ★ ★
Consistency	★ ★ ★ ★
Shareholder Perks	★ ★
NYSE: SNV	**15 points**

What do all these banks have in common: Bank of North Georgia, Citizens Bank of Cochran, the Citizens Bank of Fort Valley, the Bank of Tuscaloosa, and the Tallahassee State Bank? They are all part of the Synovus Financial family of banks. The Columbus, Georgia institution operates 36 banks in Georgia, Florida, Alabama, and South Carolina.

All 36 banks have different names—generally the same name they used prior to being acquired by Synovus—and they retain the same management and board of directors. They also make most of their banking decisions independently of the parent company. Only the back office duties, such as auditing and data processing, are rolled into the home office operations to cut costs.

The company's unique hands-off management strategy has worked well. Synovus has posted 16 consecutive years of record earnings. In

1999, Synovus was selected by *Fortune* magazine as the "best company to work for in America."

In addition to the standard banking services of checking, savings, and money market accounts, Synovus also offers some additional investment services for its customers. Its trust services division handles more than $4.2 billion in client assets. The company's Synovus Securities subsidiary offers full-service stock brokerage services to clients in 28 states and the District of Columbia.

Synovus also operates the Synovus Mortgage Corp., which offers mortgage services throughout the Southeast.

Banking services account for about 71 percent of the company's $1.3 billion in annual revenue.

The other 29 percent of revenue comes from its credit card processing subsidiary: Total System Services (of which Synovus holds an 81 percent share). Total System Services is one of the world's largest credit, debit, and private label card processing companies.

The company provides a variety of bankcard and private label credit card data processing services, including card production, international and domestic electronic clearing, cardholder statement preparation, customer service support, merchant accounting, and management information and reporting. The company primarily processes cardholder accounts for customers issuing Visa, MasterCard, and Diner's Club credit cards, along with corporate cards, private label cards, and automated teller machine cards. Among its leading customers are BankAmerica and NationsBank.

Founded in 1887 in Columbus, Georgia, Synovus has about 7,500 employees and 16,000 shareholders. It has a market capitalization of $6 billion.

EARNINGS PER SHARE GROWTH   ★ ★

Past five years: 112 percent (16 percent per year)
Past ten years: 312 percent (15 percent per year)

STOCK GROWTH ★ ★ ★ ★

Past ten years: 600 percent (21.5 percent per year)
Dollar growth: $10,000 over ten years (including reinvested dividends) would have grown to about $85,000.
Average annual compounded rate of return (including reinvested dividends): 24 percent

DIVIDEND ★ ★ ★

Dividend yield: 1.7 percent
Increased dividend: 19 consecutive years
Past five-year increase: 164 percent (21 percent per year)

CONSISTENCY ★ ★ ★ ★

Increased earnings per share: 16 consecutive years

SHAREHOLDER PERKS ★ ★

Direct purchase plan allows new investors to buy shares from the company with a minimum initial investment of $250. Dividend reinvestment and stock purchase plan allows contributions of $50 to $250,000 per year.

SYNOVUS AT A GLANCE

Fiscal year ended: Dec. 31
Total assets and net income in $ millions

	1993	1994	1995	1996	1997	1998	5-Year Growth Avg. Annual (%)	5-Year Growth Total (%)
Total assets ($)	5,627	6,115	7,928	8,612	9,260	10,498	13	87
Net income ($)	74	87	115	140	165	187	20	152
Earnings/share ($)	0.33	0.38	0.45	0.53	0.62	0.70	16	112
Dividends/share ($)	0.11	0.13	0.15	0.20	0.24	0.29	21	164
Dividend yield (%)	2.1	2.5	2.2	1.8	1.4	1.3	—	—
PE ratio range	14–19	14–17	12–20	15–28	21–36	24–37	—	—

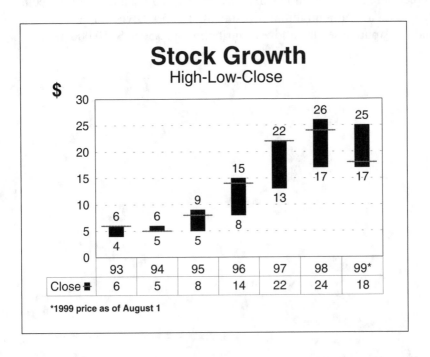

Stock Growth
High-Low-Close

	93	94	95	96	97	98	99*
Close	6	5	8	14	22	24	18

*1999 price as of August 1

Harley-Davidson, Inc.

3700 West Juneau Avenue
Milwaukee, WI 53201
414-342-4680
www.harley-davidson.com

Chairman and CEO: Jeffrey L. Bleustein

Earnings Growth	★ ★ ★ ★
Stock Growth	★ ★ ★ ★
Dividend	★
Consistency	★ ★ ★
Shareholder Perks	★ ★
NYSE: HDI	**14 points**

Harley-Davidson continues to face a dilemma few companies ever have the good fortune to encounter: The demand for its Harley motorcycles is simply too great for the company to fill.

With its emphasis on quality, Harley-Davidson has refused to accelerate its manufacturing process simply to meet demand. But the company did open two new plants recently to beef up production and get the new models to customers sooner.

Harley also added a powerful new model to its growing arsenal of motorcycles. The new 1450cc Harley Twin Cam 88–known as the "Fathead"—is the most powerful bike produced by Harley.

The Milwaukee-based operation sells more than 20 models of touring and custom heavyweight motorcycles, with suggested retail prices ranging from about $5,000 to $18,500. Its touring bikes are equipped for long-distance travel with fairings, windshields, saddlebags, and Harley Tour

Paks. The custom bikes have distinctive styling, with customized trim and accessories. The company manufactures all of its chassis and engines itself. The bikes are based on four chassis variations and are powered by one of three air-cooled, twin-cylinder engines of "V" configurations with engine displacements of 883cc, 1200cc, and 1340cc (and the new 1450cc Fathead).

The typical Harley buyer is male, early 40s, with a household income of $73,000. Only 7 percent of Harley buyers are women. About a third of Harley riders are college graduates. Harley buyers are also extremely loyal. The company's riders club, The Harley Owners Group (HOG), has about 300,000 members worldwide.

The company also manufactures the Buell line of sport and performance motorcycles.

Harley-Davidson, in its present incarnation, was incorporated in 1981 by a private investment group that purchased Harley-Davidson Motorcyle from AMF, Inc., and took it public in 1986. The reputation of the bikes—and the profits of the company—have been rising ever since. From a net profit of $4.5 million in 1986, the company's profits have soared to $214 million (in 1998).

Overseas sales are also on the rise. Foreign sales account for about 26 percent of Harley's $2.1 billion in annual revenue. Harleys enjoy their greatest popularity in Germany, Japan, Canada, and Australia, which account for about 60 percent of export sales.

Founded in 1903, Harley-Davidson has about 6,500 employees and 35,000 shareholders. It has a market capitalization of $8.6 billion.

EARNINGS PER SHARE GROWTH   ★ ★ ★ ★

Past five years: 182 percent (23 percent per year)
Past ten years: 475 percent (19 percent per year)

STOCK GROWTH   ★ ★ ★ ★

Past ten years: 2,650 percent (39 percent per year)
Dollar growth: $10,000 over ten years (including reinvested dividends) would have grown to $27,500.
Average annual compounded rate of return (including reinvested dividends): 39 percent

DIVIDEND ★

Dividend yield: 0.4 percent
Increased dividend: six consecutive years
Past five-year increase: 433 percent (40 percent per year)

CONSISTENCY ★ ★ ★

Increased earnings per share: nine of the past ten years
Increased sales: 12 consecutive years

SHAREHOLDER PERKS ★ ★

Good dividend reinvestment and stock purchase plan; voluntary stock purchase plan allows contributions of $30 to $5,000 per quarter.

HARLEY-DAVIDSON AT A GLANCE

Fiscal year ended: Dec. 31
Revenue and net income in $ millions

	1993	1994	1995	1996	1997	1998	5-Year Growth Avg. Annual (%)	Total (%)
Revenue ($)	1,217	1,542	1,351	1,531	1,763	2,064	11	70
Net income ($)	78	104	111	143	174	214	22	174
Earnings/share ($)	0.49	0.69	0.74	0.95	1.13	1.38	23	182
Dividends/share ($)	0.03	0.07	0.09	0.11	0.14	0.16	40	433
Dividend yield (%)	0.3	0.6	0.7	0.5	0.6	0.5	—	—
PE ratio range	16–23	17–23	15–20	14–26	15–27	18–34	—	—

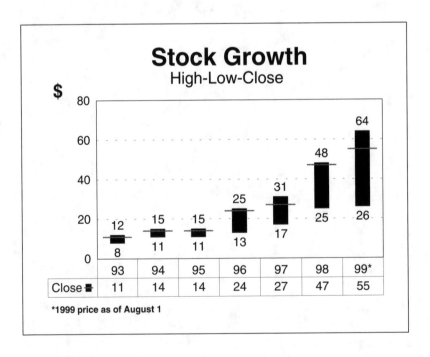

Stock Growth
High-Low-Close

	93	94	95	96	97	98	99*
Close	11	14	14	24	27	47	55

*1999 price as of August 1

Pfizer, Inc.

235 East 42nd Street
New York, NY 10017
212-573-2323
www.pfizer.com

Chairman and CEO: William C. Steere

Earnings Growth	★ ★ ★
Stock Growth	★ ★ ★ ★
Dividend	★ ★
Consistency	★ ★ ★
Shareholder Perks	★ ★
NYSE: PFE	**14 points**

Not only has Viagra added new life to the intimate relations of thousands of couples, it also has helped perk up Pfizer's bottom line. The world's first certifiably effective prescription aphrodisiac, Viagra has been one of the most successful new products ever launched by the New York–based pharmaceuticals maker.

Viagra has spawned a cottage industry of mail order doctors who sell the male potency pill through toll-free numbers and Web sites. After experiencing incredible sales of the drug in the United States, Pfizer has been introducing Viagra worldwide. In all, the company reports Viagra sales of nearly $1 billion a year.

But Viagra represents just a small part of Pfizer's extensive product line. The company produces three leading cardiovascular medications, including Norvasc, which generates about $2.6 billion in annual sales, Procardia XL ($714 million in annual sales), and Cardura ($688 million in sales). It also produces three leading medications for infectious diseases (Diflucan, Zithromax, and Trovan), which generate a total of about $2.8 billion in annual revenue, and the central nervous system disorder drug Zoloft, which generates about $1.8 billion in annual sales.

Pfizer's other two leading drugs are Glucotrol XL, which is used to treat diabetes, and Zyrtec, which is used to treat allergies. They generated about $226 million and $422 million in annual sales, respectively.

Pharmaceuticals and health care products account for 87 percent of the company's $13.5 billion in annual revenue. Consumer products, such as Visine eyedrops, BenGay topical analgesics, Cortizone cream, Rid antilice products, Unisom sleep aids, Desitin ointments, Plax prebrushing dental rinse, Barbasol shaving cream, and Bain de Soleil sun protection lotion account for about 3 percent of revenue.

Pfizer also has a line of animal health care products to treat livestock, poultry, and household pets. One of its leading products is Dectomax, a parasite control medication used to treat animals for roundworms, lung worms, lice, mange, warbles, screw worms, and ticks. Animal health care products account for about 10 percent of annual revenue.

Pfizer has sales in more than 150 countries. Foreign sales account for about 39 percent of total revenue.

The company has about 49,000 employees and 65,000 shareholders. It has a market capitalization of $148.7 billion.

EARNINGS PER SHARE GROWTH   ★ ★ ★

Past five years: 117 percent (16 percent per year)
Past ten years: 239 percent (13 percent per year)

STOCK GROWTH   ★ ★ ★ ★

Past ten years: 1,485 percent (32 percent per year)
Dollar growth: $10,000 over ten years (including reinvested dividends) would have grown to $185,000.
Average annual compounded rate of return (including reinvested dividends): 34 percent

DIVIDEND

Dividend yield: 0.8 percent
Increased dividend: 32 consecutive years
Past five-year increase: 81 percent (13 percent per year)

CONSISTENCY ★ ★ ★

Increased earnings per share: nine consecutive years
Increased sales: 49 consecutive years

SHAREHOLDER PERKS

Excellent dividend reinvestment and stock purchase plan; voluntary stock purchase plan allows contributions of $50 to $120,000 per year.

PFIZER AT A GLANCE

Fiscal year ended: Dec. 31
Revenue and net income in $ millions

	1993	1994	1995	1996	1997	1998	5-Year Growth Avg. Annual (%)	Total (%)
Revenue ($)	7,478	8,281	10,021	11,306	12,504	13,544	13	81
Net income ($)	1,180	1,298	1,554	1,929	2,213	2,627	17	123
Earnings/share ($)	0.92	1.05	1.24	1.50	1.70	2.00	16	117
Dividends/share ($)	0.42	0.47	0.52	0.60	0.68	0.76	13	81
Dividend yield (%)	2.6	2.9	2.1	1.6	1.2	0.7	—	—
PE ratio range	26–38	13–19	15–26	21–32	24–48	46–84	—	—

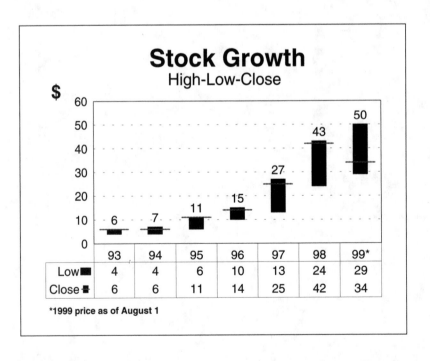

Stock Growth
High-Low-Close

	93	94	95	96	97	98	99*
Low■	4	4	6	10	13	24	29
Close ▪	6	6	11	14	25	42	34

*1999 price as of August 1

Carnival Corporation

3655 NW 87th Avenue
Miami, FL 33178
305-599-2600
www.carnivalcorp.com

Chairman and CEO: Micky Arison

Earnings Growth	★ ★ ★ ★
Stock Growth	★ ★ ★ ★
Dividend	★ ★
Consistency	★ ★ ★ ★
Shareholder Perks	
NYSE: CCL	**14 points**

It's been smooth sailing recently for Carnival. The Miami-based cruise ship operator has posted record sales and earnings for 14 consecutive years, as an increasing number of affluent Americans have taken to the high seas.

Carnival is the world's largest cruise company. The company commands more than 30 cruise ships and has about a dozen new ships under construction. Its main lines are the Carnival Cruise Lines, Holland America Lines, and Windstar Cruises. The company recently acquired majority stake in Cunard Cruise Lines and Seabourn Cruise Line. It also has a 50 percent stake in European-based Costa cruise lines.

The company's *Carnival Destiny* cruise liner is the world's largest ocean-going resort ship with a 3,400-guest capacity and a 1,050-member crew. First launched in 1996, the Destiny is valued at $400 million and weighs over 100,000 tons. It towers more than 200 feet above the water and spans a length of nearly three football fields.

Carnival's main cruise locations are the Caribbean and Alaska, although it also sails through a number of other areas around the world. In all, the company hosts more than two million cruise passengers per year.

In addition to its cruise ships, Carnival operates a tour business that markets sight-seeing tours and cruises to Alaska. It also operates 16 hotels in Alaska and the Canadian Yukon, two luxury dayboats offering tours of the glaciers of Alaska and the Yukon River, and 280 motor coaches used for sight-seeing and charters in Washington and Alaska. It also operates 13 private domed railcars on the Alaskan railroad between Anchorage and Fairbanks.

Along with its cruise line revenues, the company earns extra revenue from on-board activities such as casino gaming, liquor sales, gift shop sales, shore tours, and promotional advertising by merchants located in ports of call. The on-ship casinos feature slot machines, blackjack, craps, roulette, and stud poker.

Carnival Cruise Lines began humbly in 1972, when its only ship, the *Mardi Gras,* shoved off from the port of Miami for its maiden voyage and quickly ran aground on a sandbar. By 1974, the company was deeply in debt and near bankruptcy. The original parent company, American International Travel Service, sold the cruise line to Ted Arison for $1 and an assumed $5 million debt. Arison, who is considered the Carnival founder, turned the company around and added a second ship in 1975 and a third ship in 1978. It's been clear sailing for Carnival ever since.

The company has about 18,000 employees, including corporate staff and ship crew members. Carnival has about 4,000 shareholders. It has a market capitalization of about $26.4 billion.

EARNINGS PER SHARE GROWTH   ★ ★ ★ ★

Past five years: 150 percent (20 percent per year)
Past ten years: 300 percent (15 percent per year)

STOCK GROWTH

Past ten years: 800 percent (24.5 percent per year)
Dollar growth: $10,000 over ten years (including reinvested dividends) would have grown to $100,000.
Average annual compounded rate of return (including reinvested dividends): 26 percent

DIVIDEND

Dividend yield: 0.8 percent
Increased dividend: 11 consecutive years
Past five-year increase: 129 percent (18 percent per year)

CONSISTENCY ★ ★ ★ ★

Increased earnings per share: 14 consecutive years
Increased sales: 12 consecutive years

SHAREHOLDER PERKS

The company provides no dividend reinvestment and stock purchase plan.

CARNIVAL AT A GLANCE

Fiscal year ended: Nov. 30
Revenue and net income in $ millions

	1993	1994	1995	1996	1997	1998	5-Year Growth Avg. Annual (%)	Total (%)
Revenue ($)	1,557	1,806	1,998	2,213	2,448	3,009	14	93
Net income ($)	318	391	451	550	666	836	21	163
Earnings/share ($)	0.56	0.69	0.80	0.95	1.12	1.40	20	150
Dividends/share ($)	0.13	0.14	0.16	0.19	0.24	0.32	18	129
Dividend yield (%)	1.5	1.2	1.4	1.4	1.2	1.0	—	—
PE ratio range	13–22	14–19	13–17	12–17	14–25	14–35	—	—

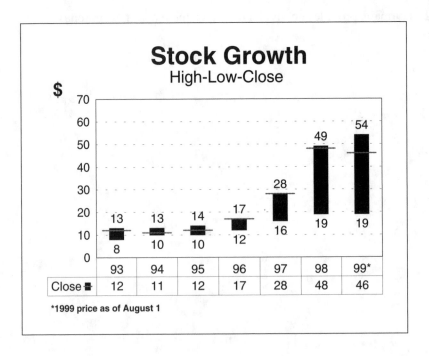

Stock Growth
High-Low-Close

	93	94	95	96	97	98	99*
Close	12	11	12	17	28	48	46

*1999 price as of August 1

19

Warner-Lambert Company

201 Tabor Road
Morris Plains, NJ 07950
973-540-2000
www.warner-lambert.com

Chairman and CEO: Melvin R. Goodes
President: Lodewijk J. R. deVink

Earnings Growth	★ ★
Stock Growth	★ ★ ★ ★
Dividend	★ ★
Consistency	★ ★ ★ ★
Shareholder Perks	★ ★
NYSE: WLA	**14 points**

Bad breath has been good business for Warner-Lambert. The company has made a mint on mints and other items intended to freshen the breath of consumers around the world. The company's product line includes Junior Mints, Freshen-Up, Trident, Dentyne, Certs, Listerine, Chewels, Chiclets, Clorets, Cinn*A*Burst, Mint*A*Burst, Clove, and Coolmint Listerine toothpaste.

The Morris Plains, New Jersey manufacturer is among the world leaders in chewing gum sales, breath fresheners, cough drops, and razors. It also manufactures a broad range of other over-the-counter and prescription medications.

Warner-Lambert has sales in more than 150 countries. International sales account for about 42 percent of the company's $10.2 billion in annual revenue.

Confectionery products account for about 18 percent of the company's total sales. In addition to its line of breath-freshening gums, the company also offers several other confectionery favorites, including Pom Poms, Sugar Daddy, Sugar Babies, and Beemans, Blackjack, and Bubblicious gums. The company also makes Halls cough drops and Celestial Seasonings Soothers.

Consumer health care products account for about 27 percent of total sales. In addition to its Listerine products, Warner-Lambert is also the maker of Rolaids, Lubriderm, Sudafed, Sinutab, Actifed, Benadryl, Anusol, Benylin, Effergrip denture adhesive, and Efferdent and Fresh 'N Brite denture cleaners. The company is also one of the world's leading razor makers, including the Wilkinson Sword and Schick brands.

Warner-Lambert's other key segment is pharmaceutical products, which accounts for 55 percent of its total revenue. The company produces a line of analgesics, anesthetics, anticonvulsants, anti-infectives, antihistamines, antiviral agents, bronchodilators, cardiovascular products, dermatologics, hemorrhoidal preparations, influenza vaccines, oral contraceptives, and other products. Its leading brand is Parke-Davis.

The company has about 41,000 employees and 48,000 shareholders. Warner-Lambert has a market capitalization of $55.7 billion.

EARNINGS PER SHARE GROWTH   ★ ★

Past five years: 91 percent (14 percent per year)
Past ten years: 252 percent (13.5 percent per year)

STOCK GROWTH   ★ ★ ★ ★

Past ten years: 750 percent (24 percent per year)
Dollar growth: $10,000 over ten years (including reinvested dividends) would have grown to $106,000.
Average annual compounded rate of return (including reinvested dividends): 27 percent

DIVIDEND

Dividend yield: 1.2 percent
Increased dividend: 23 consecutive years
Past five-year increase: 68 percent (11 percent per year)

CONSISTENCY ★ ★ ★ ★

Increased earnings per share: 12 consecutive years
Increased sales: 12 consecutive years

SHAREHOLDER PERKS

Good dividend reinvestment and stock purchase plan; voluntary stock
purchase plan allows contributions of $10 to $60,000 per year.

WARNER-LAMBERT AT A GLANCE

Fiscal year ended: Dec. 31
Revenue and net income in $ millions

	1993	1994	1995	1996	1997	1998	5-Year Growth Avg. Annual (%)	Total (%)
Revenue ($)	5,794	6,417	7,040	7,231	8,180	10,214	12	76
Net income ($)	645	694	657	694	870	1,254	14	94
Earnings/share ($)	0.80	0.86	0.90	0.95	1.04	1.48	14	91
Dividends/share ($)	0.38	0.41	0.43	0.46	0.51	0.64	11	68
Dividend yield (%)	3.3	3.4	3.1	2.4	1.3	1.0	—	—
PE ratio range	28–36	12–17	13–18	15–28	22–48	26–56	—	—

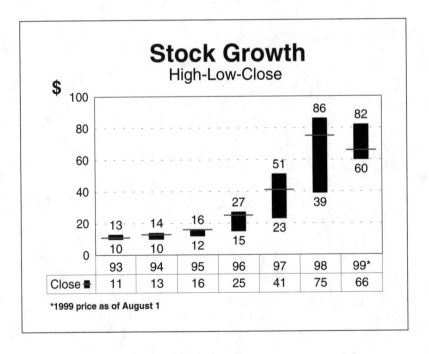

Stock Growth
High-Low-Close

	93	94	95	96	97	98	99*
Close	11	13	16	25	41	75	66

*1999 price as of August 1

The Gillette Company

Prudential Tower Building
Boston, MA 02199
617-421-7000
www.gillette.com

Chairman, President, and CEO:
Michael C. Hawley

Earnings Growth	★ ★
Stock Growth	★ ★ ★ ★
Dividend	★ ★ ★
Consistency	★ ★ ★
Shareholder Perks	★ ★
NYSE: G	**14 points**

Recognized most for its top-selling line of razor blades and shaving cream, The Gillette Company also leads the world in the sale of several other consumer staples, including toothbrushes, writing instruments, and alkaline batteries.

Gillette has long been the dominant producer of razors in both the United States and international markets. Its products account for about two-thirds of the total razor sales in the United States. With the introduction of its new triple-blade Mach3 shaver, Gillette has boosted its blades and razor sales to just over $3 billion a year worldwide. Razor sales account for about 30 percent of the company's $10.1 billion in total annual sales.

In addition to its Mach3, Gillette also offers the Sensor, SensorExcel, ContourPlus, and Agility razors.

The Boston-based operation has bought its way to the top of several other product categories through a series of major acquisitions. The latest was in 1996 when it acquired Duracell International, Inc., the maker of the world's top-selling alkaline battery. Duracell has sales in about 150 countries.

Gillette has long been focused on the global market, where it generates about 62 percent of its total revenue. The company has 50 manufacturing plants in 25 countries and markets its products in more than 200 countries and territories.

Gillette's other key segments include:

- **Toiletries** (12 percent of revenue). Gillette manufactures Right Guard, Gillette, and Soft & Dri deodorants, White Rain shampoo, Satin Care, Dry Idea, Epic Wave home permanents, Jafra skin care products, and Gillette shaving creams and gels.
- **Stationery products** (9 percent of revenue). Gillette is the world's leading manufacturer of writing instruments and correction fluid. It makes Paper Mate, Parker, Flair, Flexigrip, Dynagrip, and Waterman pens and Liquid Paper correction fluid.
- **Braun products** (17 percent of revenue). Gillette's German subsidiary is one of the leading manufacturers of electric shavers in both Europe and North America. The company also makes toasters, clocks, coffeemakers, food processors, and other household appliances.
- **Oral-B products** (6 percent of revenue). Oral-B is the leading marketer of toothbrushes in the United States and several international markets. It also manufactures dental floss and other dental care products.

Gillette was founded in 1903 by King C. Gillette, who introduced a safety razor with a compact brass shaving head and a sleek wooden handle. It came with 20 steel blades and sold for $5.

The company has about 43,000 employees and 28,500 shareholders. It has a market capitalization of about $57 billion.

EARNINGS PER SHARE GROWTH ★ ★

Past five years: 90 percent (14 percent per year)
Past ten years: 310 percent (15 percent per year)

STOCK GROWTH ★ ★ ★ ★

Past ten years: 1,080 percent (28 percent per year)
Dollar growth: $10,000 over ten years (including reinvested dividends) would have grown to $138,000.
Average annual compounded rate of return (including reinvested dividends): 30 percent

DIVIDEND ★ ★ ★

Dividend yield: 1.0 percent
Increased dividend: 21 consecutive years
Past five-year increase: 143 percent (20 percent per year)

CONSISTENCY ★ ★ ★

Increased earnings per share: nine of the past ten years
Increased sales: nine of the past ten years

SHAREHOLDER PERKS ★ ★

Good dividend reinvestment and stock purchase plan; voluntary stock purchase plan allows contributions of $100 to $120,000 a year.

Shareholders who attend the annual meeting receive an excellent selection of products. At a recent meeting, shareholder gifts included a Gillette Mach3 razor, dental floss, the new Roller Jell pen, and a pack of Duracell Ultra PowerCheck batteries.

GILLETTE AT A GLANCE

Fiscal year ended: Dec. 31
Revenue and net income in $ millions

	1993	1994	1995	1996	1997	1998	5-Year Growth Avg. Annual (%)	5-Year Growth Total (%)
Revenue ($)	5,411	6,070	6,795	9,698	10,062	10,056	13	86
Net income ($)	591	698	824	1,232	1,427	1,428	20	142
Earnings/share ($)	0.67	0.79	0.93	1.11	1.27	1.27	14	90
Dividends/share ($)	0.21	0.25	0.30	0.36	0.43	0.51	20	143
Dividend yield (%)	1.5	1.5	1.4	1.2	1.0	1.0	—	—
PE ratio range	25–33	17–23	18–29	28–46	28–42	37–65	—	—

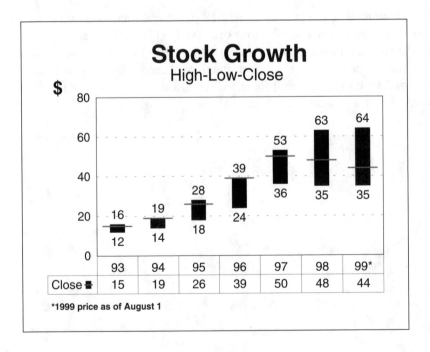

Stock Growth
High-Low-Close

	93	94	95	96	97	98	99*
Close	15	19	26	39	50	48	44

*1999 price as of August 1

Protective Life Corporation

Protective ▲

2801 Highway 280 South
Birmingham, AL 35223
205-879-9230
www.protective.com

Chairman and CEO: Drayton Nabers Jr.
President: John D. Johns

Earnings Growth	★ ★
Stock Growth	★ ★ ★ ★
Dividend	★ ★
Consistency	★ ★ ★ ★
Shareholder Perks	★ ★
NYSE: PL	**14 points**

Protective Life is a small, fast-growing insurance holding company that offers a broad range of insurance and investment products. The company has posted record earnings per share the past ten consecutive years.

Life insurance is far and away the company's biggest business segment, accounting for 50 percent of Protective's annual pretax operating income. The company sells premium term insurance, universal life, and variable universal life policies through a network of independent agents.

Protective also sells a variety of specialty insurance products. Its dental and consumer benefits division sells indemnity and prepaid dental policies and discounted fee-for-service dental programs. The division also sells group life and disability coverage. Protective also markets credit life and disability insurance policies to consumers through banks, consumer finance companies, and automobile dealers. Protective's specialty insurance group accounts for about 18 percent of pretax operating income.

The company's retirement savings and investment products division accounts for 23 percent of pretax operating income. The company markets guaranteed investment contracts to 401(k) and other qualified retirement savings plans, and it manages fixed and variable annuity products it markets through financial institutions and its own sales force.

Protective's other division is its "corporate and other" segment, which covers income earned from the company's investments. The division accounts for about 7 percent of pretax operating income.

The Birmingham, Alabama operation was founded in 1907. In addition to its principal operating subsidiary, Protective Life Insurance, the company operates several subsidiaries, including Protective Life and Annuity, CRC Protective Life, LTD, Empire General Life Assurance Corp., Financial Protection Marketing, DentiCare, ProEquities, United Dental Care, and West Coast Life.

Protective Life has about 2,500 employees and 2,000 shareholders. The company has a market capitalization of $2.3 billion.

EARNINGS PER SHARE GROWTH ★ ★

Past five years: 98 percent (14 percent per year)
Past ten years: 787 percent (24.5 percent per year)

STOCK GROWTH ★ ★ ★ ★

Past ten years: 1,035 percent (27.5 percent per year)
Dollar growth: $10,000 over ten years (including reinvested dividends) would have grown to $150,000.
Average annual compounded rate of return (including reinvested dividends): 31 percent

DIVIDEND ★ ★

Dividend yield: 1.3 percent
Increased dividend: eight consecutive years
Past five-year increase: 72 percent (11 percent per year)

CONSISTENCY

Increased earnings per share: ten consecutive years

SHAREHOLDER PERKS

Good dividend reinvestment and stock purchase plan; voluntary stock purchase plan allows contributions of $25 to $6,000 per quarter.

PROTECTIVE LIFE AT A GLANCE

Fiscal year ended: Dec. 31
Total income and net income in $ millions

	1993	1994	1995	1996	1997	1998	5-Year Growth Avg. Annual (%)	5-Year Growth Total (%)
Total income ($)	760	849	880	1,038	1,147	1,366	12	80
Net income ($)	57	70	77	89	112	131	18	130
Earnings/share ($)	1.03	1.29	1.34	1.47	1.78	2.04	14	98
Dividends/share ($)	0.25	0.28	0.31	0.35	0.39	0.43	11	72
Dividend yield (%)	2.6	2.6	2.4	1.9	1.6	1.2	—	—
PE ratio range	7–13	7–9	8–12	10–14	10–18	14–20	—	—

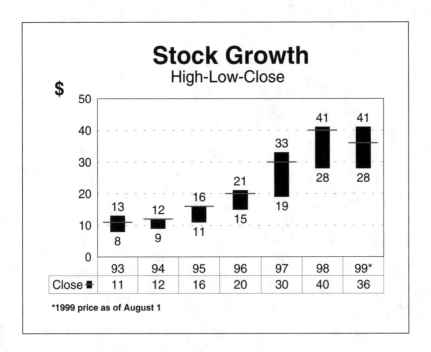

Stock Growth
High-Low-Close

	93	94	95	96	97	98	99*
Close	11	12	16	20	30	40	36

*1999 price as of August 1

M&T Bank Corporation

M&T Bank Corporation

One M&T Plaza
Buffalo, NY 14203
716-842-5445
www.mandtbank.com

Chairman: Robert J. Bennett
President and CEO: Robert G. Wilmers

Earnings Growth	★ ★
Stock Growth	★ ★ ★ ★
Dividend	★ ★
Consistency	★ ★ ★ ★
Shareholder Perks	★ ★
NYSE: MTB	**14 points**

Formerly known as First Empire State Corporation, M&T Bank Corporation has been one of the nation's fastest growing banking institutions. The Buffalo, New York operation is a holding company of banks in several states, including Pennsylvania, Ohio, Oregon, Utah, Colorado, Massachusetts, Washington, and its home state of New York.

The company does most of its business through two wholly owned banking subsidiaries, Manufacturers and Traders Trust Company and the M&T Bank, National Association.

M&T recently acquired ONBANcorp, a Syracuse, New York–based bank with 59 branch offices in the Syracuse, Rochester, and Albany areas and 19 branches in Pennsylvania.

In all, M&T operates more than 200 branch offices in eight states, although the core of its business is in upstate New York.

M&T offers the standard banking services such as savings, checking, and loan services for consumers, businesses, and other clients.

M&T also conducts business through a number of subsidiaries, including M&T Capital Corp., which provides equity capital and long-term credit to small businesses; M&T Credit Corp., which offers credit services for consumers; M&T Mortgage, which has offices in several states and specializes in residential home mortgage loans and mortgage services; M&T Financial, which specializes in capital equipment leasing; M&T Real Estate, which specializes in commercial real estate lending and servicing; and M&T Securities, which provides securities brokerage and advisory services for bank customers.

The company has established a solid presence in New York City, particularly in the area of multiple-unit housing financing.

The company's loan portfolio breaks down this way: commercial loans, 19 percent; commercial real estate, 58 percent; consumer, 16 percent; leases, 4 percent; and construction, 3 percent.

M&T has about 5,500 employees and 5,200 shareholders. It has a market capitalization of about $4.2 billion.

EARNINGS PER SHARE GROWTH ★ ★

Past five years: 101 percent (16 percent per year)
Past ten years: 364 percent (16.5 percent per year)

STOCK GROWTH ★ ★ ★ ★

Past ten years: 796 percent (24.5 percent per year)
Dollar growth: $10,000 over ten years (including reinvested dividends) would have grown to $100,000.
Average annual compounded rate of return (including reinvested dividends): 26 percent

DIVIDEND

Dividend yield: 0.8 percent
Increased dividend: More than 18 consecutive years
Past five-year increase: 100 percent (15 percent per year)

CONSISTENCY

Increased earnings per share: 11 consecutive years

SHAREHOLDER PERKS

Dividend reinvestment and stock purchase plan; voluntary stock purchase plan allows contributions of $10 to $1,000 per quarter.

M&T BANK AT A GLANCE

Fiscal year ended: Dec. 31
Total assets and net income in $ millions

	1993	1994	1995	1996	1997	1998	5-Year Growth Avg. Annual (%)	Total (%)
Total assets ($)	10,365	10,529	11,956	12,944	14,003	20,584	15	99
Net income ($)	102	117	131	151	176	222	17	118
Earnings/share ($)	13.87	16.35	18.79	21.31	25.26	27.92	16	101
Dividends/share ($)	1.90	2.20	2.50	2.80	3.20	3.80	15	100
Dividend yield (%)	1.3	1.5	1.4	1.1	0.9	0.8	—	—
PE ratio range	9–11	8–10	7–11	9–13	11–18	15–21	—	—

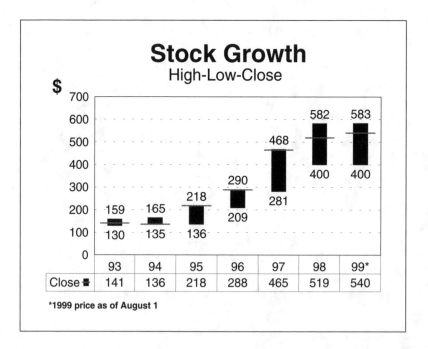

Stock Growth
High-Low-Close

$	93	94	95	96	97	98	99*
Close	141	136	218	288	465	519	540

*1999 price as of August 1

Interpublic Group of Companies, Inc.

THE INTERPUBLIC GROUP OF COMPANIES, INC.
Partners in Global Communications

1271 Avenue of the Americas
New York, NY 10020
212-399-8000
www.interpublic.com

Chairman, President, and CEO: Philip H. Geier, Jr.

Earnings Growth	★ ★
Stock Growth	★ ★ ★ ★
Dividend	★ ★
Consistency	★ ★ ★ ★
Shareholder Perks	★ ★
NYSE: IPG	**14 points**

Interpublic Group is the imagemaker behind some of world's biggest commercial icons, including Coca-Cola, Unilever, Nestlé, and Chevrolet. The agency has been pitching General Motors cars since 1916.

Interpublic is the parent company of a worldwide network of more than 40 agencies and related companies involved in producing and placing advertising. It is the world's second largest advertising group.

McCann-Erickson Worldwide Advertising, which is the crown jewel of the Interpublic kingdom, has operations in 110 countries and agencies in 67 countries. It handles more global advertising accounts than any other agency.

Interpublic's other leading agencies include Ammirati Puris Lintas, The Lowe Group, Campbell Mithun Esty, Daily and Associates, Draft-Worldwide, Allied Communications Group, and Hill, Holliday, Connors, Cosmopulos.

In all, Interpublic Group has more than 4,000 advertising clients. The New York–based operation is the world's second largest organization of advertising agencies. About half of the company's income comes from foreign operations.

Interpublic has done advertising campaigns for Levi-Strauss, Nestle, GMAC, Camel cigarettes, L'Oreal, Gillette, Mennen, Black & Decker, Delta faucets, Johnson & Johnson, Maybelline, Goodyear, Exxon, Casio, Microsoft, and Del Monte fruits. Interpublic gave Chevrolet the "Heartbeat of America," deemed Coke "the Real Thing," and made UPS the "tightest ship in the shipping business."

In addition to advertising creations, Interpublic agencies plan campaigns and place advertising on TV and radio and in magazines, newspapers, and direct response mailers. It also offers related services such as corporate identity promotions, graphic design, management consulting, marketing research, sales promotion, interactive services, sales meetings and events, and brand equity promotion.

Interpublic was founded in 1902 by A.W. Erickson (and in 1911 by Harrison K. McCann). It was first incorporated in 1930 as McCann-Erickson and has been operating under the name Interpublic Group since 1961.

The agency has about 22,000 employees and 3,500 shareholders. It has a market capitalization of $10.8 billion.

EARNINGS PER SHARE GROWTH ★ ★

Past five years: 106 percent (16 percent per year)
Past ten years: 268 percent (14 percent per year)

STOCK GROWTH ★ ★ ★ ★

Past ten years: 654 percent (22.5 percent per year)
Dollar growth: $10,000 over ten years (including reinvested dividends) would have grown to $86,000.
Average annual compounded rate of return (including reinvested dividends): 24 percent

DIVIDEND

Dividend yield: 0.9 percent
Increased dividend: 15 consecutive years
Past five-year increase: 76 percent (12 percent per year)

CONSISTENCY

Increased earnings per share: 17 consecutive years
Increased sales: nine of the past ten years

SHAREHOLDER PERKS ★ ★

Good dividend reinvestment and stock purchase plan; voluntary stock
purchase plan allows contributions of $10 to $3,000 per quarter.

INTERPUBLIC GROUP AT A GLANCE

Fiscal year ended: Dec. 31
Revenue and net income in $ millions

	1993	1994	1995	1996	1997	1998	5-Year Growth Avg. Annual (%)	Total (%)
Revenue ($)	1,794	1,984	2,180	2,538	3,126	3,969	17	121
Net income ($)	125	152	168	205	239	331	21	165
Earnings/share ($)	1.11	1.34	1.43	1.71	1.90	2.29	16	106
Dividends/share ($)	0.33	0.37	0.41	0.45	0.50	0.58	12	76
Dividend yield (%)	1.6	1.7	1.6	1.5	1.2	0.7	—	—
PE ratio range	14–21	17–23	19–25	16–20	20–34	20–35	—	—

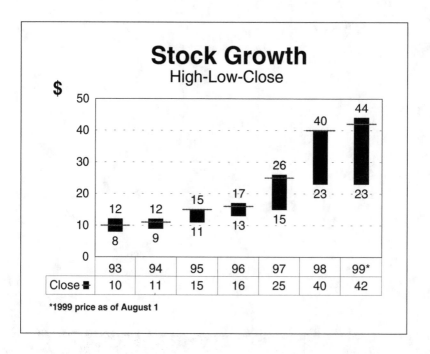

Stock Growth
High-Low-Close

	93	94	95	96	97	98	99*
Close	10	11	15	16	25	40	42

*1999 price as of August 1

Donaldson Company, Inc.

1400 West 94th Street
Minneapolis, MN 55431
612-887-3131
www.donaldson.com

Chairman, President, and CEO:
William G. Van Dyke

Earnings Growth	★ ★ ★
Stock Growth	★ ★ ★
Dividend	★ ★
Consistency	★ ★ ★ ★
Shareholder Perks	★ ★
NYSE: DCI	**14 points**

Dust is the enemy. So are grime, slime, and flying particles. But it's a battle that the Donaldson Company usually wins. The Minneapolis-based operation manufactures filters and purifiers for trucks, turbines, and a broad range of industrial and agricultural equipment.

The company's biggest market is engine filtration and exhaust products, which account for about 36 percent of its total revenue. Donaldson makes liquid filters, air cleaners and accessories, and exhaust products such as mufflers for the construction, industrial, mining, agricultural, and transportation markets.

Its other key segments include:

- **Dust collection** (16 percent of revenue). The company's Torit Products division makes dust, fume, and mist collectors for manufacturing and assembly plants.
- **Gas turbine systems** (9 percent of revenue). Donaldson manufactures static and pulse-clean air filter systems, replacement filters, exhaust silencers, chiller coils, and anti-icing systems for turbine engines used in the electric power generation and the oil and gas industries.
- **High purity products** (9 percent of revenue). The firm makes specialized air filtration systems for computer disk drives, aircraft and automotive cabins, industrial and hospital cleanrooms, business machines, room air cleaners, personal respirators, and for air emission control.
- **Aftermarket** (30 percent of revenue). The company makes a variety of filtration products for several aftermarket distributors, including automotive jobbers, fleets, national buying groups, specialty installers, and hydraulic distributors.

Donaldson is well positioned overseas, with 11 foreign manufacturing plants and joint ventures in India, China, and Indonesia, and subsidiaries in the Netherlands, France, Italy, Japan, Hong Kong, Mexico, South Africa, and Australia. About 32 percent of its $940 million in annual revenue comes from foreign sales.

Donaldson was founded in 1915 by Frank Donaldson, whose first filter was a tin can and Spanish moss air filter he made for a farmer's tractor. By the late 1920s, Donaldson had developed a spark-arresting muffler designed to cut the incidence of crop fires from engine sparks. From that beginning, the company expanded to the wide range of filter systems it offers today.

Donaldson has about 6,900 employees and 1,500 shareholders. It has a market capitalization of about $1 billion.

EARNINGS PER SHARE GROWTH   ★ ★ ★

Past five years: 124 percent (17 percent per year)
Past ten years: 307 percent (15 percent per year)

STOCK GROWTH ★ ★ ★

Past ten years: 547 percent (21 percent per year)
Dollar growth: $10,000 over ten years (including reinvested dividends) would have grown to $73,000.
Average annual compounded rate of return (including reinvested dividends): 22 percent

DIVIDEND ★ ★

Dividend yield: 1.1 percent
Increased dividend: 11 consecutive years
Past five-year increase: 100 percent (15 percent per year)

CONSISTENCY ★ ★ ★ ★

Increased earnings per share: 11 consecutive years
Increased sales: 13 consecutive years

SHAREHOLDER PERKS ★ ★

Good dividend reinvestment and stock purchase plan; voluntary stock purchase plan allows contributions of $10 to $1,000 per month.

DONALDSON AT A GLANCE

Fiscal year ended: July 31
Revenue and net income in $ millions

	1993	1994	1995	1996	1997	1998	5-Year Growth Avg. Annual (%)	Total (%)
Revenue ($)	533	594	704	759	833	940	12	76
Net income ($)	28	32	39	43	51	57	15	102
Earnings/share ($)	0.51	0.59	0.73	0.84	0.99	1.14	17	124
Dividends/share ($)	0.10	0.13	0.14	0.15	0.18	0.20	15	100
Dividend yield (%)	1.2	1.1	1.2	1.2	1.1	0.9	—	—
PE ratio range	16–22	17–22	16–19	14–20	15–28	12–23	—	—

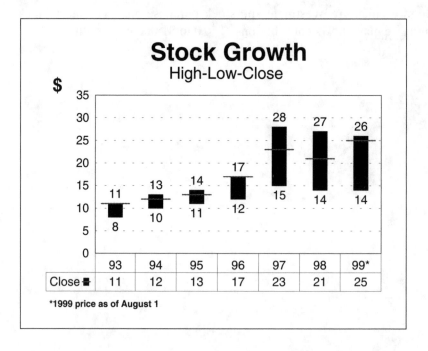

Stock Growth
High-Low-Close

	93	94	95	96	97	98	99*
Close	11	12	13	17	23	21	25

*1999 price as of August 1

Illinois Tool Works, Inc.

3600 West Lake Avenue
Glenview, IL 60025
847-724-7500
www.itwinc.com

Chairman, President, and CEO:
W. James Farrell

Earnings Growth	★ ★ ★ ★
Stock Growth	★ ★ ★
Dividend	★ ★
Consistency	★ ★ ★
Shareholder Perks	★ ★
NYSE: ITW	**14 points**

Illinois Tool Works (ITW) operates 400 separate business divisions that churn out a wide range of engineered goods, such as nails, nuts, bolts, adhesives, resealable packaging, and electronic component packaging. The company sells its products primarily to companies in the automotive, construction, and manufacturing industries.

ITW has established a solid track record of growth, with increased earnings per share 11 of the past 12 years.

The company's 400 business units are small and decentralized, operating without stringent controls from the parent company. ITW breaks its operations into four key segments: (1) engineered products–North America, which makes up 31 percent of the company's $5.6 billion in annual revenue; (2) engineered products–international (16 percent); (3) specialty systems–North America (35 percent); and (4) specialty systems–international (18 percent).

The company has grown through a very aggressive acquisition policy. ITW generally gives its division a high level of autonomy, allowing them to maintain the same name, management staff, and product line. ITW simply tries to help the acquired divisions increase their earnings and cut costs. "We don't even require them to have ITW on their letterhead or their brochures," says company Chairman W. James Farrell in a recent media interview. "Our customers know us as those brand names—they don't know us as ITW. We're not trying to make everybody look like everybody else."

ITW has operations in about 35 countries. Its international operations account for about 34 percent of total revenue.

In addition to fasteners, adhesives, and packaging, the company makes specialty equipment for such applications as industrial spray coating, quality measurement, and static control. In addition to its core customer base of automotive, construction, and industrial companies, ITW also markets products to food and beverage producers, paper products makers, and electronics, consumer durables, and industrial capital goods manufacturers.

Founded in 1912, ITW went public with its initial stock offering in 1973. The company has about 29,000 employees and 4,500 shareholders. It has a market capitalization of about $16 billion.

EARNINGS PER SHARE GROWTH   ★ ★ ★ ★

Past five years: 190 percent (24 percent per year)
Past ten years: 299 percent (15 percent per year)

STOCK GROWTH

Past ten years: 524 percent (20 percent per year)
Dollar growth: $10,000 over ten years (including reinvested dividends) would have grown to $67,000.
Average annual compounded rate of return (including reinvested dividends): 21 percent

DIVIDEND

Dividend yield: 0.9 percent
Increased dividend: 15 consecutive years
Past five-year increase: 116 percent (16.5 percent per year)

CONSISTENCY ★ ★ ★

Increased earnings per share: nine of the past ten years
Increased sales: 15 consecutive years

SHAREHOLDER PERKS ★ ★

Good dividend reinvestment and stock purchase plan; voluntary stock purchase plan allows contributions of $25 to $5,000 per quarter.

ILLINOIS TOOL WORKS AT A GLANCE

Fiscal year ended: Dec. 31
Revenue and net income in $ millions

	1993	1994	1995	1996	1997	1998	5-Year Growth Avg. Annual (%)	5-Year Growth Total (%)
Revenue ($)	3,159	3,461	4,152	4,997	5,220	5,648	12	79
Net income ($)	207	278	388	486	587	673	27	225
Earnings/share ($)	0.92	1.23	1.65	1.97	2.33	2.67	24	190
Dividends/share ($)	0.25	0.28	0.31	0.36	0.46	0.54	16	116
Dividend yield (%)	1.3	1.4	1.2	1.0	1.0	0.9	—	—
PE ratio range	18–22	15–19	12–20	13–22	16–26	17–27	—	—

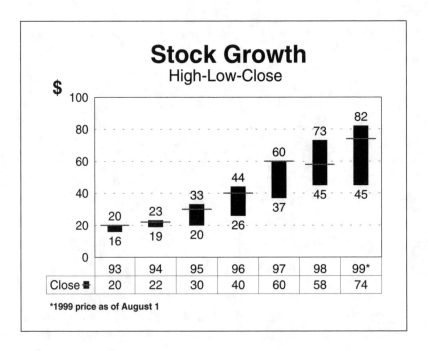

Dollar General Corp.

104 Woodmont Boulevard, Suite 500
Nashville, TN 37205
615-783-2000
www.dollargeneral.com

Chairman and CEO: Cal Turner, Jr.

Earnings Growth	★ ★ ★
Stock Growth	★ ★ ★
Dividend	★
Consistency	★ ★ ★
Shareholder Perks	
NYSE: DG	**13 points**

Dollar General has become one of the fastest growing retailers in America by filling a gaping niche in the market that Wal-Mart and Kmart have left largely unattended. While the large discounters are quietly fleeing to the suburbs to attract a more affluent customer base, Dollar General is making its stand in small towns, urban strip malls, and poorer neighborhoods closer to the center of town.

The Nashville-based convenience discount retailer has smaller stores—less than one-tenth the size of a typical Wal-Mart—but it still offers low prices on a wide range of merchandise. The stores feature both name brand and generic products, including household items, foods, and toiletries. They offer more than 1,000 items for $1 or less.

A recent flyer from Dollar General advertised plastic chairs for $3.50 a piece, planters for $1, knit shirts for $5, sandals for $3.50, a garden hose for $5, a four-pack of light bulbs for $1, and dozens of food products, cleaning supplies, towels, health and beauty aids, and other household items at discount prices.

Dollar General has about 3,700 stores in 24 states and has been opening about 500 new stores each year. Most of its stores are located in the South, East, and Midwest. It has 432 stores in Texas, 214 in Tennessee, 185 in Florida, and 173 in Kentucky. The company restocks its stores at least once a week, facilitated by its seven distribution centers scattered throughout its primary market.

Dollar General was founded in 1939 by the father and grandfather of current chairman and CEO Cal Turner, Jr. At first, their company, J. L. Turner and Son, worked as wholesalers selling basic dry goods to stores in the Kentucky area. They opened their first retail store in 1946, initially to unload an oversupply of ladies lingerie. By 1955, the company had grown to 35 stores. The Turners introduced their dollar store concept in 1956. Its marketing slogan, "Nothing over a dollar," helped pack the aisles with curious bargain hunters. Over the next decade, the chain grew to more than 250 stores.

Dollar General has about 28,000 employees and 4,000 shareholders. The company has a market capitalization of $7.9 billion.

EARNINGS PER SHARE GROWTH ★ ★ ★ ★

Past five years: 254 percent (29 percent per year)
Past ten years: 1,699 percent (33 percent per year)

STOCK GROWTH ★ ★ ★ ★

Past ten years: 3,233 percent (42 percent per year)
Dollar growth: $10,000 over ten years (including reinvested dividends) would have grown to $355,000.
Average annual compounded rate of return (including reinvested dividends): 43.5 percent

DIVIDEND ★

Dividend yield: 0.4 percent
Increased dividend: six consecutive years
Past five-year increase: 250 percent (29 percent per year)

CONSISTENCY

Increased earnings per share: 12 consecutive years
Increased sales: 12 consecutive years

SHAREHOLDER PERKS

The company offers no dividend reinvestment and stock purchase plan.

DOLLAR GENERAL AT A GLANCE

Fiscal year ended: Jan. 31
Revenue and net income in $ millions

	1994	1995	1996	1997	1998	1999	5-Year Growth Avg. Annual (%)	Total (%)
Revenue ($)	1,449	1,764	2,134	2,627	3,219	3,221	17	122
Net income ($)	49	74	88	115	145	182	30	274
Earnings/share ($)	0.24	0.35	0.41	0.53	0.67	0.85	29	254
Dividends/share ($)	0.04	0.05	0.07	0.08	0.10	0.14	29	250
Dividend yield (%)	0.7	0.8	0.7	0.7	0.7	0.6	—	—
PE ratio range	12–31	15–23	13–23	10–22	15–32	20–37	—	—

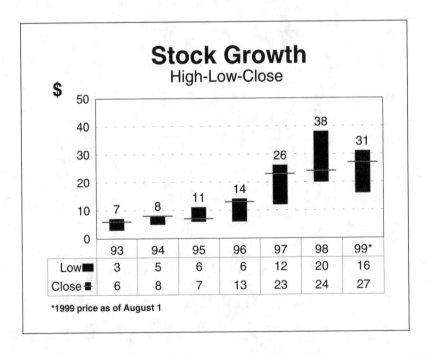

Stock Growth
High-Low-Close

$	93	94	95	96	97	98	99*
Low	3	5	6	6	12	20	16
Close	6	8	7	13	23	24	27

*1999 price as of August 1

Omnicom Group, Inc.

Omnicom

437 Madison Avenue
New York, NY 10022
212-415-3600
www.omnicomny.com

Chairman: Bruce Crawford
President and CEO: John D. Wren

Earnings Growth	★ ★ ★ ★
Stock Growth	★ ★ ★ ★
Dividend	★
Consistency	★ ★ ★ ★
Shareholder Perks	
NYSE: OMC	**13 points**

Got milk? You can thank Omnicom Group for that advertising master-piece for the National Dairy Association.

Gonna be awhile? Grab a Snickers. That's also Omnicom. Bud-weiser's Louie the Lizard–that's Omnicom, too. The agency also created the flying geese commercial for PepsiCo that was rated the most popular ad of the 1998 Super Bowl. At the recent Clio awards, Omnicom's leading subsidiary, BBDO Worldwide, dominated the event by winning 58 awards.

Omnicom is the world's largest advertising group, based on billings. Its BBDO subsidiary has 291 offices in 73 countries.

Another Omnicom subsidiary, DDB Needham Worldwide, has 206 offices in 96 countries. Among its clients are Volkswagen, Compaq Computer, U.S. West, Epson, Polo Ralph Lauren, Merck, and Heinz Weight Watchers.

Omnicom is also the parent company of TBWA Worldwide, which has 136 offices in 63 countries, and Goodby Silverstein & Partners, which counts among its clients Mattel, Intel, Pacific Bell, Breyer's, Hewlett Packard, Nike, Pepsi, and Budweiser.

Omnicom also owns a number of other advertising and public relations firms. The New York–based operation offers a wide range of advertising and marketing services, including creation and production of advertising, marketing consultation, strategic media planning and buying, financial and business-to-business advertising, directory advertising, health care communications, managed care consultancy, recruitment communications, branding consultancy, digital communications, and contract publishing.

The company also offers direct database marketing, field marketing, integrated promotional marketing, public affairs, corporate and financial public relations, reputation management, sports and event marketing, telemarketing, and Internet and digital media development.

With offices and customers worldwide, Omnicom generates about 50 percent of its revenue from its international operations.

The company has 36,000 employees and 3,700 shareholders. It has a market capitalization of $12.5 billion.

EARNINGS PER SHARE GROWTH ★ ★ ★ ★

Past five years: 140 percent (19 percent per year)
Past ten years: 320 percent (15.5 percent per year)

STOCK GROWTH ★ ★ ★ ★

Past ten years: 1,221 percent (29.5 percent per year)
Dollar growth: $10,000 over ten years (including reinvested dividends) would have grown to $141,000.
Average annual compounded rate of return (including reinvested dividends): 32 percent

DIVIDEND ★

Dividend yield: 0.9 percent
Increased dividend: four consecutive years
Past five-year increase: 71 percent (11.5 percent per year)

CONSISTENCY ★ ★ ★ ★

Increased earnings per share: 13 consecutive years
Increased sales: 12 consecutive years

SHAREHOLDER PERKS

The company does not offer a dividend reinvestment and stock purchase plan, nor does it provide other shareholder perks.

OMNICOM GROUP AT A GLANCE

Fiscal year ended: Dec. 31
Revenue and net income in $ millions

	1993	1994	1995	1996	1997	1998	5-Year Growth Avg. Annual (%)	Total (%)
Revenue ($)	1,517	1,756	2,258	2,642	3,125	4,092	22	170
Net income ($)	85	108	140	176	222	285	27	235
Earnings/share ($)	0.70	0.79	0.95	1.15	1.37	1.68	19	140
Dividends/share ($)	0.31	0.31	0.33	0.37	0.45	0.53	11	71
Dividend yield (%)	2.9	2.5	2.2	1.7	1.5	1.0	—	—
PE ratio range	18–23	14–17	13–20	15–22	16–30	22–34	—	—

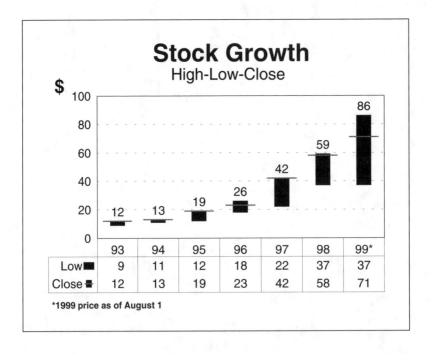

Stock Growth
High-Low-Close

	93	94	95	96	97	98	99*
Low	9	11	12	18	22	37	37
Close	12	13	19	23	42	58	71

*1999 price as of August 1

Walgreen Company

Walgreens

200 Wilmot Road
Deerfield, IL 60015
847-940-2500
www.walgreens.com

Chairman: Charles R. Walgreen III
CEO: L. Daniel Jorndt
President: David W. Bernauer

Earnings Growth	★ ★
Stock Growth	★ ★ ★ ★
Dividend	★
Consistency	★ ★ ★ ★
Shareholder Perks	★ ★
NYSE: WAG	**13 points**

Walgreen's target market is growing older—and that's just fine with the Chicago-based retailer. Consumers over 50 tend to use more prescriptions and over-the-counter medications, a trend that should help Walgreen continue to grow. Americans also are living longer, which means Walgreen is keeping its best customers for more years.

With nearly 3,000 stores across America, Walgreen is the nation's largest drugstore chain. The company plans to double that figure to 6,000 stores by 2010. Walgreen is committed to opening an average of one store a day—at least 365 per year—for the foreseeable future.

The company's popularity with consumers is the result in large part of Walgreen's focus on service and selection. Its nationwide computer database allows customers to refill their prescriptions at any Walgreen's store across the country. And to make it even easier, the company has added drive-through windows at more than 1,200 stores that allow customers to pick up prescriptions without leaving their car.

The company also has been pulling its stores out of the big shopping malls—where parking and access can be difficult—and relocating them at freestanding locations that provide quicker, easier access for busy consumers.

Walgreen's stores average about 10,000 square feet per store and carry a wide range of merchandise, including clocks, calculators, jewelry, artwork, lunch buckets, wastebaskets, coffeemakers, mixers, telephones, tape decks, and TV sets, along with the usual line of cosmetics, toiletries, and tobacco. Many Walgreen's also carry dairy products, frozen foods, and a large selection of other grocery items.

The company's newest stores are more than 13,000 square feet and often include pharmacy waiting areas, consultation windows, fragrance bars, and one-hour photofinishing services.

Prescription drugs account for 50 percent of the company's $15.3 billion in annual revenue. Nonprescription drugs account for 12 percent; liquor and beverages, 5 percent; cosmetics and toiletries, 8 percent; and general merchandise, 25 percent.

Walgreen's greatest concentration of stores is around its Chicago home base, with 330 stores in Illinois, 119 in Wisconsin, and 103 in Indiana. Other leading areas are Florida, with 412 stores; Arizona, 137; California, 196; Texas, 261; Massachusetts, 73; Minnesota, 64; Missouri, 82; and Tennessee, 85.

All of the company's stores are linked by satellite dish to Walgreen's home office, enabling the company to track inventory, monitor sales levels, and provide prescription histories for Walgreen's customers.

Walgreen was founded in 1901 by Charles Walgreen. The company has posted 23 consecutive years of record sales and earnings.

Walgreen has 90,000 employees and 45,000 shareholders. It has a market capitalization of $27 billion.

EARNINGS PER SHARE GROWTH   ★ ★

Past five years: 104 percent (15 percent per year)
Past ten years: 292 percent (15 percent per year)

STOCK GROWTH

Past ten years: 1,020 percent (27 percent per year)
Dollar growth: $10,000 over ten years (including reinvested dividends) would have grown to $125,000.
Average annual compounded rate of return (including reinvested dividends): 29 percent

DIVIDEND

Dividend yield: 0.6 percent
Increased dividend: 12 consecutive years
Past five-year increase: 63 percent (10 percent per year)

CONSISTENCY

Increased earnings per share: 23 consecutive years
Increased sales: 23 consecutive years

SHAREHOLDER PERKS ★ ★

The company offers a direct purchase plan with a minimum $50 initial investment (plus a $10 new account fee). Dividend reinvestment and stock purchase plan allows voluntary contributions of $50 to $60,000 per year.

Shareholders who attend the Walgreen annual meeting usually receive one or two Walgreen products, such as vitamins or other personal care products.

WALGREEN AT A GLANCE

Fiscal year ended: Aug. 31
Revenue and net income in $ millions

	1993	1994	1995	1996	1997	1998	5-Year Growth Avg. Annual (%)	5-Year Growth Total (%)
Revenue ($)	8,295	9,235	10,395	11,778	13,363	15,307	13	84
Net income ($)	245	282	321	372	437	514	16	110
Earnings/share ($)	0.25	0.29	0.33	0.38	0.44	0.51	15	104
Dividends/share ($)	0.08	0.09	0.10	0.11	0.12	0.13	10	63
Dividend yield (%)	1.5	1.7	1.7	1.4	1.1	0.7	—	—
PE ratio range	15–22	15–20	17–24	19–29	22–38	27–56	—	—

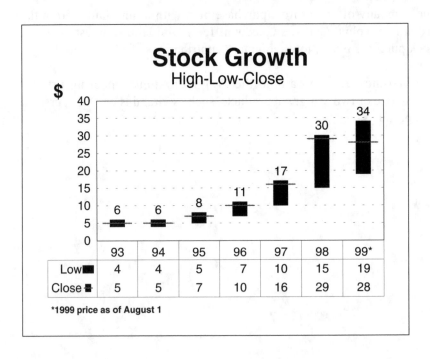

Stock Growth
High-Low-Close

	93	94	95	96	97	98	99*
Low■	4	4	5	7	10	15	19
Close ▆	5	5	7	10	16	29	28

*1999 price as of August 1

Wal-Mart Stores, Inc.

WAL★MART ®

702 SW Eighth Street
Bentonville, AR 72716
501-273-4000
www.wal-mart.com

Chairman: S. Robson Walton
President and CEO: David D. Glass

Earnings Growth	★ ★
Stock Growth	★ ★ ★ ★
Dividend	★
Consistency	★ ★ ★ ★
Shareholder Perks	★ ★
NYSE: WMT	**13 points**

Now that Wal-Mart has established a prominent presence across America—from rural towns to major urban centers—the company has begun to push aggressively into the international market. The Bentonville, Arkansas retailer has opened more than 700 stores outside the United States.

Most of the expansion has come just across the border. In Mexico, Wal-Mart operates about 350 discount stores, 27 Supercenters, and 28 Sam's Club stores. In Canada, it has 144 discount stores. The company also has 9 stores in Argentina, 8 stores in Brazil, 13 in Puerto Rico, 3 in China, and 21 in Germany.

Wal-Mart is the world's largest retail chain, with total annual revenue of $139 billion. The company has nearly 3,500 stores in all, including 2,421 Wal-Mart discount stores, 502 Supercenters, and 483 Sam's Club warehouse stores.

Wal-Mart's Supercenter stores are its fastest growing segment. Wal-Mart opened its first Supercenter in 1989 and has added about 50 new stores a year ever since. The Supercenters range in size from about 170,000 to 200,000 square feet and offer food, general merchandise, and a wide range of services, including pharmacy, dry cleaning, portrait studios, photo finishing, hair salons, and optical shops.

Wal-Mart's product sales break down this way: soft goods (apparel, towels, sheets, etc.), 21 percent of sales; hard goods (hardware, housewares, auto supplies, and small appliances), 23 percent; grocery, candy, and tobacco, 11 percent; pharmaceuticals, 9 percent; sporting goods and toys, 8 percent; health and beauty aids, 7 percent; records and electronics, 9 percent; stationery, 5 percent; shoes, 2 percent; and jewelry, 2 percent.

The company has posted consistent earnings and revenue growth for many years, including 29 consecutive years of record sales and earnings dating back to 1969, the year the company went public.

Wal-Mart was founded in 1962 by Sam Walton, who ultimately became a legend of American business and the nation's richest man before his death in 1992. Walton entered the retailing business in 1945 when he opened a Ben Franklin variety store franchise in Newport, Arkansas. His first Wal-Mart store (called Wal-Mart Discount City) was opened in Rogers, Arkansas, in 1962.

Walton achieved his early success largely by locating stores in rural locations like Rogers, where there was no competition from other discounters. The retailer's "everyday low prices" attracted throngs of shoppers wherever the new stores appeared. The company has been able to keep its prices low by buying its merchandise in large volume and turning it over quickly, incurring a minimum of overhead in the process.

Wal-Mart stores have since invaded the urban areas en masse, where they compete toe-to-toe with Target, Kmart, and the other discounters. While the competition is stiffer, the urban-based Wal-Marts have still proven very profitable.

Wal-Mart has 875,000 employees and 260,000 shareholders. The company has a market capitalization of $205 billion.

EARNINGS PER SHARE GROWTH ★ ★

Past five years: 94 percent (14 percent per year)
Past ten years: 421 percent (18 percent per year)

STOCK GROWTH ★ ★ ★ ★

Past ten years: 921 percent (26 percent per year)
Dollar growth: $10,000 over ten years (including reinvested dividends) would have grown to about $105,000.
Average annual compounded rate of return (including reinvested dividends): 26.5 percent

DIVIDEND ★

Dividend yield: 0.4 percent
Increased dividend: 21 consecutive years
Past five-year increase: 129 percent (18 percent per year)

CONSISTENCY ★ ★ ★ ★

Increased earnings per share: 29 consecutive years (every year since going public in 1969)
Increased sales: 29 consecutive years

SHAREHOLDER PERKS ★ ★

Excellent dividend reinvestment and stock purchase program; voluntary stock purchase plan allows contributions of $50 to $150,000 per year. Investors also may elect to have $25 a month (or more) automatically deducted from their checking account and invested in Wal-Mart stock. Persons who are not shareholders also may enroll in the program, either by investing as little as $250 or by authorizing automatic monthly withdrawals of at least $25.

WAL-MART AT A GLANCE

Fiscal year ended: Jan. 31
Revenue and net income in $ millions

	1994	1995	1996	1997	1998	1999	5-Year Growth Avg. Annual (%)	Total (%)
Revenue ($)	67,345	82,494	93,627	104,859	119,300	139,208	15	107
Net income ($)	2,333	2,681	2,740	3,056	3,526	4,583	14	96
Earnings/share ($)	0.51	0.58	0.60	0.67	0.78	0.99	14	94
Dividends/share ($)	0.07	0.09	0.10	0.11	0.14	0.16	18	129
Dividend yield (%)	0.5	0.7	0.8	0.9	0.8	0.5	—	—
PE ratio range	23–36	18–25	17–23	14–21	14–27	19–42	—	—

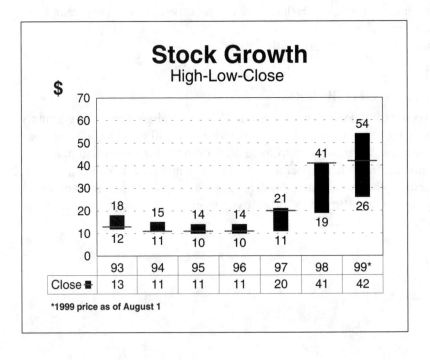

Stock Growth
High-Low-Close

	93	94	95	96	97	98	99*
Close	13	11	11	11	20	41	42

*1999 price as of August 1

Freddie Mac

8200 Jones Branch Drive
McLean, VA 22102
703-903-3725
www.freddiemac.com

Chairman and CEO: Leland C. Brendsel
President: David W. Glenn

Earnings Growth	★ ★ ★
Stock Growth	★ ★ ★ ★
Dividend	★ ★
Consistency	★ ★ ★ ★
Shareholder Perks	
NYSE: FRE	**13 points**

Known as Freddie Mac, the Federal Home Loan Mortgage Corporation has been helping consumers achieve the American dream of home ownership for 29 years. During that period, Freddie Mac has indirectly financed one out of every six home purchases in America.

Freddie Mac was established by Congress in 1970 to provide a continuous flow of funds for residential mortgages by buying mortgage loans and mortgage-related securities in the secondary market.

Congress stipulated four mandates for Freddie Mac: (1) to provide stability in the secondary market for residential mortgages; (2) to respond appropriately to the private capital market; (3) to provide ongoing assistance to the secondary market for residential mortgages—including low- and moderate-income families; and (4) to promote access to mortgage credit throughout the United States by increasing the liquidity of mortgage investments and improving the distribution of investment capital available for residential mortgage financing.

Freddie Mac purchases residential mortgages and mortgage-related securities from lenders, other mortgage sellers, and securities dealers. To fund its activities, the company sells mortgage-related securities, and debt and equity securities.

The McLean, Virginia operation has been very profitable, posting a return on equity in excess of 20 percent for 17 consecutive years.

In all, Freddie Mac has financed homes for 23 million families, including nearly three million homes a year in recent years.

Through its activities, Freddie Mac helps facilitate home purchases by less affluent buyers. The company offers special mortgages designed to help homebuyers who need assistance with down payments and closing costs. It also sets underwriting guidelines to help lenders work with government agencies, nonprofit organizations, and other housing finance agencies to create secondary financing programs for potential borrowers. Freddie Mac tries to establish public-private relationships designed to increase access to mortgage credit for low- to moderate-income and minority households.

Freddie Mac has about 3,000 employees and a market capitalization of about $42 billion.

EARNINGS PER SHARE GROWTH ★ ★ ★

Past five years: 126 percent (18 percent per year)
Past ten years: 381 percent (17 percent per year)

STOCK GROWTH ★ ★ ★ ★

Past ten years: 900 percent (26 percent per year)
Dollar growth: $10,000 over ten years (including reinvested dividends) would have grown to $118,000.
Average annual compounded rate of return (including reinvested dividends): 28 percent

DIVIDEND

Dividend yield: 0.9 percent
Increased dividend: nine consecutive years
Past five-year increase: 105 percent (15 percent per year)

CONSISTENCY ★ ★ ★ ★

Increased earnings per share: ten consecutive years

SHAREHOLDER PERKS

Freddie Mac offers no dividend reinvestment plan, nor does it offer other
shareholder perks.

FREDDIE MAC AT A GLANCE

Fiscal year ended: Dec. 31
Mortgage loans and net income in $ millions

	1993	1994	1995	1996	1997	1998	5-Year Growth Avg. Annual (%)	Total (%)
Mortgage loans ($)	55,476	72,693	107,424	137,755	164,421	255,009	33	306
Net income ($)	786	983	1,091	1,243	1,395	1,700	17	116
Earnings/share ($)	1.02	1.27	1.42	1.65	1.90	2.31	18	126
Dividends/share ($)	0.22	0.26	0.30	0.35	0.40	0.45	15	105
Dividend yield (%)	1.7	1.9	1.8	1.5	1.2	0.9	—	—
PE ratio range	11–14	9–12	9–15	11–17	14–23	17–29	—	—

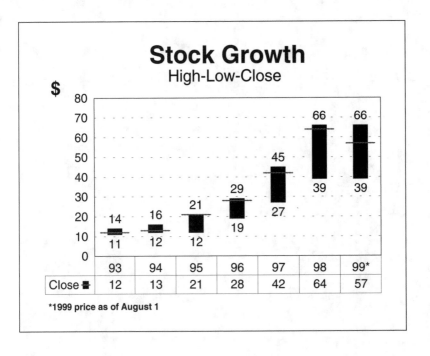

Stock Growth
High-Low-Close

Close	93	94	95	96	97	98	99*
	12	13	21	28	42	64	57

*1999 price as of August 1

Albertson's, Inc.

250 Parkcenter Boulevard
Boise, ID 83726
208-395-6200
www.albertsons.com

Chairman and CEO: Gary G. Michael
President: Richard L. Kling

Earnings Growth	★
Stock Growth	★ ★ ★
Dividend	★ ★ ★
Consistency	★ ★ ★ ★
Shareholder Perks	★ ★
NYSE: ABS	**13 points**

Albertson's has been filling its grocery cart in recent years with a series of smaller grocery and drug store chains. The company acquired 74 stores in 1998, including the 43-store Buttrey Food and Drug Store chain, the 10-store Smitty's Super Market chain in Missouri, 15 Bruno's stores, and 10 Seessel's stores in the Memphis, Tennessee, area. Albertson's also opened about 50 new supermarkets during the year.

But all those mergers pale compared with its 1999 acquisition of the 1,558-store American Stores Company drug and food store chain. With the acquisition, Albertson's adds five chains formerly owned by American, including Jewel (184 stores), Osco Drug (438 stores), Sav-On drug stores (312 stores), Lucky Stores (447 stores), and Acme Markets (177 stores).

In all, the Boise, Idaho grocer operates about 2,600 stores in 37 states. Most of its stores are located in western, midwestern, and southern states. Albertson's, which is one of the nation's largest grocery store chains, has posted 29 consecutive years of record sales and earnings.

The company has been successful in increasing its sales and earnings by expanding its stores both in size and number. The company operates about 800 Albertson's food and drug stores, which average about 50,000 square feet each. It also operates about 69 conventional supermarkets that range in size from 15,000 to 35,000 square feet and 34 Max Food and Drug warehouse-style stores that range in size from 17,000 to 73,000 square feet. Max stores offer substantial discounts over other grocers, with special emphasis on discounted meat and produce. The firm has 11 distribution centers across the country.

Many of the larger Albertson's stores provide not only the standard offering of grocery items, but also include a floral center, pharmacy, video rental, deli, and full-service bakery.

In addition to its standard grocery offerings, many of Albertson's larger stores have five special service departments:

1. **Pharmacy.** Grocery customers can pick up prescription drugs at low-cost pharmacies in many Albertson's stores.
2. **Lobby departments.** Most Albertson's stores offer a variety of special services for customers, such as money orders, bus passes, lottery tickets, stamps, camera supplies, film developing, and video rental.
3. **Service deli.** Delicatessens in about 500 of its stores offer take-home foods, meats, cheeses, fresh salads, and fried chicken. Salad bars have been added to many stores.
4. **Service fish and meat departments.** Most of the larger Albertson's stores have specialty departments with a full array of fresh fish, shell fish, premium cuts of meat, and semiprepared items such as stuffed pork chops.
5. **Bakeries.** The company offers a full range of baked goods in its in-store bakeries.

The company was founded in 1939 by the late Joe Albertson, whose first store opened in Bosie. Although he retired from management in 1976, Albertson remained a director of the company's executive committee until his death in 1993 at age 86. Albertson's has 218,000 employees and 18,000 shareholders. It has a market capitalization of about $14 billion (not counting the American Stores acquisition).

EARNINGS PER SHARE GROWTH ★

Past five years: 66 percent (11 percent per year)
Past ten years: 289 percent (14.5 percent per year)

STOCK GROWTH ★ ★ ★

Past ten years: 575 percent (21 percent per year)
Dollar growth: $10,000 over ten years (including reinvested dividends)
would have grown to $75,000.
Average annual compounded rate of return (including reinvested dividends): 22.5 percent

DIVIDEND ★ ★ ★

Dividend yield: 1.4 percent
Increased dividend: 28 consecutive years
Past five-year increase: 89 percent (13.5 percent per year)

CONSISTENCY ★ ★ ★ ★

Increased earnings per share: 29 consecutive years
Increased sales: 29 consecutive years

SHAREHOLDER PERKS ★ ★

Good dividend reinvestment and stock purchase plan; shareholders of
record owning at least 15 shares may contribute $30 to $30,000 per quarter.

ALBERTSON'S AT A GLANCE

Fiscal year ended: Jan. 31
Revenue and net income in $ millions

	1993	1994	1995	1996	1997	1998	5-Year Growth Avg. Annual (%)	Total (%)
Revenue ($)	11,284	11,895	12,585	13,777	14,690	16,005	7	42
Net income ($)	352	417	465	494	517	567	10	61
Earnings/share ($)	1.39	1.65	1.84	1.96	2.09	2.31	11	66
Dividends/share ($)	0.36	0.42	0.52	0.60	0.64	0.68	14	89
Dividend yield (%)	1.4	1.5	1.7	1.6	1.7	1.3	—	—
PE ratio range	18–22	15–19	14–19	16–22	15–23	19–29	—	—

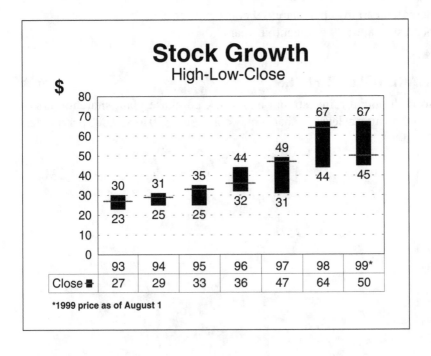

Stock Growth
High-Low-Close

	93	94	95	96	97	98	99*
Close	27	29	33	36	47	64	50

*1999 price as of August 1

AFLAC, Inc.

1932 Wynnton Road
Columbus, GA 31999
706-323-3431
www.aflac.com

Chairman: Paul Amos
President and CEO: Daniel Amos

Earnings Growth	★
Stock Growth	★ ★ ★ ★
Dividend	★ ★
Consistency	★ ★ ★ ★
Shareholder Perks	★ ★
NYSE: AHP	**13 points**

This is one of the few American companies that does better in Japan than it does here. AFLAC is an insurance carrier that specializes in supplemental cancer coverage to help fill the gaps in its customers' primary policies. The company also sells life, accident, Medicare supplement, and long-term convalescent care policies.

About 80 percent of AFLAC's revenue comes from its Japanese operations—most of it from supplemental cancer insurance policies. AFLAC is the leading foreign insurance carrier in Japan. Japanese are attracted to AFLAC policies because of the company's solid financial standing. By contrast, many of its Japanese competitors are strapped with large holdings of low-priced stocks and bad loans.

Japan is also a prime target for AFLAC's supplemental coverage, because most Japanese are covered by the national health insurance system, which is not particularly comprehensive. The AFLAC policies cover medical and nonmedical costs that are not reimbursed under the national system.

AFLAC's cancer life insurance, which is the main product offered by the company, provides a fixed daily indemnity benefit for hospitalization and outpatient services related to cancer, and a lump-sum benefit on initial diagnosis of internal cancer. The policies also provide a death benefit and cash surrender value.

One of every five Japanese is insured by AFLAC, and its policies are offered to employees of 96 percent of the companies listed on the Tokyo Stock Exchange.

In the United States, AFLAC is the leading provider of supplemental insurance at the worksite. Its policies are offered to more than 130,000 payroll groups.

In all, AFLAC insures more than 40 million people worldwide, the vast majority of whom hold supplemental insurance policies. The policies are marketed through about 60,000 independent sales associates.

AFLAC also sells various life insurance policies, including whole life, limited pay life, voluntary group term life, and term life coverage.

The Columbus, Georgia operation was incorporated in 1973. AFLAC has about 4,000 employees and 89,000 shareholders. The company has a market capitalization of about $14 billion.

EARNINGS PER SHARE GROWTH   ★

Past five years: 103 percent (15 percent per year)
Past ten years: 333 percent (16 percent per year)

STOCK GROWTH   ★ ★ ★ ★

Past ten years: 1,004 percent (27 percent per year)
Dollar growth: $10,000 over ten years (including reinvested dividends) would have grown to $118,000.
Average annual compounded rate of return (including reinvested dividends): 28 percent

DIVIDEND

Dividend yield: 0.6 percent
Increased dividend: 16 consecutive years
Past five-year increase: 92 percent (14 percent per year)

CONSISTENCY

Increased earnings per share: nine consecutive years

SHAREHOLDER PERKS

AFLAC offers a direct purchase plan for new investors with a minimum initial investment of $750 and a minimum contribution of $50 thereafter. The dividend reinvestment and stock purchase plan allows voluntary contributions of $50 to $120,000 per year.

AFLAC AT A GLANCE

Fiscal year ended: Dec. 31
Premium income and net income in $ millions

	1993	1994	1995	1996	1997	1998	5-Year Growth Avg. Annual (%)	5-Year Growth Total (%)
Premium income ($)	5,001	6,111	7,191	7,100	6,984	7,104	7	42
Net income ($)	244	293	349	358	374	432	11	77
Earnings/share ($)	0.77	0.95	1.17	1.20	1.33	1.56	15	103
Dividends/share ($)	0.13	0.15	0.17	0.19	0.22	0.25	14	92
Dividend yield (%)	1.3	1.4	1.3	1.1	0.9	0.8	—	—
PE ratio range	10–14	9–12	9–12	10–16	9–13	12–25	—	—

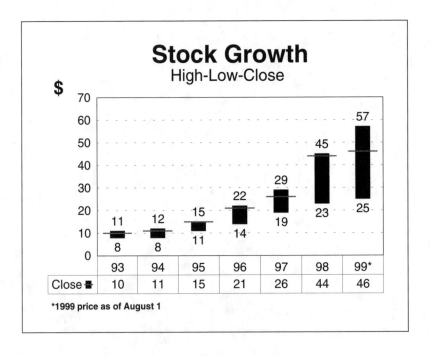

Stock Growth
High-Low-Close

	93	94	95	96	97	98	99*
Close	10	11	15	21	26	44	46

*1999 price as of August 1

33

American Home Products Corporation

Five Giralda Farms
Madison, NJ 07940
973-660-5000
www.ahp.com

Chairman, President, and CEO: John R. Stafford

Earnings Growth	★
Stock Growth	★ ★ ★ ★
Dividend	★ ★
Consistency	★ ★ ★ ★
Shareholder Perks	★ ★
NYSE: AHP	**13 points**

Despite its name, American Home Products (AHP) is finding its way into homes all over the world. About 43 percent of the company's $13.5 billion in revenue comes from sales outside the United States. The company has sales in about 145 countries.

The Madison, New Jersey operation is recognized most for its consumer health care products, including Advil, Anacin, Robitussin, Dristan, Dimetapp, and Chap Stick. It is the world's leading producer of nonprescription drugs.

Among its other leading over-the-counter remedies are Anbesol, which is the leading topical analgesic for both babies and adults; Preparation H, which is the top-selling product in the hemorrhoidal relief category; and Primatene, which is the largest-selling nonprescription asthma medication. It also makes Centrum and Solgar vitamins and herbal products. Consumer health products account for about 16 percent of the company's total revenue.

Most of the company's revenues are generated by its prescription medications, which account for 66 percent of total revenue. Its leading areas are women's health medications, cardiovascular drugs, neuroscience therapies, pain and arthritis medications, vaccines, oncology therapies, anti-infectives, and infant nutritionals.

AHP is also one of the world's leading producers of agricultural products. The company makes herbicides (including Pursuit, Prowl, and Raptor), insecticides (including Counter), fungicides, and plant growth regulators. Agricultural products account for about 16 percent of total revenue.

AHP recently sold off its food unit (including Chef Boyarde and Palaner jellies) and its medical devices division.

AHP has never been known for spectacular growth, but its growth has certainly been steady, with a streak of 47 consecutive years of increased earnings.

The company was founded in 1926. It has about 53,000 employees and 65,000 shareholders. AHP has a market capitalization of $79 billion.

EARNINGS PER SHARE GROWTH   ★

Past five years: 59 percent (10 percent per year)
Past ten years: 125 percent (8.5 percent per year)

STOCK GROWTH   ★ ★ ★ ★

Past ten years: 667 percent (23 percent per year)
Dollar growth: $10,000 over ten years (including reinvested dividends) would have grown to $94,000.
Average annual compounded rate of return (including reinvested dividends): 25 percent

DIVIDEND   ★ ★

Dividend yield: 1.4 percent
Increased dividend: 46 consecutive years
Past five-year increase: 21 percent (3 percent per year)

CONSISTENCY

Increased earnings per share: 47 consecutive years
Increased sales: nine of the past ten years

SHAREHOLDER PERKS

Good dividend reinvestment and stock purchase plan; voluntary stock purchase plan allows contributions of $50 to $10,000 per month. Occasionally, the company also sends out coupons for some of its foods and health care products along with dividend checks.

AMERICAN HOME PRODUCTS AT A GLANCE

Fiscal year ended: Dec. 31
Revenue and net income in $ millions

	1993	1994	1995	1996	1997	1998	5-Year Growth Avg. Annual (%)	Total (%)
Revenue ($)	8,305	8,966	13,375	14,085	14,196	13,463	10	62
Net income ($)	1,469	1,528	1,338	1,883	2,160	2,474	11	68
Earnings/share ($)	1.18	1.24	1.10	1.48	1.67	1.88	10	59
Dividends/share ($)	0.72	0.74	0.76	0.79	0.86	0.87	3	21
Dividend yield (%)	4.5	4.9	3.8	2.8	2.3	1.8	—	—
PE ratio range	12–15	11–14	11–18	16–22	18–27	20–31	—	—

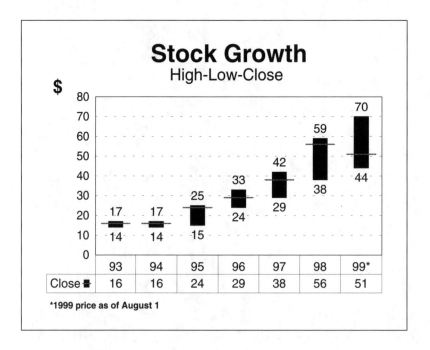

Stock Growth
High-Low-Close

Close ■	93	94	95	96	97	98	99*
	16	16	24	29	38	56	51

*1999 price as of August 1

Abbott Laboratories

100 Abbott Park Road
Abbott Park, IL 60064-3500
847-937-6100
www.abbott.com

Chairman and CEO: Duane L. Burnham
President: Thomas R. Hodgson

Earnings Growth	★
Stock Growth	★ ★ ★
Dividend	★ ★ ★
Consistency	★ ★ ★ ★
Shareholder Perks	★ ★
NYSE: ABT	**13 points**

Abbott Laboratories is a 109-year-old medical manufacturer that specializes in products that detect diseases and those that treat them. The Chicago-area operation is one of the world's leading makers of diagnostic testing products and drug delivery systems.

Abbott also produces a growing line of nutritional products, including Similac, Isomil, and Alimentum infant formulas, and Ensure, Jevity, Glucerna, PediaSure, and Pulmocare adult and pediatric nutritional formulas. Abbott is also the maker of Murine eye drops, Selsun Blue dandruff shampoo, and Tronolane hemorrhoid medication. Abbott's nutritional segment accounts for about 15 percent of the company's $12.5 billion in annual sales.

With 28 consecutive years of increased sales and earnings, Abbott is one of the nation's most consistent companies.

Abbott is probably most widely recognized for its diagnostic products. It is among the world leaders in blood screening equipment and was the first company to introduce an AIDS antibody test. It is also among the leaders in tests for hepatitis, sexually transmitted diseases, cancer, thyroid function, pregnancy, illicit drugs, and drug monitoring. Diagnostics account for about 22 percent of total revenue.

Pharmaceuticals account for about 21 percent of revenue. Among its leading pharmaceuticals are clarithromycin, an anti-infective, and drugs used for the treatment of epilepsy, migraine, and bipolar disorder. It is a leading producer of antibiotics, and it manufactures a broad line of cardiovascular products, cough and cold formulas, and vitamins.

Hospital products account for about 15 percent of revenue. Leading products include critical care monitoring instruments, intravenous and irrigation fluids (and the equipment to administer them), drug delivery devices, and multiple-application diagnostic machines.

Abbott is also a leading producer of biological pesticides, plant growth regulators, herbicides, and related agricultural products, although those products account for only 3 percent of the company's total revenue.

The firm boasts a strong international business, which accounts for about 24 percent of total revenue. It has sales or operations in more than 130 countries.

Abbott Laboratories was founded in 1888 by Dr. Wallace C. Abbott, who began the business as a sideline venture in his small Chicago apartment making pills from the alkaloid of plants.

Abbott has grown to about 56,000 employees and 103,000 shareholders. It has a market capitalization of $71 billion.

EARNINGS PER SHARE GROWTH   ★

Past five years: 78 percent (12 percent per year)
Past ten years: 260 percent (14 percent per year)

STOCK GROWTH

Past ten years: 516 percent (20 percent per year)
Dollar growth: $10,000 over ten years (including reinvested dividends) would have grown to $75,000.
Average annual compounded rate of return (including reinvested dividends): 22 percent

DIVIDEND

Dividend yield: 1.6 percent
Increased dividend: every year since 1971
Past five-year increase: 76 percent (12 percent per year)

CONSISTENCY ★★★★

Increased earnings per share: 28 consecutive years (since 1971)
Increased sales: 28 consecutive years

SHAREHOLDER PERKS

Good dividend reinvestment and stock purchase plan; voluntary stock purchase plan allows contributions of $10 to $5,000 per quarter.

Shareholders who attend the annual meeting receive a sampling of Abbott's consumer products, such as Selsun Blue, Murine, Tronolane, and Ensure nutritional drink.

ABBOTT LABORATORIES AT A GLANCE

Fiscal year ended: Dec. 31
Revenue and net income in $ millions

	1993	1994	1995	1996	1997	1998	5-Year Growth Avg. Annual (%)	5-Year Growth Total (%)
Revenue ($)	8,408	9,156	10,012	11,013	11,883	12,477	8	48
Net income ($)	1,399	1,517	1,689	1,882	2,095	2,333	11	67
Earnings/share ($)	0.85	0.94	1.06	1.21	1.34	1.51	12	78
Dividends/share ($)	0.34	0.38	0.42	0.48	0.54	0.60	12	76
Dividend yield (%)	2.5	2.6	2.2	2.1	1.7	1.5	—	—
PE ratio range	13–18	14–18	14–21	16–24	18–26	21–33	—	—

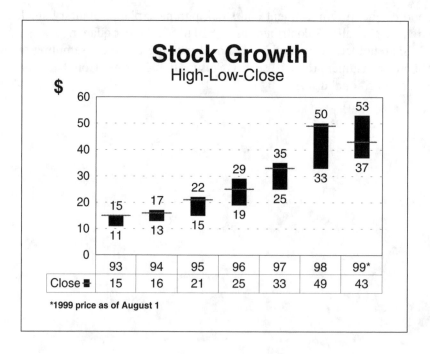

Stock Growth
High-Low-Close

	93	94	95	96	97	98	99*
Close ■	15	16	21	25	33	49	43

*1999 price as of August 1

SouthTrust Corporation

SouthTrust Corporation ≋

420 North 20th Street
Birmingham, AL 35203
205-254-5509
www.southtrust.com

Chairman, President, and CEO: William D. Malone, Jr.

Earnings Growth	★
Stock Growth	★ ★ ★
Dividend	★ ★ ★ ★
Consistency	★ ★ ★
Shareholder Perks	★ ★
Nasdaq: SOTR	**13 points**

SouthTrust has been one of the fastest growing banks in the South over the past decade. The Birmingham-based institution operates more than 600 banking offices and several bank-related affiliates in Alabama, Florida, Georgia, Mississippi, North Carolina, South Carolina, Texas, and Tennessee.

It is the 22nd largest banking organization in the country and the fifth largest in the Southeast. Its customer base includes 1.3 million households and 110,000 businesses. The company has posted increased loan totals 12 straight years and increased earnings 9 of the past 10 years.

SouthTrust has grown quickly through internal expansion and acquisitions. In 1998, the company acquired nine banking organizations, including five Florida operations (First of America, American National Bank of Florida, Home Savings of America, Marine Bank, and First American Bank of Indian River County); three Texas companies (Gardner Mortgage Services, Partners Mortgage Services, and Security Bank Texas); and the Georgia National Bank.

Commercial banking is the bread and butter of SouthTrust's business. Its banks offer a broad range of standard services, such as checking and savings accounts, cash management, lending and credit services, discount brokerage accounts, corporate and trust accounts, and data processing services. The company also offers Visa and MasterCard merchant credit card processing services.

The firm operates a number of bank-related subsidiaries, including SouthTrust Mortgage Corp., SouthTrust Data Services, SouthTrust Life Insurance Company, SouthTrust Insurance Agency, SouthTrust Securities, and SouthTrust Asset Management Company.

SouthTrust has been modernizing its operations through several technological initiatives. For instance, it now offers online banking services to small businesses and retailers who use their personal computers to handle many of their financial tasks. The company also has set up a centralized call center for all telecommunications interaction with customers and prospects. The centers provide account information by phone 24 hours a day.

SouthTrust was among the first banks to offer corporate imaging technology for cash management customers. Using software provided by SouthTrust, customers can access check images online or on CD-ROM and electronically store those images, providing them with a permanent record of all of their canceled checks.

The company has about 12,000 employees and 15,000 shareholders. It has a market capitalization of $6.6 billion.

EARNINGS PER SHARE GROWTH   ★

Past five years: 74 percent (12 percent per year)
Past ten years: 196 percent (11.5 percent per year)

STOCK GROWTH

Past ten years: 488 percent (19 percent per year)
Dollar growth: $10,000 over ten years (including reinvested dividends)
would have grown to about $80,000.
Average annual compounded rate of return (including reinvested dividends): 23 percent

DIVIDEND

Dividend yield: 2.5
Increased dividend: 29 consecutive years
Past five-year increase: 90 percent (14 percent per year)

CONSISTENCY

Increased earnings per share: nine of the past ten years
Increased loans: 12 consecutive years

SHAREHOLDER PERKS

Good dividend reinvestment and stock purchase plan; voluntary stock
purchase plan allows contributions of $25 to $10,000 per quarter.

SOUTHTRUST AT A GLANCE

Fiscal year ended: Dec. 31
Total assets and net income in $ millions

	1993	1994	1995	1996	1997	1998	5-Year Growth Avg. Annual (%)	Total (%)
Total assets ($)	14,708	17,632	20,787	26,223	30,906	38,134	21	159
Net income ($)	151	173	199	255	307	370	19	146
Earnings/share ($)	1.29	1.43	1.57	1.79	2.03	2.25	12	74
Dividends/share ($)	0.40	0.45	0.53	0.59	0.67	0.76	14	90
Dividend yield (%)	3.1	3.5	3.5	3.0	2.3	2.0	—	—
PE ratio range	6–8	5–7	5–8	6–9	7–21	11–20	—	—

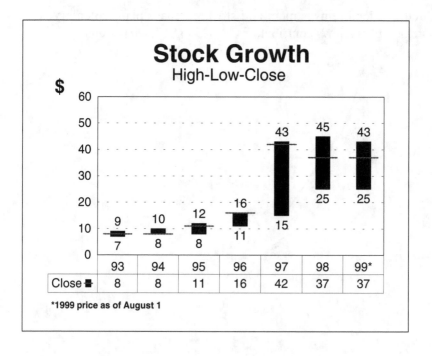

Stock Growth
High-Low-Close

	93	94	95	96	97	98	99*
Close	8	8	11	16	42	37	37

*1999 price as of August 1

Becton Dickinson
and Company

One Becton Drive
Franklin Lakes, NJ 07417
800-284-6845
www.bd.com

Chairman, President, and CEO:
Clateo Castellini

Earnings Growth	★ ★
Stock Growth	★ ★ ★
Dividend	★ ★
Consistency	★ ★ ★ ★
Shareholder Perks	★ ★
NYSE: BDX	**13 points**

It's a throw-away society, and Becton Dickinson and Company (BD) is in the right place at the right time. The Franklin Lakes, New Jersey operation is one of the world's leading suppliers of disposable syringes, hypodermic needles, and other single-use medical devices.

Becton Dickinson is also the leading maker of insulin injection systems and holds strong positions in a number of other drug-delivery and infusion-therapy-related products. The company also manufactures thermometers, disposable scrubs, surgical blades, and other surgical products.

Medical supplies and devices account for about 55 percent of BD's $3.1 billion in annual revenue. The company spends about $200 million a year on research and development.

Becton Dickinson also makes a line of clinical and industrial microbiology products, sample collection products, flow cytometry systems, tissue culture labware, hematology instruments, immunodiagnostic test kits, and other diagnostic systems. Diagnostic products account for about 45 percent of the company's revenue.

In recent years, the company has grown through acquisitions and international expansion. Becton Dickinson made several acquisitions in 1998, including Tru Fit Marketing Corp., which manufactures sports heath care products; Concepts in Healthcare, which offers consulting services; Boin Medica Company, which is a Korean medical device manufacturer; and the Medical Devices Division, which is a European maker of intravenous catheters.

BD's products are manufactured and marketed worldwide. Foreign sales account for about 46 percent of the company's revenue. The company has manufacturing operations in Australia, Brazil, France, Germany, Ireland, Japan, Mexico, Singapore, Spain, China, India, and the United Kingdom.

Overseas growth has been spurred by strong sales of the company's Vacutainer blood collection products and Hypak prefillable syringe systems and infusion therapy products.

Becton Dickinson was founded more than a century ago in 1897, when Maxwell W. Becton and Fairleigh S. Dickinson opened a small medical supply business. Their first product was a Luer all-glass syringe that sold for $2.50.

Becton Dickinson has about 22,000 employees and 10,000 shareholders. The company has a market capitalization of about $9.6 billion.

EARNINGS PER SHARE GROWTH ★★

Past five years: 101 percent (15 percent per year)
Past ten years: 198 percent (11.5 percent per year)

STOCK GROWTH ★★★

Past ten years: 444 percent (18.5 percent per year)
Dollar growth: $10,000 over ten years (including reinvested dividends) would have grown to $62,000.
Average annual compounded rate of return (including reinvested dividends): 20 percent

DIVIDEND

Dividend yield: 1.0 percent
Increased dividend: 17 consecutive years
Past five-year increase: 71 percent (11.5 percent per year)

CONSISTENCY

Increased earnings per share: 15 consecutive years
Increased sales: 15 consecutive years

SHAREHOLDER PERKS ★ ★

Becton Dickinson offers a direct stock purchase program that allows new investors to buy shares directly from the company with a minimum initial investment of $250. Its dividend reinvestment and stock purchase plan for existing shareholders allows voluntary investments of a minimum of $50. There are no maximum investment limitations.

BECTON DICKINSON AT A GLANCE

Fiscal year ended: Sept. 30
Revenue and net income in $ millions

	1993	1994	1995	1996	1997	1998	5-Year Growth Avg. Annual (%)	Total (%)
Revenue ($)	2,465	2,560	2,713	2,770	2,811	3,117	5	26
Net income ($)	213	224	252	283	315	360	11	69
Earnings/share ($)	0.68	0.75	0.90	1.06	1.21	1.37	15	101
Dividends/share ($)	0.17	0.19	0.21	0.23	0.28	0.29	11	71
Dividend yield (%)	1.8	1.9	1.5	1.2	1.1	0.9	—	—
PE ratio range	12–15	11–16	13–21	16–21	17–23	26–52	—	—

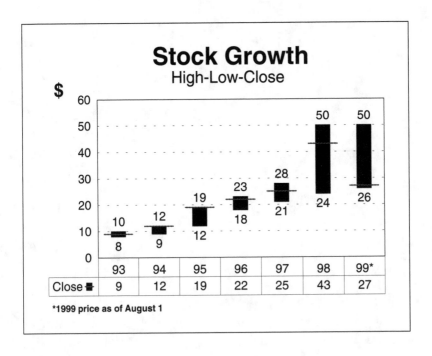

Stock Growth
High-Low-Close

Close ■	9	12	19	22	25	43	27
	93	94	95	96	97	98	99*

*1999 price as of August 1

William Wrigley, Jr. Company

410 North Michigan Avenue
Chicago, IL 60611
312-644-2121
www.wrigley.com

President and CEO: William Wrigley

Earnings Growth	★
Stock Growth	★ ★ ★
Dividend	★ ★ ★
Consistency	★ ★ ★ ★
Shareholder Perks	★ ★
NYSE: WWY	**13 points**

The taste of Wrigley's gum goes a long way–all the way around the world, in fact, with sales in more than 140 countries. And nowhere is the popularity of Wrigley's growing faster than in China, where sales volume has been growing at nearly 50 percent per year since 1993 when the company opened a manufacturing facility in the Guangdong province.

The Chicago-based manufacturer recently expanded the China factory to try to keep up with the growing popularity of gum in China. Wrigley also has factories in Russia, India, the Czech Republic, Kenya, Poland, Japan, and more than 20 other countries.

International sales account for about 62 percent of the company's $2 billion in total annual sales. For Wrigley, it's a good thing that international sales are growing, because sales growth in the U.S. market has been stagnate in recent years. In fact, Wrigley sold more gum in Europe in 1998 than it did in the United States for the first time ever. With its international growth, Wrigley has managed to extend its string of record sales and earnings to 16 consecutive years.

In the United States, Wrigley is the leading gum producer, with about a 50 percent share of the total gum market.

Brand extension has paid big dividends for Wrigley. The company has added about 15 new brands in recent years. Wrigley's top-grossing brands continue to be Spearmint, Doublemint, Juicy Fruit, Big Red, and Winterfresh. Its Extra sugarfree gum (available in several flavors and as bubble gum) is the nation's top-selling sugarfree brand. The sugarfree line is also beginning to sell well in European markets. Other Wrigley brands include Freedent, Orbit, Hubba Bubba, and Sugarfree Hubba Bubba.

Wrigley also owns Amurol Products, which manufactures children's novelty bubble gum and other confectionery products, including Big League Chew, Bubble Tape gum, BubbleJug, SqueezePop, OUCH!, and Bubble Beeper.

Wrigley was founded in 1891 by William Wrigley, Jr., the late grandfather of current president William Wrigley, who is 65. Wrigley was a baking soda salesman who first offered gum as a premium to customers who bought his baking soda. The gum quickly became more in demand than the baking soda, so Wrigley did what any smart marketer would do— he switched products. In 1893, he introduced his first flavors of Wrigley's gum, Spearmint and Juicy Fruit, and an American institution was born.

As Will Rogers once put it, "All Wrigley had was an idea. He was the first man to discover that American jaws must wag, so why not give them something to wag against." Now jaws all over the world are wagging with Wrigley's.

The Wrigley Company has 9,200 employees, and 38,000 shareholders. It has a market capitalization of $8.2 billion.

EARNINGS PER SHARE GROWTH   ★

Past five years: 71 percent (11 percent per year)
Past ten years: 252 percent (13 percent per year)

STOCK GROWTH

Past ten years: 486 percent (19 percent per year)
Dollar growth: $10,000 over ten years (including reinvested dividends) would have grown to $70,000.
Average annual compounded rate of return (including reinvested dividends): 21.5 percent

DIVIDEND

Dividend yield: 1.6 percent
Increased dividend: 17 consecutive years
Past five-year increase: 12 percent (73 percent per year)

CONSISTENCY ★ ★ ★ ★

Increased earnings per share: 16 consecutive years
Increased sales: 16 consecutive years

SHAREHOLDER PERKS ★ ★

Good dividend reinvestment and stock purchase plan; voluntary stock purchase plan allows contributions of $50 to $5,000 per month. More than 17,000 shareholders participate in the company's dividend reinvestment program.

WRIGLEY AT A GLANCE

Fiscal year ended: Dec. 31
Revenue and net income in $ millions

	1993	1994	1995	1996	1997	1998	5-Year Growth Avg. Annual (%)	5-Year Growth Total (%)
Revenue ($)	1,429	1,597	1,755	1,836	1,937	2,005	7	40
Net income ($)	175	201	224	243	274	298	11	70
Earnings/share ($)	1.50	1.73	1.93	2.10	2.36	2.57	11	71
Dividends/share ($)	0.75	0.90	0.96	1.02	1.17	1.30	12	73
Dividend yield (%)	2.0	1.9	2.1	1.8	1.7	1.5	—	—
PE ratio range	20–31	19–27	22–28	24–32	23–35	27–40	—	—

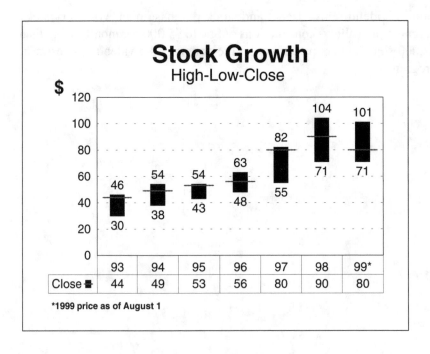

Stock Growth
High-Low-Close

	93	94	95	96	97	98	99*
Close ■	44	49	53	56	80	90	80

*1999 price as of August 1

38
Jefferson Pilot Corp.

100 North Greene Street
Greensboro, NC 27401
336-691-3382
www.jpfinancial.com

Chairman: Robert H. Spilman
President and CEO: David A. Stonecipher

Earnings Growth	★ ★
Stock Growth	★ ★ ★
Dividend	★ ★
Consistency	★ ★ ★ ★
Shareholder Perks	★ ★
NYSE: JP	**13 points**

It's a strange mix of holdings, but Jefferson-Pilot's combination of insurance groups and TV and radio stations has helped keep the company's bottom line booming. The firm has posted 11 consecutive years of record earnings.

Jefferson-Pilot is best known for its insurance products, but the company also owns three television stations in Charlotte, Charleston, and Richmond (Virginia), and 17 radio stations in Atlanta, Charlotte, Denver, Miami, and San Diego. The communications division, which also produces television sports programs covering college basketball and football and professional motor sports, generates about 9 percent of Jefferson-Pilot's operating income.

The vast share of the company's profits come from its insurance groups. Founded in 1890, Jefferson-Pilot offers a broad range of life insurance, group health insurance, and other types of insurance policies and investment products.

Through its Jefferson-Pilot and Alexander Hamilton life insurance companies, the Greensboro, North Carolina operation offers continuous and limited-pay life and endowment policies, universal life policies and annuity contracts, retirement income plans, and level and decreasing term insurance.

Life insurance products account for about 68 percent of Jefferson-Pilot's operating income.

Jefferson-Pilot also offers a range of investment products and services, including several types of annuities and mutual funds. Annuities and investment products generate about 20 percent of operating income. (The other 3 percent comes from a combination of other sources.)

The company's life insurance and investment products are marketed by a staff of more than 400 full-time agents and thousands of independent agents. They also are sold by 60 financial institutions and 36 brokerage companies.

Jefferson-Pilot has about 3,000 employees and 10,000 shareholders. The company has a market capitalization of $7.1 billion.

EARNINGS PER SHARE GROWTH

Past five years: 102 percent (15 percent per year)
Past ten years: 428 percent (18 percent per year)

STOCK GROWTH ★ ★ ★

Past ten years: 528 percent (20 percent per year)
Dollar growth: $10,000 over ten years (including reinvested dividends) would have grown to $62,000.
Average annual compounded rate of return (including reinvested dividends): 20 percent

DIVIDEND

Dividend yield: 1.9 percent
Increased dividend: 17 consecutive years
Past five-year increase: 68 percent (11 percent per year)

CONSISTENCY

Increased earnings per share: 11 consecutive years

SHAREHOLDER PERKS

Good dividend reinvestment and stock purchase plan; voluntary stock purchase plan allows contributions of $20 to $2,000 per month.

JEFFERSON PILOT AT A GLANCE

Fiscal year ended: Dec. 31
Revenue and net income in $ millions

	1993	1994	1995	1996	1997	1998	5-Year Growth Avg. Annual (%)	Total (%)
Revenue ($)	1,247	1,207	1,521	2,125	2,578	2,610	16	109
Net income ($)	219	230	255	294	396	444	15	103
Earnings/share ($)	1.94	2.10	2.37	2.73	3.47	3.91	15	102
Dividends/share ($)	0.69	0.75	0.83	0.93	1.04	1.16	11	68
Dividend yield (%)	3.1	3.3	3.1	2.6	2.3	1.9	—	—
PE ratio range	11-14	9-12	9-14	11-15	10-17	12-20	—	—

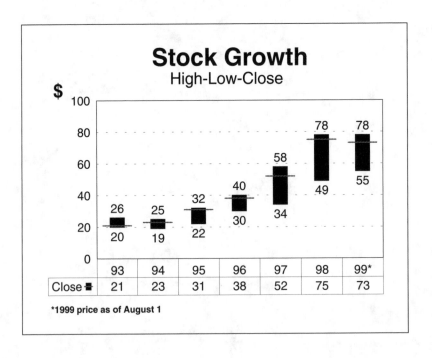

Stock Growth
High-Low-Close

	93	94	95	96	97	98	99*
Close	21	23	31	38	52	75	73

*1999 price as of August 1

Wells Fargo & Company

WELLS FARGO

420 Montgomery Street
San Francisco, CA 94163
800-411-4932
www.wellsfargo.com

President, Chairman, and CEO:
Richard Kovacevich

Earnings Growth	★
Stock Growth	★ ★ ★ ★
Dividend	★ ★ ★
Consistency	★ ★ ★
Shareholder Perks	★ ★
NYSE: WFC	**13 points**

The merger of Norwest Corp. and Wells Fargo in 1998 brought together two of the nation's largest banking organizations. The combined company is the nation's seventh largest banking institution with assets of about $200 billion. The company claims some 15 million customers and has operations in all 50 states.

The megamerger between Wells Fargo and Norwest is part of a long trend by the two banks. In all, the combined company has been involved in about 1,500 mergers and acquisitions over the past 147 years.

Wells Fargo has a total of 2,900 banking offices in 21 states (mostly in the West and Midwest); 1,350 consumer finance offices in 47 states, Canada, the Caribbean, and Central America; and 850 mortgage offices in 50 states.

The merged company, based in San Francisco, has carried on part of the philosophy that was key to Norwest's success prior to the merger. The company refers to its banking offices as "stores," and it approaches the business as a retailer rather than a traditional bank. Its focus is on "cross-selling"—selling multiple services such as savings, checking, CDs, consumer loans, mortgages, credit cards, and investment services. A high percentage of its customers use several of its banking services.

In addition to its consumer services, the bank also offers community and corporate banking, trust, capital management, and credit card services. The company operates several related subsidiaries, including investment services, insurance, and venture capital companies.

Wells Fargo's community banking segment accounts for about 42 percent of after-tax profit. Other segments include specialized lending, 14 percent; investments and insurance, 11 percent; consumer finance, 9 percent; home mortgages, 9 percent; business banking, 9 percent; and commercial real estate, 6 percent.

Wells Fargo was founded in 1852 by Henry Wells and William G. Fargo and is best known in Old West folklore as a stage coach operator. The company operated the westernmost leg of the Pony Express and ran stagecoach lines in the western United States. The banking business was separated from the express business in 1905.

Wells Fargo has 102,000 employees and about 50,000 shareholders. The company has a market capitalization of $69 billion.

EARNINGS PER SHARE GROWTH   ★

Past five years: 67 percent (11 percent per year)
Past ten years: 207 percent (12 percent per year)

STOCK GROWTH   ★ ★ ★ ★

Past ten years: 720 percent (23 percent per year)
Dollar growth: $10,000 over ten years (including reinvested dividends) would have grown to about $105,000.
Average annual compounded rate of return (including reinvested dividends): 26.5 percent

DIVIDEND

Dividend yield: 2.1 percent
Increased dividend: 12 consecutive years
Past five-year increase: 119 percent (17 percent per year)

CONSISTENCY

Increased earnings per share: nine of the past ten years

SHAREHOLDER PERKS ★ ★

Good dividend reinvestment and stock purchase plan; voluntary stock purchase plan allows contributions of up to $10,000 per month.

WELLS FARGO AT A GLANCE

Fiscal year ended: Dec. 31
Total assets and net income in $ millions

	1993	1994	1995	1996	1997	1998	5-Year Growth Avg. Annual (%)	5-Year Growth Total (%)
Total assets ($)	50,782	59,316	72,134	80,175	88,540	202,475	33	299
Net income ($)	654	800	956	1,154	1,351	2,909	35	345
Earnings/share ($)	1.05	1.21	1.37	1.54	1.75	1.75	11	67
Dividends/share ($)	0.32	0.38	0.45	0.5	30.62	0.70	17	119
Dividend yield (%)	2.6	3.1	3.2	2.8	2.1	1.9	—	—
PE ratio range	11–15	9–11	8–12	11–17	14–26	23–37	—	—

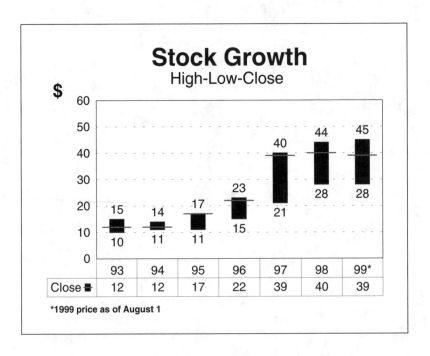

Stock Growth
High-Low-Close

	93	94	95	96	97	98	99*
Close	12	12	17	22	39	40	39

*1999 price as of August 1

ReliaStar Financial Corporation

RELIASTAR

20 Washington Avenue South
Minneapolis, MN 55401
612-372-5432
www.reliastar.com

Chairman and CEO: John Turner
President: John Flittie

Earnings Growth	★ ★ ★
Stock Growth	★ ★
Dividend	★ ★ ★
Consistency	★ ★ ★
Shareholder Perks	★ ★
NYSE: RLR	**13 points**

Formerly known as Norwestern National Life, ReliaStar is an insurance company that is steadily adding other financial products to its mix of offerings.

The company operates in four key operating segments: personal financial services, worksite financial services, tax-sheltered and fixed annuities, and reinsurance.

The leading segment of the Minneapolis-based operation is its personal financial services division, which accounts for 35 percent of operating income. The division sells insurance and investment products through a nationwide network of independent personal financial planners, agents, and brokers. It sells a wide range of life insurance products, including term life, universal life, variable life, and variable and fixed annuities.

Tax-sheltered and fixed annuities account for 28 percent of operating income. ReliaStar's products are geared almost exclusively to school teacher retirement funds, known as 403(b) plans. The annuities are marketed through a network of independent agents. The company also has developed some annuities that can be used in IRAs and other qualified plans, as well as nonqualified plans.

ReliaStar's worksite financial services division, which accounts for 22 percent of operating income, provides employee benefits and financial services for employees of medium-size and large businesses. The company offers employee life insurance, excess risk medical insurance, long-term disability, and 401(k) retirement plans. ReliaStar provides worksite services for about 4,000 organizations and four million individuals.

Reinsurance—both life and health—makes up 15 percent of operating income. The company sells group and special risk reinsurance in the United States and international markets to other insurance carriers.

ReliaStar, which is the nation's 11th largest publicly held life insurance holding company, traces its founding to 1885.

The company has 3,500 employees and 50,000 shareholders. It has a market capitalization of $3.6 billion.

EARNINGS PER SHARE GROWTH   ★ ★ ★

Past five years: 139 percent (19 percent per year)
Past ten years: 242 percent (13 percent per year)

STOCK GROWTH   ★ ★

Past ten years: 383 percent (17 percent per year)
Dollar growth: $10,000 over ten years (including reinvested dividends) would have grown to about $65,000.
Average annual compounded rate of return (including reinvested dividends): 20.5 percent

DIVIDEND

Dividend yield: 1.5 percent
Increased dividend: 13 consecutive years
Past five-year increase: 82 percent (13 percent per year)

CONSISTENCY

Increased earnings per share: nine of the past ten years
Increased total income: eight consecutive years

SHAREHOLDER PERKS ★ ★

Good dividend reinvestment and stock purchase plan; voluntary stock purchase plan allows contributions of $50 to $5,000 per month. Dividend reinvestment participants receive a 4 percent discount to the market price, and stock purchase participants receive a 1 percent discount.

RELIASTAR AT A GLANCE

Fiscal year ended: Dec. 31
Total income and net income in $ millions

	1993	1994	1995	1996	1997	1998	5-Year Growth Avg. Annual (%)	5-Year Growth Total (%)
Total income ($)	1,490	1,571	2,090	2,191	2,510	2,848	14	91
Net income ($)	83	108	169	193	222	279	27	236
Earnings/share ($)	1.26	1.54	2.05	2.37	2.55	3.01	19	139
Dividends/share ($)	0.39	0.44	0.49	0.55	0.61	0.71	13	82
Dividend yield (%)	2.5	2.8	2.6	2.3	1.8	1.6	—	—
PE ratio range	9–15	8–10	7–10	8–11	11–16	11–20	—	—

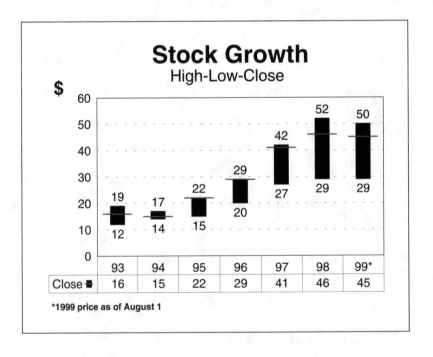

Stock Growth
High-Low-Close

	93	94	95	96	97	98	99*
Close	16	15	22	29	41	46	45

*1999 price as of August 1

Microsoft Corporation

Microsoft ®

One Microsoft Way
Redmond, VA 98052
612-574-4000
www.microsoft.com

Chairman and CEO: William H. Gates
President: Steven A. Ballmer

Earnings Growth	★ ★ ★ ★
Stock Growth	★ ★ ★ ★
Dividend	
Consistency	★ ★ ★ ★
Shareholder Perks	
Nasdaq: MSFT	**12 points**

Microsoft is the biggest success story in the history of corporate America.

Brash assertion, but the evidence is lock-tight. At the still youthful age of 43, Microsoft founder and chairman Bill Gates has amassed a personal fortune well in excess of $100 billion. He owns about 1.3 billion shares of the company stock, valued recently at about $115 billion. That makes Gates far and away the richest person on earth—and perhaps the richest of all time.

He did it by turning a complex and powerful new technology into a useful, multifaceted tool consumers the world over could use. Through Microsoft, Gates has introduced a long line of software products, such as

Windows, DOS, Word, and Explorer, that have made computer technology easily accessible to the average consumer.

Founded in 1975, Microsoft is the worldwide leader in software for personal computers. The Redmond, Washington manufacturer helps maintain its edge on the market by spending generously on product development. It spends about $2.5 billion a year on research and development.

Microsoft has market or support operations in more than 60 countries. Foreign sales account for about 33 percent of total revenue.

Microsoft divides its products into several key categories, including:

- **Platforms** (computer operating systems). Includes Windows, Windows 98, Windows 95, Windows NT Workstation, and Windows NT Server.
- **Desktop applications.** Includes Microsoft Office (a software package with a wide range of business-related applications), Word (word processing), Excel (spreadsheet), PowerPoint (presentations), Access (database management), and Outlook (Internet e-mail).
- **Server applications.** Includes Windows NT Server for office networks, Microsoft Exchange Server, and SQL Server.
- **Developer tools.** Used by software developers to create new applications.
- **Interactive media.** Includes interactive entertainment and information products such as Microsoft Encarta encyclopedia, Microsoft Bookshelf, and other Internet and CD-ROM products.

The company has about 27,000 employees and 71,000 shareholders. It has a market capitalization of $395 billion.

EARNINGS PER SHARE GROWTH ★ ★ ★ ★

Past five years: 345 percent (35 percent per year)
Past ten years: 2,866 percent (41 percent per year)

STOCK GROWTH ★ ★ ★ ★

Past ten years: 9,344 percent (58 percent per year)
Dollar growth: $10,000 over ten years would have grown to about $940,000.
Average annual compounded rate of return: 58 percent

DIVIDEND

Microsoft pays no dividends.

CONSISTENCY ★ ★ ★ ★

Increased earnings per share: 16 consecutive years
Increased sales: 16 consecutive years

SHAREHOLDER PERKS

The company offers no dividend reinvestment and stock purchase plan, nor does it provide other shareholder perks.

MICROSOFT AT A GLANCE

Fiscal year ended: June 30
Revenue and net income in $ millions

	1993	1994	1995	1996	1997	1998	5-Year Growth Avg. Annual (%)	5-Year Growth Total (%)
Revenue ($)	3,753	4,649	5,937	8,671	11,358	14,484	32	286
Net income ($)	953	1,210	1,453	2,176	3,454	4,786	38	402
Earnings/share ($)	0.20	0.25	0.29	0.43	0.66	0.89	35	345
Dividends/share ($)	—	—	—	—	—	—	—	—
Dividend yield (%)	—	—	—	—	—	—	—	—
PE ratio range	22–31	21–35	25–48	22–46	28–52	34–79	—	—

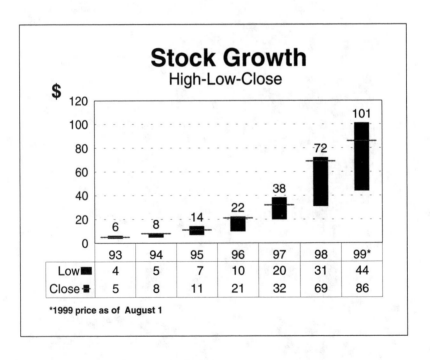

Stock Growth
High-Low-Close

	93	94	95	96	97	98	99*
Low	4	5	7	10	20	31	44
Close	5	8	11	21	32	69	86

*1999 price as of August 1

Cisco Systems, Inc.

170 West Tasman Drive
San Jose, CA 95134
408-526-4000
www.cisco.com

Chairman: John Morgridge
President and CEO: John T. Chambers

Earnings Growth	★ ★ ★ ★
Stock Growth	★ ★ ★ ★
Dividend	
Consistency	★ ★ ★ ★
Shareholder Perks	
Nasdaq: CSCO	**12 points**

The World Wide Web is strung together by the cables, routers, switches, bridges, and servers manufactured by Cisco Systems. The San Jose, California manufacturer is far and away the dominant player in the Internet industry. Nearly all the information on the Internet travels across Cisco Systems products.

The company's hardware and software products are designed to link computers and networks in such a way that they can transcend time, space, and differences in computer operating systems.

Cisco is the leading global supplier of networking products for corporate intranets and the global Internet. Cisco markets its products to four types of buyers: Its leading buyers are large organizations with complex networking needs, such as corporations, government agencies, and universities. It also sells to service providers such as telecommunications carriers, cable companies, and Internet service providers; volume markets such as small businesses, home offices, and residential users; and other suppliers who license features of Cisco software for inclusion in their products or services.

Cisco's end-to-end networking products help clients build their own network infrastructure and gain access to their suppliers' or vendors' networks. The Cisco networking products provide a common technical architecture that allows network services to be provided to all computer users on the network.

Cisco's routers are used to move data from one network to another, and its switches are designed to help users migrate from traditional shared local area networks to fully switched networks.

The company spends about $1 billion a year on research and development.

Cisco sells its products through a direct sales force of 5,000 representatives and technical support personnel. The company has operations worldwide, with about 200 offices in 55 countries. Foreign sales account for about 40 percent of the company's $8.5 billion in annual revenue.

Cisco was formed in 1984 by a group of Stanford University scientists who were interested in developing a way to link the computer world together. The company brought its first product to market in 1986, and sales have been soaring ever since.

The company has about 15,000 employees and 17,000 shareholders. It has a market capitalization of about $190 billion.

EARNINGS PER SHARE GROWTH ★ ★ ★ ★

Past five years: 638 percent (49 percent per year)
Past eight years: 11,600 percent (80 percent per year)

STOCK GROWTH ★ ★ ★ ★

Past nine years: 26,567 percent (85 percent per year)
Dollar growth: $10,000 over nine years would have grown to about $2.7 million.
Average annual compounded rate of return: 85 percent

DIVIDEND

The company pays no dividends.

CONSISTENCY

Increased earnings per share: nine consecutive years
Increased sales: 11 consecutive years

SHAREHOLDER PERKS

The company provides no stock purchase plan, nor does it offer other perks for its shareholders.

CISCO SYSTEMS AT A GLANCE

Fiscal year ended: July 31
Revenue and net income in $ millions

	1993	1994	1995	1996	1997	1998	5-Year Growth Avg. Annual (%)	5-Year Growth Total (%)
Revenue ($)	649	1,243	1,979	4,096	6,440	8,459	68	1,203
Net income ($)	172	315	479	913	1,414	1,873	61	989
Earnings/share ($)	0.8	0.13	0.19	0.30	0.45	0.59	49	638
Dividends/share ($)	—	—	—	—	—	—	—	—
Dividend yield (%)	—	—	—	—	—	—	—	—
PE ratio range	29–49	17–38	22–62	22–48	28–57	39–111	—	—

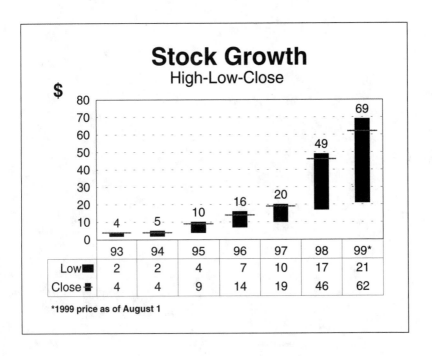

Stock Growth
High-Low-Close

$	93	94	95	96	97	98	99*
Low	2	2	4	7	10	17	21
Close	4	4	9	14	19	46	62

*1999 price as of August 1

43

Staples, Inc.

STAPLES

500 Staples Drive
Framingham, MA 01702
508-253-5000
www.staples.com

Chairman and CEO: Thomas Stemberg
President: Richard Gentry

Earnings Growth	★ ★ ★ ★
Stock Growth	★ ★ ★ ★
Dividend	
Consistency	★ ★ ★ ★
Shareholder Perks	
Nasdaq: SPLS	**12 points**

Staples has become one of the fastest growing retailers in America by marketing its huge offering of office products and equipment to a wide range of businesses, from the mom-and-pop home office to Fortune 500 conglomerates.

The Framingham, Massachusetts retailer has more than 900 retail outlets, plus a catalog operation and an Internet business. It has about 850 stores in 37 states and Canada, plus 48 stores in the United Kingdom and 25 in Germany. Foreign sales account for just 4 percent of the company's total revenue.

The company's prototype store is about 24,000 square feet and sells a broad range of office supplies at discount prices. Most of its stores also offer copying, faxing, and overnight mailing services. The company also operates some Stables Express stores in urban areas that range from 6,000 to 10,000 square feet.

Staples has marketing initiatives that target four key groups of office products users: (1) home office owners, (2) small businesses and organizations, (3) medium-size businesses, and (4) large businesses with more than 1,000 office workers. To reach the smaller groups it uses radio, television, newspapers, the Internet, and direct mail catalogs. For the larger organizations, Staples uses direct mail catalogs, customized catalogs, and a field sales force.

Office and related supplies and services account for 46 percent of the company's $7.1 billion in annual sales; equipment and business machines make up 24 percent; computers and related products account for 22 percent; and office furniture accounts for 8 percent.

Staples is growing quickly with plans to add at least 150 new stores per year in North America and 20 in Germany and the UK.

In addition to its stores, the company operates Staples National Advantage, a nationwide contract stationer business that focuses on selling to large multiregional businesses. Staples also operates Staples.com, a Web-based superstore that offers more than 6,000 products online, with free delivery for orders over $50.

Founded in 1985, Staples opened its first store in 1986 in Brighton, Massachusetts. The company has about 44,000 employees and a market capitalization of about $15 billion.

EARNINGS PER SHARE GROWTH ★ ★ ★ ★

Past five years: 489 percent (42 percent per year)
Past nine years: 1,667 percent (33 percent per year)

STOCK GROWTH ★ ★ ★ ★

Past ten years: 2,400 percent (37 percent per year)
Dollar growth: $10,000 over ten years would have grown to $250,000.
Average annual compounded rate of return: 37 percent

DIVIDEND

Staples pays no dividends.

CONSISTENCY ★ ★ ★ ★

Increased earnings per share: ten consecutive years
Increased sales: ten consecutive years

SHAREHOLDER PERKS

The company offers no stock purchase plan, nor does it provide other shareholder perks.

STAPLES AT A GLANCE

Fiscal year ended: Jan. 31
Revenue and net income in $ millions

	1993	1994	1995	1996	1997	1998	5-Year Growth Avg. Annual (%)	5-Year Growth Total (%)
Revenue ($)	1,122	2,000	3,068	3,968	5,181	7,123	44	535
Net income ($)	25	40	74	106	149	243	58	872
Earnings/share ($)	0.09	0.13	0.20	0.28	0.39	0.53	42	489
Dividends/share ($)	—	—	—	—	—	—	—	—
Dividend yield (%)	—	—	—	—	—	—	—	—
PE ratio range	32–58	23–39	20–40	17–31	20–36	25–72	—	—

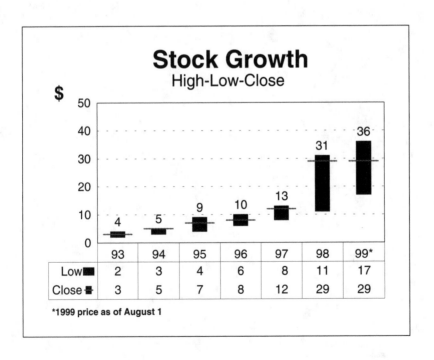

Stock Growth
High-Low-Close

$							
	93	94	95	96	97	98	99*
Low■	2	3	4	6	8	11	17
Close ▬	3	5	7	8	12	29	29

*1999 price as of August 1

44

Cardinal Health, Inc.

5555 Glendon Court
Dublin, OH 43016
614-717-5000
www.cardhealth.com

Chairman and CEO: Robert D. Walter
President: John C. Kane

Earnings Growth	★ ★ ★ ★
Stock Growth	★ ★ ★ ★
Dividend	
Consistency	★ ★ ★ ★
Shareholder Perks	
NYSE: CAH	**12 points**

Cardinal Health is one of the nation's leading distributors of pharmaceuticals and related health care products to drugstores, hospitals, care centers, and pharmacy departments of supermarkets and mass merchandisers.

Founded originally as a food wholesaler in 1971, the Dublin, Ohio operation abandoned the food business long ago to focus solely on the health care business. The company has grown quickly through a series of acquisitions. Since its initial public offering in 1983, Cardinal has acquired more than 20 other companies.

Cardinal now operates a small group of subsidiaries that provide a wide range of products and services to health care customers. Its leading divisions include:

- **Cardinal Distribution and National Specialty Services.** A pharmaceutical distributor to retailers and health care facilities.
- **Pyxis Corp.** The nation's largest manufacturer of point-of-use systems that automate the distribution, management, and control of medications and supplies in hospitals and alternate care facilities.
- **Allegiance Corp.** Leading manufacturer and supplier of health care products and a provider of cost-management services for hospitals, laboratories, and other health care facilities.
- **R.P. Scherer.** Develops drug delivery products, including soft gelatin capsules.
- **PCI Services.** Provides integrated packaging services to pharmaceutical manufacturers.
- **MediQual Systems.** Offers clinical information management systems for medical care facilities.
- **Owen Healthcare.** Provides pharmacy management and information services to hospitals.

Cardinal also owns Medicine Shoppe International, which is the nation's largest franchiser of independent retail pharmacies.

About 53 percent of the company's operating earnings comes from its distribution business, while the other 47 percent comes from services for the health care industry.

Cardinal's full-service national coverage and its integrated inventory management and marketing systems, coupled with guaranteed next-day delivery, have helped strengthen its relationship with customers. Cardinal's innovations also have caught the attention of drug manufacturers who increasingly prefer to work with technologically sophisticated distributors that can take larger, more diversified product lines to market.

The company has about 11,000 employees and a market capitalization of $16.5 billion.

EARNINGS PER SHARE GROWTH ★ ★ ★ ★

Past five years: 213 percent (26 percent per year)
Past ten years: 735 percent (22 percent per year)

STOCK GROWTH

Past ten years: 1,350 percent (31 percent per year)
Dollar growth: $10,000 over ten years (including reinvested dividends) would have grown to $148,000.
Average annual compounded rate of return (including reinvested dividends): 31 percent

DIVIDEND

Dividend yield: 0.2 percent
Increased dividend: two consecutive years (through fiscal 1999)
Past five-year increase: 133 percent (18 percent per year)

CONSISTENCY ★ ★ ★ ★

Increased earnings per share: ten consecutive years
Increased sales: nine of the past ten years

SHAREHOLDER PERKS

Cardinal offers no dividend reinvestment plan, nor does it offer other perks for its shareholders.

CARDINAL HEALTH AT A GLANCE

Fiscal year ended: June 30
Revenue and net income in $ millions

	1993	1994	1995	1996	1997	1998	Avg. Annual (%)	Total (%)
							5-Year Growth	
Revenue ($)	1,967	5,790	7,806	8,862	10,968	12,927	46	557
Net income ($)	31	63	85	160	221	283	56	813
Earnings/share ($)	0.54	0.71	0.89	1.10	1.35	1.69	26	213
Dividends/share ($)	0.03	0.04	0.05	0.05	0.06	0.07	18	133
Dividend yield (%)	0.3	0.3	0.3	0.2	0.2	0.1	—	—
PE ratio range	18–35	26–37	20–27	29–48	30–46	31–51	—	—

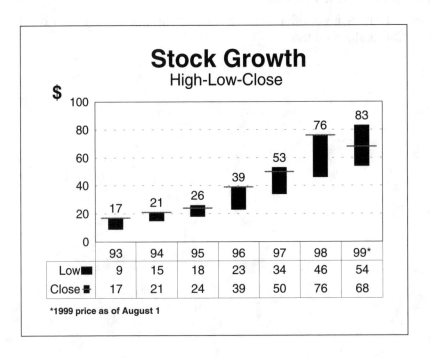

Stock Growth
High-Low-Close

	93	94	95	96	97	98	99*
Low	9	15	18	23	34	46	54
Close	17	21	24	39	50	76	68

*1999 price as of August 1

Maxim Integrated Products

120 San Gabriel Drive
Sunnyvale, CA 94086
408-737-7600
www.maxim-ic.com

Chairman, President, and CEO: John Gifford

Earnings Growth	★ ★ ★ ★
Stock Growth	★ ★ ★ ★
Dividend	
Consistency	★ ★ ★ ★
Shareholder Perks	
Nasdaq: MXIM	**12 points**

Maxim Integrated Products helps link the real world with the digital world. It produces computer circuits that use digital technology to detect, measure, amplify, and convert real world measures, such as temperature, pressure, speed, and sound, into digital signals that can be stored and processed on a computer.

Among its leading products are data converters, interface circuits, microprocessor supervisors, operational amplifiers, power supplies, multiplexers, switches, battery chargers, battery management circuits, fiber optic transceivers, and voltage references.

In all, the Sunnyvale, California operation markets more than 1,500 products. Many of its products are used on microprocessor-based electronics equipment, such as personal computers and peripherals, test equipment, handheld devices, wireless phones and pagers, and video displays.

The company produces products for four key industries. In the communications industry, its products are used for broadband networks, cable systems, central office switches, direct broadcast TV, fiber optics, pagers, cellular phones, satellite communications, and video communications.

In the industrial control industry, its products are used to control temperature, velocity, flow, pressure, and position. In the instrumentation industry, Maxim circuits are used for automatic test equipment, analyzers, data recorders, and instruments used to measure electricity, light, pressure, sound, speed, and temperature. In the data processing area, its circuits are used for bar code readers, disk drives, mainframes, minicomputers, personal computers, printers, point of sale terminals, tape drives, and workstations.

The company also produces products for military and medical equipment applications.

Maxim markets its products worldwide. International sales account for about 56 percent of its $560 million in annual revenue.

The company spends more than $70 million a year on research and development and introduces about 250 new products a year.

Founded in 1983, Maxim has about 3,000 employees and 950 shareholders. It has a market capitalization of about $8 billion.

EARNINGS PER SHARE GROWTH   ★ ★ ★ ★

Past five years: 743 percent (54 percent per year)
Past ten years: 2,067 percent (36 percent per year)

STOCK GROWTH   ★ ★ ★ ★

Past ten years: 5,900 percent (50 percent per year)
Dollar growth: $10,000 over ten years would have grown to about $600,000.
Average annual compounded rate of return: 50 percent

DIVIDEND

The company pays no dividends.

CONSISTENCY ★ ★ ★ ★

Increased earnings per share: ten consecutive years
Increased sales: ten consecutive years

SHAREHOLDER PERKS

The company offers no dividend reinvestment and stock purchase plan.

MAXIM AT A GLANCE

Fiscal year ended: June 30
Revenue and net income in $ millions

	1993	1994	1995	1996	1997	1998	5-Year Growth Avg. Annual (%)	5-Year Growth Total (%)
Revenue ($)	110	154	251	422	434	560	38	409
Net income ($)	17	24	39	123	137	178	60	947
Earnings/share ($)	0.14	0.19	0.29	0.87	0.94	1.18	54	743
Dividends/share ($)	—	—	—	—	—	—	—	—
Dividend yield (%)	—	—	—	—	—	—	—	—
PE ratio range	21–43	26–42	21–62	10–24	19–35	16–33	—	—

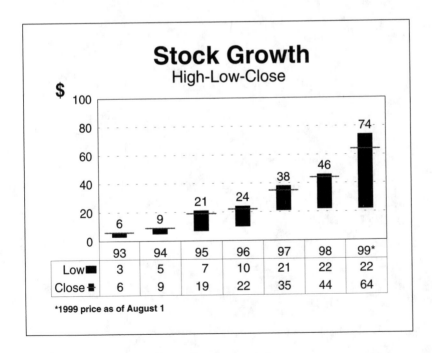

Stock Growth
High-Low-Close

	93	94	95	96	97	98	99*
Low	3	5	7	10	21	22	22
Close	6	9	19	22	35	44	64

*1999 price as of August 1

The Charles Schwab Corporation

Charles Schwab

120 Kearny Street
San Francisco, CA 94104
415-627-7000
www.schwab.com

Chairman and Co-CEO: Charles Schwab
President and Co-CEO: David Pottruck

Earnings Growth	★ ★ ★ ★
Stock Growth	★ ★ ★ ★
Dividend	
Consistency	★ ★ ★ ★
Shareholder Perks	
NYSE: SCH	**12 points**

Charles Schwab has been trying to capture the attention of investors for many years, but only after the company went online did the trading public really stand up and take notice. Its stock price went from a low of $3.38 (split-adjusted) prior to launching its Web-based service in 1997 to $77 a share in early 1999 after the service was up and running.

Schwab is a hybrid among brokerage services. The commissions it charges to buy and sell stocks, bonds, and options are lower than the full-service brokers, but higher than almost all discount brokers. While Schwab's customers don't get the personal attention that full-service brokers offer, they can take advantage of a wide array of research services that most other discounters don't offer.

Schwab is the nation's largest discount broker, with about six million customers and customer assets of about $500 million. The company has 290 branch offices.

With the company's foray into online trading, Schwab reduced its commission fees to about $30 per trade (for online customers only) and added a number of new services: the Analyst Center, which connects customers to proprietary and third-party investment research, guidance, and decision-making tools; the Positions Monitor, which tracks the historic performance of stocks and mutual funds; a mutual fund tracking feature; a stock screening feature; and a money transfer feature that allows customers to transfer funds electronically from their Schwab account to other financial institutions.

Over the past few years, Schwab has tried to position itself as more than just a discount broker. It offers a range of services for independent investment managers, including custodial, trading, and support services. Money managers can call up information about their customers' accounts directly from Schwab's computer system and handle their customers' trades online. Schwab refers more than 12,000 investors each year to independent investment managers.

Schwab also offers retirement plan services and performs market-making activities, making markets for about 1,000 small stocks on the Pacific and Boston regional stock exchanges.

Schwab was founded in 1971 by Charles Schwab and went into the discount brokerage business in 1974. Schwab has about 13,000 employees and 2,700 shareholders. The company has a market capitalization of about $42 billion.

EARNINGS PER SHARE GROWTH ★ ★ ★ ★

Past five years: 175 percent (22 percent per year)
Past ten years: 2,100 percent (36 percent per year)

STOCK GROWTH ★ ★ ★ ★

Past ten years: 5,100 percent (48 percent per year)
Dollar growth: $10,000 over ten years (including reinvested dividends) would have grown to $555,000.
Average annual compounded rate of return (including reinvested dividends): 49 percent

DIVIDEND

Dividend yield: 0.2
Increased dividend: ten consecutive years
Past five-year increase: 400 percent (38 percent per year)

CONSISTENCY

Increased earnings per share: 12 consecutive years
Increased sales: 12 consecutive years

SHAREHOLDER PERKS

The company does not offer a dividend reinvestment and stock purchase plan.

CHARLES SCHWAB AT A GLANCE

Fiscal year ended: Dec. 31
Revenue and net income in $ millions

	1993	1994	1995	1996	1997	1998	5-Year Growth Avg. Annual (%)	Total (%)
Revenue ($)	1,097	1,263	1,777	2,277	2,845	3,388	25	209
Net income ($)	124	135	173	234	270	349	23	181
Earnings/share ($)	0.16	0.17	0.22	0.30	0.34	0.44	22	175
Dividends/share ($)	0.01	0.02	0.03	0.04	0.05	0.05	38	400
Dividend yield (%)	0.7	1.0	0.7	0.7	0.5	0.4	—	—
PE ratio range	8–18	10–16	11–29	13–24	20–43	21–78	—	—

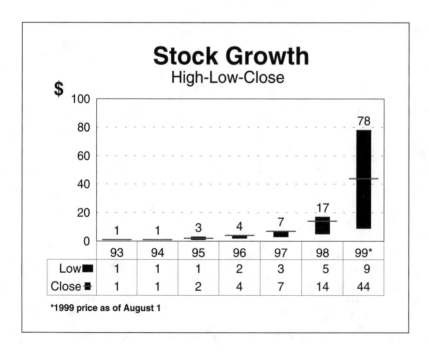

Stock Growth
High-Low-Close

$

	93	94	95	96	97	98	99*
Low	1	1	1	2	3	5	9
Close	1	1	2	4	7	14	44

*1999 price as of August 1

Fiserv, Inc.

255 Fiserv Drive
Brookfield, WI 53045
414-879-5000
www.fiserv.com

Chairman and CEO: George D. Dalton
President: Leslie M. Muma

Earnings Growth	★ ★ ★ ★
Stock Growth	★ ★ ★ ★
Dividend	
Consistency	★ ★ ★ ★
Shareholder Perks	
Nasdaq: FISV	**12 points**

Fiserv knows where the money is. That's why the Milwaukee-area operation has developed a data processing business geared to banks, credit unions, and other financial organizations. Bankers are also money savvy, which is why they have turned their data processing chores over to Fiserv. Fiserv is equipped to handle the data processing duties more effectively and inexpensively than the financial institutions it serves.

In all, Fiserv provides a wide range of data processing services for 7,000 financial clients, including banks, brokerage companies, credit unions, financial planners and investment advisers, insurance companies, leasing companies, mortgage banks, and savings institutions.

Fiserv was formed in 1984 by George Dalton (who continues to serve as chairman and CEO) and Leslie Muma through the merger of two regional data processing firms. Since then, the company has made about

80 acquisitions, which helped turn it into the nation's largest data processing provider for banks and savings institutions.

Fiserv claims customers in more than 70 countries, although its U.S. operations still generate the vast majority of its $1.2 billion in annual revenue.

The company provides a wide range of data processing services, including software systems for account, item, and financial transaction processing and recordkeeping, regulatory reporting, electronic funds transfer, and related database management.

It also offers account processing services, administration and trusteeship of self-directed retirement plans, marketing communications and graphic design services, plastic card products and services, and disaster recovery services.

Fiserv provides backroom automation software systems, self-directed retirement plan processing, network installation and integration services, human resource outsourcing, and delivery and support of third-party software and hardware products.

The company recently introduced a new service for discount brokers that will enable them to do business with customers through voice recognition technology.

Fiserv has about 13,000 employees and 20,000 shareholders. The company has a market capitalization of about $3 billion.

EARNINGS PER SHARE GROWTH ★ ★ ★ ★

Past five years: 155 percent (20 percent per year)
Past ten years: 500 percent (19.5 percent per year)

STOCK GROWTH ★ ★ ★ ★

Past ten years: 1,233 percent (29.5 percent per year)
Dollar growth: $10,000 over ten years would have grown to $134,000.
Average annual compounded rate of return: 29.5 percent

DIVIDEND

Fiserv pays no dividends.

CONSISTENCY

Increased earnings per share: 13 consecutive years
Increased sales: 13 consecutive years

SHAREHOLDER PERKS

The company offers no stock purchase plan, nor does it provide other shareholder perks.

FISERV AT A GLANCE

Fiscal year ended: Dec. 31
Revenue and net income in $ millions

	1993	1994	1995	1996	1997	1998	5-Year Growth Avg. Annual (%)	Total (%)
Revenue ($)	455	537	703	798	974	1,234	22	171
Net income ($)	31	38	50	62	91	114	30	272
Earnings/share ($)	0.53	0.63	0.75	0.89	1.13	1.35	20	155
Dividends/share ($)	—	—	—	—	—	—	—	—
Dividend yield (%)	—	—	—	—	—	—	—	—
PE ratio range	20–29	18–24	—	16–26	19–30	22–38	—	—

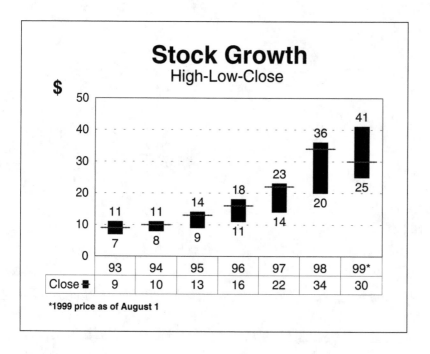

Stock Growth
High-Low-Close

	93	94	95	96	97	98	99*
Close	9	10	13	16	22	34	30

*1999 price as of August 1

Intel Corporation

2200 Mission College Boulevard
Santa Clara, CA 95052
408-765-8080
www.intel.com

Chairman: Andrew S. Grove
President and CEO: Craig R. Barrett

Earnings Growth	★ ★ ★ ★
Stock Growth	★ ★ ★ ★
Dividend	
Consistency	★ ★
Shareholder Perks	★ ★
Nasdaq: INTC	**12 points**

Intel has been supplying the brains of the computer revolution. The company is the world's leading manufacturer of microprocessors, which act as the brain of a computer, processing system data and controlling other devices in the system.

The more advanced the microprocessing chips, the faster and more power the computer. Intel's ability to develop faster and faster chips has kept it at the forefront of the computer revolution—and has kept its profits growing rapidly. The company has grown at a dizzying pace the past decade, with revenues surging from $3.1 billion in 1989 to $26.3 billion a decade later.

Intel's computer microchips process system data and control input, output, and peripheral and memory devices in the PC. With its Pentium III chips, Intel continues to be the dominant player in the worldwide microprocessor market.

Founded in 1968, the Santa Clara, California company has been the world leader in the microchip market since the mid-1980s, after designing the original microprocessor for the IBM PC. It has maintained its lead by first turning out its popular 286 chip, followed by the 386, then the 486, and finally the Pentium generation of chips. Worldwide, well over 100 million PCs are based on Intel architecture. Intel's primary customers are manufacturers of microcomputers.

The U.S. market accounts for about 44 percent of Intel's $26.3 billion in annual revenue. Its other leading markets are Europe (28 percent of revenue), Asia-Pacific (20 percent), and Japan (7 percent).

Microprocessor sales account for about 82 percent of Intel's total revenue.

In addition to its standard microprocessing chips, Intel produces a line of related products, including:

- **Microcontrollers.** Intel produces a wide range of single-chip computers (also called embedded controllers) used to control the operation of communications systems, automobile control applications, robotics, electronic instrumentation, keyboards, home video machines, and other high-tech products.
- **Computer modules and boards.** These are sold to manufacturers who integrate them into their products.
- **Network and communications products.** Intel's products help computers communicate with each other and provide access to online services.
- **Personal conferencing products.** PC users can install Intel software and cards that allow two users to view and manipulate the same documents simultaneously.
- **Parallel supercomputers.** The company's high performance computer systems use multiple microprocessors to speed up the processing function and solve complex computational problems.
- **Semiconductor products.** Intel's flash memory products provide easily reprogrammable memory for cellular phones, computers, and other systems.

Intel's computing enhancement group, including chipsets, embedded processors, microcontrollers, flash memory, and graphics products, accounts for about 15 percent of total revenue. Its network communications group, which makes network and Internet connectivity products, accounts for about 3 percent of revenue.

Intel has about 65,000 employees and 200,000 shareholders. It has a market capitalization of $189 billion.

EARNINGS PER SHARE GROWTH

Past five years: 172 percent (22 percent per year)
Past ten years: 1,006 percent (26 percent per year)

STOCK GROWTH   ★ ★ ★ ★

Past ten years: 2,981 percent (41 percent per year)
Dollar growth: $10,000 over ten years (including reinvested dividends) would have grown to $300,000.
Average annual compounded rate of return (including reinvested dividends): 41 percent

DIVIDEND

Dividend yield: 0.2 percent
Increased dividend: seven consecutive years
Past five-year increase: 67 percent (11 percent per year)

CONSISTENCY   ★ ★

Increased earnings per share: eight of the past ten years
Increased sales: 12 consecutive years

SHAREHOLDER PERKS

Excellent dividend reinvestment and stock purchase plan; voluntary stock purchase plan allows contributions of $25 to $15,000 per month.

INTEL AT A GLANCE

Fiscal year ended: Dec. 31
Revenue and net income in $ millions

	1993	1994	1995	1996	1997	1998	5-Year Growth Avg. Annual (%)	Total (%)
Revenue ($)	8,782	11,521	16,202	20,847	25,070	26,273	25	199
Net income ($)	2,277	2,563	3,491	5,157	6,945	6,178	22	171
Earnings/share ($)	0.65	0.73	0.99	1.45	1.94	1.77	22	172
Dividends/share ($)	0.03	0.03	0.04	0.05	0.06	0.05	11	67
Dividend yield (%)	0.3	0.4	0.3	0.2	0.1	0.1	—	—
PE ratio range	9–14	11–14	7–18	8–23	15–24	18–35	—	—

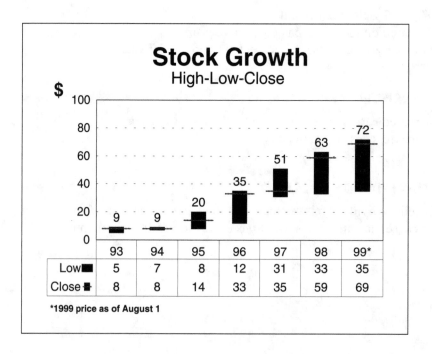

Stock Growth
High-Low-Close

$	93	94	95	96	97	98	99*
	9	9	20	35	51	63	72
Low■	5	7	8	12	31	33	35
Close ▪	8	8	14	33	35	59	69

*1999 price as of August 1

Fastenal Company

FASTENAL COMPANY

2001 Theurer Boulevard
Winona, MN 55987
507-454-5374
www.fastenal.com

Chairman, President, and CEO: Robert A. Kierlin

Earnings Growth	★ ★ ★ ★
Stock Growth	★ ★ ★ ★
Dividend	
Consistency	★ ★ ★ ★
Shareholder Perks	
Nasdaq: FAST	**12 points**

Fasten it with Fastenal. The company sells 59,000 different types of nuts, bolts, screws, studs, washers, and other threaded fasteners and industrial and construction supplies.

The Winona, Minnesota operation also sells 30,000 different types of tools and safety supplies through its FastTool division, 16,000 different types of metal cutting tool blades under the SharpCut brand, and 14,000 types of fluid transfer components and accessories for hydraulic and pneumatic power under the PowerFlow brand.

Fastenal also markets EquipRite handling and storage products, CleanChoice janitorial and paper products, PowerPhase electrical supplies, and FastArc welding supplies.

Fastenal, which went public with its initial stock offering in 1987, has posted record sales and earnings per share every year since then, with double-digit earnings growth each of the past seven years. It has been named to the Forbes list of the "best small companies in America" every year since 1987.

The company sells its products through nearly 800 branch stores in small to medium-size cities in 48 states and Canada. Unlike the typical supply store, Fastenal makes a significant share of its sales through direct calls on customers by store personnel. Most of its customers are in the construction or manufacturing businesses, including plumbers, electricians, sheet metal contractors, and road construction companies.

Threaded fasteners account for about 55 percent of Fastenal's $503 million in annual sales. At one time, the company only sold the Fastenal line of threaded fasteners and industrial supplies, but it added seven other product lines (such as FastTool, SharpCut, and CleanChoice) to its list of offerings from 1993 to 1997.

In addition to its product offerings, the company operates a special manufacturing division that can, as the company puts it, "produce anything that can be cut, machined, or formed from metal bars." It also can modify standard fasteners to meet customer specifications.

Fastenal was founded in 1967 by company president Bob Kierlin, whose original concept was to make a vending machine that would dispense nuts and washers to customers.

The company has about 5,000 customers and 2,200 shareholders. Fastenal has a market capitalization of about $1.5 billion.

EARNINGS PER SHARE GROWTH   ★ ★ ★ ★

Past five years: 338 percent (34 percent per year)
Past ten years: 1,650 percent (38 percent per year)

STOCK GROWTH   ★ ★ ★ ★

Past ten years: 1,158 percent (29 percent per year)
Dollar growth: $10,000 over ten years (including reinvested dividends) would have grown to $127,000.
Average annual compounded rate of return (including reinvested dividends): 29 percent

DIVIDEND

Dividend yield: 0.05 percent
Increased dividend: no increase since 1992
Past five-year increase: 0 percent

CONSISTENCY

Increased earnings per share: 11 consecutive years
Increased sales: 11 consecutive years

SHAREHOLDER PERKS

The company offers no dividend reinvestment and stock purchase plan.

FASTENAL AT A GLANCE

Fiscal year ended: Dec. 31
Revenue and net income in $ millions

	1993	1994	1995	1996	1997	1998	5-Year Growth Avg. Annual (%)	5-Year Growth Total (%)
Revenue ($)	110	162	223	288	398	503	36	357
Net income ($)	12	19	27	33	41	53	35	342
Earnings/share ($)	0.32	0.49	0.72	0.86	1.08	1.40	34	338
Dividends/share ($)	0.02	0.02	0.02	0.02	0.02	0.02	0	0
Dividend yield (%)	0.1	0.1	0.1	0.0	0.0	0.05	—	—
PE ratio range	30–51	29–47	27–59	34–58	29–56	15–41	—	—

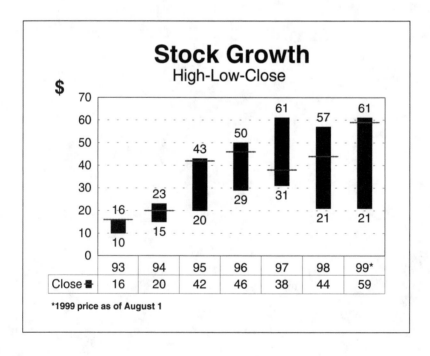

Stock Growth
High-Low-Close

	93	94	95	96	97	98	99*
Close	16	20	42	46	38	44	59

*1999 price as of August 1

Stryker Corporation

stryker

2725 Fairfield Road
Kalamazoo, MI 49002
616-385-2600
www.med.strykercorp.com

Chairman, President, and CEO: John W. Brown

Earnings Growth	★ ★ ★ ★
Stock Growth	★ ★ ★ ★
Dividend	
Consistency	★ ★ ★ ★
Shareholder Perks	
NYSE: SYK	**12 points**

Among Stryker's growing line of medical products is the InfraVision Imaging System, a tiny video camera with an infrared light that surgeons can use during internal surgery to get a broadcast-quality image inside the patient's body. The system often is used with Stryker's "video endosuite," a fully functional operating room that enables the surgical team to control all its equipment through a routing device and to view the patient's internal parts through the special remote video equipment inserted into the body.

Stryker is a leader in the development of a wide range of surgical instruments that facilitate minimally invasive surgery. The Kalamazoo,

Michigan operation is also a leading manufacturer of artificial limbs and other reconstructive products.

Medical and surgical equipment accounts for about 52 percent of Stryker's $1.1 billion in annual revenue. In addition to its medical video equipment, the company makes powered drills, saws, fixation and reaming equipment, and other surgical instruments. It also makes micropowered tools for more delicate operations such as spinal surgery, neurosurgery, and plastic surgery.

Stryker makes a line of specialty stretchers and beds and other patient-handling equipment. Its critical care beds enable physicians to weigh patients, take X-rays, and perform other functions without removing the patient from the bed.

The company is a leading maker of orthopedic implants, which account for about 37 percent of its total revenue. Stryker's line of artificial limbs gives renewed mobility to thousands of injured and arthritis-riddled patients. In addition to artificial limbs, the company makes knee and hip replacements and spinal implant systems used to treat degenerative spinal diseases and related ailments.

The company also offers physical, occupational, and speech therapy services to patients recovering from orthopedic or neurological illness and injury through a network of 222 outpatient physical therapy centers in 23 states. Physical therapy services account for about 11 percent of the company's total revenue.

Stryker markets its products in more than 100 countries. Foreign operations and exports make up 34 percent of total revenue.

Stryker was founded in 1941 by Dr. Homer H. Stryker, a prominent orthopedic surgeon and the inventor of several leading orthopedic products. The company has about 11,000 employees and 3,100 shareholders. It has a market capitalization of $5.9 billion.

EARNINGS PER SHARE GROWTH   ★ ★ ★ ★

Past five years: 143 percent (20 percent per year)
Past ten years: 800 percent (25 percent per year)

STOCK GROWTH

Past ten years: 1,100 percent (28 percent per year)
Dollar growth: $10,000 over ten years (including reinvested dividends) would have grown to $120,000.
Average annual compounded rate of return (including reinvested dividends): 28 percent

DIVIDEND

Dividend yield: 0.2 percent
Increased dividend: seven consecutive years
Past five-year increase: 300 percent (33 percent per year)

CONSISTENCY

Increased earnings per share: 21 consecutive years
Increased sales: 21 consecutive years

SHAREHOLDER PERKS

Stryker does not offer a dividend reinvestment plan, nor does it provide other shareholder perks.

STRYKER AT A GLANCE

Fiscal year ended: Dec. 31
Revenue and net income in $ millions

	1993	1994	1995	1996	1997	1998	5-Year Growth Avg. Annual (%)	Total (%)
Revenue ($)	557	682	872	910	980	1,103	14	98
Net income ($)	60	72	87	101	125	151	20	152
Earnings/share ($)	0.63	0.75	0.90	1.04	1.28	1.53	20	143
Dividends/share ($)	0.04	0.04	0.05	0.10	0.11	0.12	33	300
Dividend yield (%)	0.3	0.3	0.2	0.4	0.3	0.3	—	—
PE ratio range	17–32	16–25	20–33	18–30	19–35	75–136	—	—

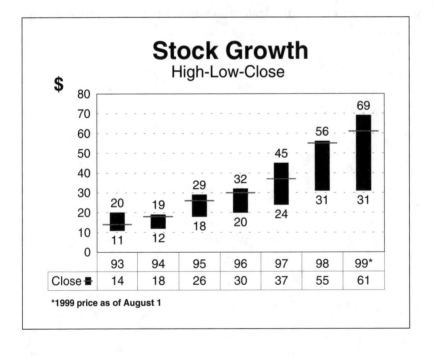

Stock Growth
High-Low-Close

$	93	94	95	96	97	98	99*
Close	14	18	26	30	37	55	61

*1999 price as of August 1

Tyco International, Ltd.

One Tyco Park
Exeter, NH 03833
603-778-9700
www.tyco.com

Chairman, President, and CEO:
L. Dennis Kozlowski

Earnings Growth	★ ★ ★ ★
Stock Growth	★ ★ ★ ★
Dividend	
Consistency	★ ★
Shareholder Perks	★ ★
NYSE: TYC	**12 points**

Tyco International is the world leader in one of the hottest markets around. The company manufactures, installs, and services fire detection equipment and sprinkler systems. Tyco is also the world's largest provider of electronic security systems.

In all, the New Hampshire–based operation generates about 39 percent of its $12.3 billion annual revenue from its fire and security services division. The firm also operates divisions involved in a diverse mix of other areas, from pipes and plastics to electronics and medical supplies.

Tyco has operations in more than 50 countries around the world. Foreign sales account for about 27 percent of the company's total revenue.

The company makes fire extinguishers, fire hydrants, firefighting hose, alarms, detection and fire suppression systems, sprinklers, and electronic security systems. It also installs, maintains, and monitors its electronic security systems, which are used for both commercial and residential customers.

Tyco's other leading divisions include:

- **Disposal and specialty products** (28 percent of revenue). The company makes disposable medical supplies, including gauze and other wound care products, wound closure products, vascular therapy products, and infant medical accessories. It also makes urological, incontinence, and anesthetic supplies; medical stress and resting electrode sensors; and medical and industrial chart paper. The division also makes polyethylene film; coated, laminated, and printed packaging materials; garment hangers; pipeline coatings for the oil, gas, and water distribution industries; and pressure-sensitive adhesives and coatings.
- **Flow control products** (19 percent of revenue). Tyco makes a full line of valves for industrial and process control systems for liquids, gases, and other substances. It also makes pipes, pipe fittings, meters, and pipe hangers.
- **Electrical and electronic components** (14 percent of revenue). The firm makes undersea fiber-optic communications cable, cable assemblies, and underwater electric power cables. The division also makes high-precision printed circuit boards and related products.

Tyco has about 90,000 employees and 6,200 shareholders. It has a market capitalization of about $53 billion.

EARNINGS PER SHARE GROWTH ★ ★ ★ ★

Past five years: 248 percent (28 percent per year)
Past ten years: 359 percent (16.5 percent per year)

STOCK GROWTH ★ ★ ★ ★

Past ten years: 673 percent (23 percent per year)
Dollar growth: $10,000 over ten years (including reinvested dividends) would have grown to about $85,000.
Average annual compounded rate of return (including reinvested dividends): 24 percent

DIVIDEND

Dividend yield: 0.1 percent
Increased dividend: unchanged in six years
Past five-year increase: none

CONSISTENCY

Increased earnings per share: eight of the past ten years
Increased sales: nine of the past ten years

SHAREHOLDER PERKS   ★ ★

Good dividend reinvestment and stock purchase plan; voluntary stock
purchase plan allows cash contributions of $25 to $10,000 per month.

TYCO AT A GLANCE

Fiscal year ended: Sept. 30
Revenue and net income in $ millions

	1993	1994	1995	1996	1997	1998	5-Year Growth Avg. Annual (%)	Total (%)
Revenue ($)	3,115	3,263	4,535	5,090	6,598	12,311	31	295
Net income ($)	100	125	248	310	419	1,117	62	1,020
Earnings/share ($)	0.58	0.68	0.82	1.02	1.31	2.02	28	248
Dividends/share ($)	0.10	0.10	0.10	0.10	0.10	0.10	0	0
Dividend yield (%)	1.0	0.8	0.8	0.6	0.4	0.2	—	—
PE ratio range	46–64	83–108	28–56	—	—	19–38	—	—

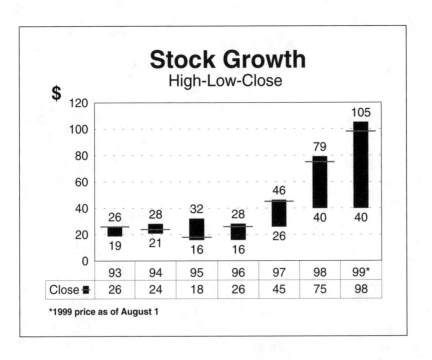

Stock Growth
High-Low-Close

	93	94	95	96	97	98	99*
Close	26	24	18	26	45	75	98

*1999 price as of August 1

Cintas Corporation

Chairman: Richard Farmer
CEO: Robert Kolhepp
President: Scott Farmer

Earnings Growth	★ ★ ★
Stock Growth	★ ★ ★ ★
Dividend	★
Consistency	★ ★ ★ ★
Shareholder Perks	
Nasdaq: CTAS	**12 points**

Cintas supplies the work clothes for more than three million Americans. The company leases and sells uniforms for a wide range of businesses, from delivery services and airlines to service stations and retail chains.

The Cincinnati-based operation has been one of the most consistent companies in America, with 29 consecutive years of record sales and earnings.

Cintas operates about 200 uniform rental centers in 154 cities throughout North America.

It also has four garment manufacturing plants and three distribution centers. The company's customer base extends from coast to coast. It is the largest public company in the uniform business.

The company rents or sells the uniforms to customer companies and typically provides laundry services as well. Cintas designs and manufactures most of the uniforms it supplies for customers.

Much of the company's growth has come through acquisitions. Since going public in 1983, Cintas has acquired nearly 90 smaller regional uniform companies. And with more than 700 mostly family-owned uniform rental companies still operating in the United States, Cintas plans to continue its aggressive acquisition policy. Recent acquisitions include Uniforms to You in Chicago and Mechanics Uniform Service in Indianapolis.

The uniform rental service accounts for about 72 percent of the firm's $1.2 billion in annual revenue. Other services make up the other 28 percent.

Cintas launched a first aid and safety division in 1997 that provides first aid supplies for companies throughout the United States. The company has 28 first aid supply operations in 33 major cities.

In addition to uniforms, the company also supplies rain gear, caps, gloves, long underwear, socks, and work shoes.

Founded in 1929, Cintas has about 17,000 employees and 1,900 shareholders. The company has a market capitalization of $6.7 billion.

EARNINGS PER SHARE GROWTH ★ ★ ★

Past five years: 133 percent (19 percent per year)
Past ten years: 418 percent (18 percent per year)

STOCK GROWTH ★ ★ ★ ★

Past ten years: 884 percent (26 percent per year)
Dollar growth: $10,000 over ten years (including reinvested dividends) would have grown to $105,000.
Average annual compounded rate of return (including reinvested dividends): 26.5 percent

DIVIDEND ★

Dividend yield: 0.3 percent
Increased dividend: 14 consecutive years
Past five-year increase: 157 percent (21 percent per year)

CONSISTENCY

Increased earnings per share: 29 consecutive years
Increased sales: 29 consecutive years

SHAREHOLDER PERKS

The company offers no dividend reinvestment and stock purchase plan, nor does it provide other shareholder perks.

CINTAS AT A GLANCE

Fiscal year ended: May 31
Revenue and net income in $ millions

	1993	1994	1995	1996	1997	1998	5-Year Growth Avg. Annual (%)	Total (%)
Revenue ($)	453	523	615	730	840	1,198	22	165
Net income ($)	459	53	63	75	91	118	21	163
Earnings/share ($)	0.49	0.57	0.67	0.80	0.96	1.14	19	133
Dividends/share ($)	0.07	0.09	0.10	0.13	0.15	0.18	21	157
Dividend yield (%)	0.5	0.6	0.6	0.6	0.5	0.4	—	—
PE ratio range	22–30	22–27	19–27	20–30	21–35	21–46	—	—

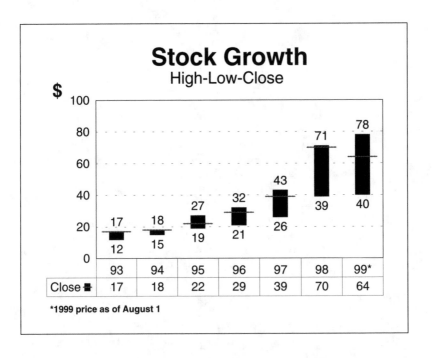

Stock Growth
High-Low-Close

$	93	94	95	96	97	98	99*
Close	17	18	22	29	39	70	64

*1999 price as of August 1

53

Automatic Data Processing, Inc.

One ADP Boulevard
Roseland, NJ 07068
973-994-5000
www.adp.com

Chairman and CEO: Arthur F. Weinbach
President: Gary C. Butler

Earnings Growth	★ ★
Stock Growth	★ ★ ★ ★
Dividend	★ ★
Consistency	★ ★ ★ ★
Shareholder Perks	
NYSE: AUD	**12 points**

Automatic Data Processing (ADP) has been one of the most consistent companies in the world since it opened for business in 1949. The Roseland, New Jersey operation has posted record sales and earnings every year for 49 consecutive years.

ADP provides paycheck processing and other transaction processing, and data communications and information services for about 425,000 corporate clients. The company processes the paychecks for 26 million workers, which represent a total annual payout of more than $3 billion.

The company is the nation's largest payroll and tax filing processor and is credited with pioneering "outsourcing," in which companies farm out tasks that don't directly relate to their core competencies.

ADP's oldest business is Employer Services, which generates 58 percent of the company's $4.8 billion in annual revenue. The division provides a comprehensive range of payroll, tax deposit and reporting, benefits outsourcing, 401(k) recordkeeping, and unemployment compensation management services.

Its employer services also are offered throughout Europe, where the company has more than 20,000 corporate clients.

ADP also operates in three other key segments, including:

1. **Brokerage services** (23 percent of revenue). ADP provides data services, recordkeeping, order entry, proxy processing, and other services for the financial services industry. ADP is the leading provider of third-party processing and retail equity information in North America. It processes more than 15 percent of the retail equity brokerage transactions in the United States and Canada, handling more than 600,000 trades per day.

2. **Dealer services** (14 percent). The company provides some computing, data, and professional services to more than 18,000 automobile, truck, and farm equipment dealers and manufacturers in the United States, Canada, Europe, Asia, and Latin America. Auto dealers use ADP's on-site systems to manage their accounting, factory communications, inventory, sales, and service activities. To help auto dealers eliminate paperwork, ADP systems can digitize and store records that can be retrieved from workstations for viewing, faxing, or printing.

3. **Claims services and other income** (5 percent). The company provides auto collision estimates and parts availability services to insurance companies, claims adjusters, repair shops, and salvage yards.

ADP has 30,000 employees and about 25,000 shareholders. The company has a market capitalization of $27 billion.

EARNINGS PER SHARE GROWTH ★ ★

Past five years: 90 percent (14 percent per year)
Past ten years: 254 percent (13 percent per year)

STOCK GROWTH

Past ten years: 743 percent (23.5 percent per year)
Dollar growth: $10,000 over ten years (including reinvested dividends) would have grown to $86,500.
Average annual compounded rate of return (including reinvested dividends): 24.5 percent

DIVIDEND

Dividend yield: 0.8 percent
Increased dividend: 23 consecutive years
Past five-year increase: 117 percent (17 percent per year)

CONSISTENCY ★ ★ ★ ★

Increased earnings per share: 49 consecutive years
Increased sales: 49 consecutive years

SHAREHOLDER PERKS

The company provides no dividend reinvestment and stock purchase plan, nor does it offer other perks for its shareholders.

AUTOMATIC DATA PROCESSING AT A GLANCE

Fiscal year ended: June 30
Revenue and net income in $ millions

	1993	1994	1995	1996	1997	1998	5-Year Growth Avg. Annual (%)	Total (%)
Revenue ($)	2,223	2,469	2,894	3,567	4,112	4,798	17	116
Net income ($)	294	334	395	455	524	605	16	106
Earnings/share ($)	0.52	0.59	0.69	0.79	0.90	0.99	14	90
Dividends/share ($)	0.12	0.14	0.12	0.20	0.22	0.26	17	117
Dividend yield (%)	1.0	1.0	0.8	1.1	1.0	0.9	—	—
PE ratio range	23–27	20–25	21–30	23–29	22–36	28–41	—	—

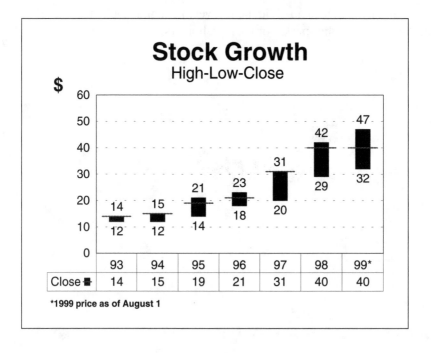

Stock Growth
High-Low-Close

Close	93	94	95	96	97	98	99*
	14	15	19	21	31	40	40

*1999 price as of August 1

Xerox Corporation

800 Long Ridge Road
Stamford, CT 06904
203-968-3000
www.xerox.com

Chairman: Paul A. Allaire
President and CEO: G. Richard Thoman

Earnings Growth	★ ★ ★ ★
Stock Growth	★ ★ ★
Dividend	★
Consistency	★ ★
Shareholder Perks	★ ★
NYSE: XRX	**12 points**

It's no exaggeration to say that Xerox has long been synonymous with photocopying. The company invented the process–introducing its first copier half a century ago in 1949–and has been ringing up profits from the process ever since.

Xerox makes a full line of both color and black-and-white copy machines and other document processing and printing equipment.

The company's largest and fastest growing segment is its digital copy group, which now accounts for about 46 percent of its $19.4 billion in total annual sales. Its light lens copiers, which had once accounted for well over half of the company's revenue, have dropped to about 41 percent of total revenue. Paper, ink, and other related products account for about 13 percent of sales.

In terms of its customer base, the company's fastest growing segment is the small business and home office market. The company has released a line of lower-priced copiers aimed at the small business market.

Xerox markets the broadest line of black-and-white copiers and duplicators in the industry, ranging from a 3-copies-per-minute personal copier to a 150-copies-per-minute duplicator to special copiers designed for large engineering and architectural drawings of up to four feet long.

Xerox also manufactures a family of Docutech digital publishing systems. The systems can scan hard copy and convert it into digital documents, or accept digital documents directly from networked personal computers or workstations. Its newest models print high-resolution pages at up to 180 impressions per minute, and the in-line finisher staples completed sets or finishes booklets with covers and thermal-adhesive bindings.

Xerox has been a pioneer in electronic laser printing, which combines computer, laser, communications, and xerographic technologies. The company markets a line of electronic printers with speeds ranging from five pages per minute to more than 400 pages per minute.

The company entered the digital color copier market in 1991 and currently offers several high-end color copiers.

Xerox is worldwide in scope, generating about 48 percent of total revenue through foreign sales, including about 28 percent from Europe.

The company was founded in 1906 as the Haloid Company. It introduced its first copier in 1949 and its first plain paper copier in 1959. The company changed its name to Xerox in 1961. The New York–based operation has about 93,000 employees and 70,000 shareholders. It has a market capitalization of $38.7 billion.

EARNINGS PER SHARE GROWTH   ★ ★ ★ ★

Past five years: 174 percent (22 percent per year)
Past ten years: 137 percent (9 percent per year)

STOCK GROWTH   ★ ★ ★

Past ten years: 453 percent (19 percent per year)
Dollar growth: $10,000 over ten years (including reinvested dividends) would have grown to $83,000.
Average annual compounded rate of return (including reinvested dividends): 23.5 percent

DIVIDEND ★

Dividend yield: 1.4 percent
Increased dividend: four consecutive years
Past five-year increase: 40 percent (7 percent per year)

CONSISTENCY ★ ★

Increased earnings per share: eight of the past ten years
Increased sales: nine of the past ten years

SHAREHOLDER PERKS ★ ★

Good dividend reinvestment and stock purchase plan; voluntary stock purchase plan allows contributions of $10 to $5,000 per month.

XEROX AT A GLANCE

Fiscal year ended: Dec. 31
Revenue and net income in $ millions

	1993	1994	1995	1996	1997	1998	5-Year Growth Avg. Annual (%)	5-Year Growth Total (%)
Revenue ($)	14,437	15,088	16,611	17,378	18,166	19,449	6	35
Net income ($)	580	794	1,076	1,206	1,452	1,692	24	192
Earnings/share ($)	0.85	1.07	1.47	1.66	2.02	2.33	22	174
Dividends/share ($)	0.50	0.50	0.50	0.56	0.63	0.70	7	40
Dividend yield (%)	3.8	3.0	2.5	2.3	1.8	1.4	—	—
PE ratio range	—	13–17	9–14	11–16	12–20	40–74	—	—

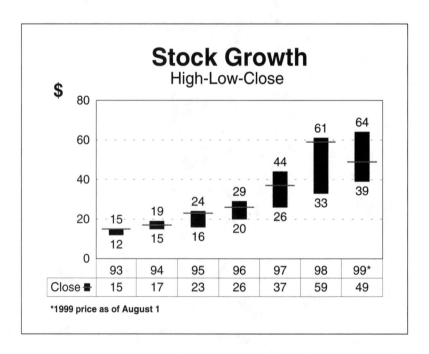

Stock Growth
High-Low-Close

	93	94	95	96	97	98	99*
Close	15	17	23	26	37	59	49

*1999 price as of August 1

COMPUTER® ASSOCIATES
Software superior by design.

Computer Associates International, Inc.

One Computer Associates Plaza
Islandia, NY 11788
516-342-5224
www.cai.com

Chairman and CEO: Charles B. Wang
President: Sanjay Kumar

Earnings Growth	★ ★ ★ ★
Stock Growth	★ ★ ★ ★
Dividend	
Consistency	★ ★
Shareholder Perks	★ ★
NYSE: CA	**12 points**

Among the broad range of software products Computer Associates offers for its corporate clients is a program called Unicenter TNG. The program uses 3D animation and elements of virtual reality to help organizations visualize and control their information technology infrastructure—applications, databases, systems, and networks.

The Unicenter TNG, which is the company's top-selling software product among its library of more than 500 software offerings, helps organizations define their business policies, map those polices to particular resource management requirements, and then monitor resources for their support of specific business processes.

Computer Associates is one of the world's largest business software manufacturers. It designs software for more than 40 different desktop, midrange, and mainframe operating systems and platforms.

Much of the company's recent growth has come through acquisitions, as it continues to buy companies with leading-edge business software.

Originally, Computer Associates developed operating software exclusively for large IBM mainframe computers. But as American industry shifted increasingly to smaller computers, Computer Associates began expanding its product base to include applications for smaller computers as well.

Most of the company's software is designed to enhance data processing functions by providing tools to measure and improve computer hardware and software performance and programmer productivity.

The company also makes database management, business applications, and graphics software for mainframe, midrange, and desktop computers from a variety of vendors, including IBM, DEC, Hewlett-Packard, Amdahl, Data General, Sun, Sequent, Tandem, Compaq, and Apple.

Computer Associates markets its products through a sales and support staff of about 5,300 people, plus a network of independent resellers, distributors, and dealers.

The Islandia, New York operation has subsidiaries in 43 foreign countries. Foreign sales account for about 36 percent of total revenue.

First incorporated in 1974, Computer Associates has about 12,000 employees and 10,000 shareholders. It has a market capitalization of about $24 billion.

EARNINGS PER SHARE GROWTH   ★ ★ ★ ★

Past five years: 235 percent (27 percent per year)
Past ten years: 670 percent (23 percent per year)

STOCK GROWTH

Past ten years: 828 percent (25 percent per year)
Dollar growth: $10,000 over ten years (including reinvested dividends) would have grown to $95,000.
Average annual compounded rate of return (including reinvested dividends): 25.5 percent

DIVIDEND

Dividend yield: 0.2 percent
Increased dividend: three of the past five years
Past five-year increase: 100 percent (15 percent per year)

CONSISTENCY

Increased earnings per share: eight consecutive years
Increased sales: 17 consecutive years

SHAREHOLDER PERKS   ★ ★

Good dividend reinvestment and stock purchase plan; voluntary stock
purchase plan allows contributions of $25 to $3,000 per month.

COMPUTER ASSOCIATES AT A GLANCE

Fiscal year ended: March 31
Revenue and net income in $ millions

	1993	1994	1995	1996	1997	1998	5-Year Growth Avg. Annual (%)	5-Year Growth Total (%)
Revenue ($)	2,149	2,623	3,505	4,040	4,719	5,253	20	144
Net income ($)	401	586	752	964	1,190	1,300	26	224
Earnings/share ($)	0.69	1.03	1.32	1.69	2.10	2.31	27	235
Dividends/share ($)	0.04	0.06	0.06	0.07	0.08	0.08	15	100
Dividend yield (%)	0.4	0.4	0.3	0.2	0.2	0.2	—	—
PE ratio range	9–19	11–20	—	34–68	12–27	23–54	—	—

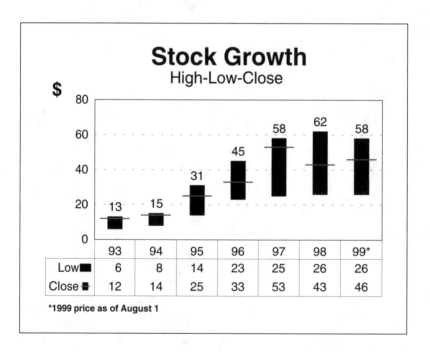

Stock Growth
High-Low-Close

	93	94	95	96	97	98	99*
Low	6	8	14	23	25	26	26
Close	12	14	25	33	53	43	46

*1999 price as of August 1

The Clorox Company

1221 Broadway
Oakland, CA 94612
510-271-7000
www.clorox.com

Chairman, President, and CEO:
G. Craig Sullivan

Earnings Growth	★ ★
Stock Growth	★ ★ ★
Dividend	★ ★
Consistency	★ ★ ★
Shareholder Perks	★ ★
NYSE: CLX	**12 points**

Clorox Company offers a lot more than bleach. The Oakland-based operation sells a long line of cleaning products, cat litter, charcoal, foods, and other household products.

Many of its leading brands have come through acquisitions, including the 1999 acquisition of First Brands, which is the maker of Glad bags, GladWare, Jonny Cat, EverFresh, Scoop Away, StarterLogg, and Hearth-Logg brands.

Other recent acquisitions include Black Flag insecticides, Lestoil household cleaning products, and the Armor All line of automotive cleaning products. The company typically introduces 10 to 20 new products each year.

Other leading Clorox products include Clorox toilet bowl cleanser, Clorox Clean-Up household spray cleaner, Formula 409 cleaning spray,

Liquid Plumr, Pine-Sol spray cleaner, S.O.S. soap pads, Tackle cleaner, Tilex tile cleaner, and Tuffy mesh scrubber.

The company also makes Kingsford charcoal, Combat insecticides, Control and Fresh Step cat litters, Hidden Valley dressings, and Brita water filtration systems.

Clorox also offers a line of professional cleaning products that it markets to contract cleaners, maid services, building contractors, and small business owners. It also sells its salad dressings in gallon containers to restaurants nationwide.

Clorox has been expanding its marketing worldwide. It sells its products in more than 80 countries throughout Europe, Asia, and North and South America. Foreign sales account for about 17 percent of the company's $2.7 billion in total revenue.

Clorox bleach has been a laundry room fixture in homes across America for most of this century. The firm was founded in 1913 as the Electro-Alkaline Company, then changed its name to the Clorox Chemical Corporation in 1922. In 1957, the Oakland-based bleach maker was acquired by Procter & Gamble, which held onto it for a dozen years before divesting it in 1969.

Clorox has been a very steady performer, posting increased earnings 16 of the past 17 years.

Clorox has 35 manufacturing plants throughout the United States and abroad.

The company has 6,600 employees and 13,000 shareholders. It has a market capitalization of $13 billion.

EARNINGS PER SHARE GROWTH   ★ ★

Past five years: 83 percent (13 percent per year)
Past ten years: 129 percent (8.5 percent per year)

STOCK GROWTH   ★ ★ ★

Past ten years: 474 percent (19 percent per year)
Dollar growth: $10,000 over ten years (including reinvested dividends) would have grown to $74,000.
Average annual compounded rate of return (including reinvested dividends): 22 percent

DIVIDEND ★ ★

Dividend yield: 1.3 percent
Increased dividend: 18 consecutive years
Past five-year increase: 49 percent (8 percent per year)

CONSISTENCY ★ ★ ★

Increased earnings per share: nine of the past ten years
Increased sales: nine of the past ten years

SHAREHOLDER PERKS ★ ★

Outstanding dividend reinvestment and stock purchase plan; voluntary stock purchase plan allows contributions of a minimum of $10 to a maximum of $60,000 a year.

CLOROX AT A GLANCE

Fiscal year ended: June 30
Revenue and net income in $ millions

	1993	1994	1995	1996	1997	1998	5-Year Growth Avg. Annual (%)	5-Year Growth Total (%)
Revenue ($)	1,634	1,837	1,984	2,218	2,533	2,741	11	68
Net income ($)	168	180	201	222	249	298	12	77
Earnings/share ($)	1.54	1.68	1.89	2.14	2.41	2.82	13	83
Dividends/share ($)	0.86	0.93	0.96	1.06	1.16	1.28	8	49
Dividend yield (%)	3.7	3.6	3.4	2.8	2.1	1.7	—	—
PE ratio range	14–18	14–18	15–21	16–26	20–33	26–41	—	—

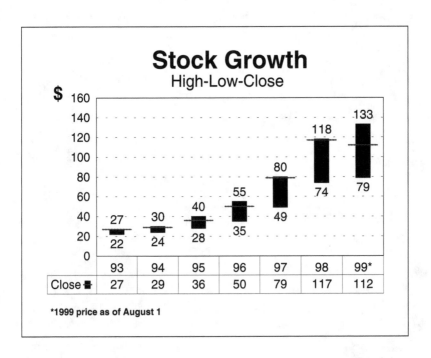

Stock Growth
High-Low-Close

	93	94	95	96	97	98	99*
Close	27	29	36	50	79	117	112

*1999 price as of August 1

Pitney Bowes, Inc.

Pitney Bowes

1 Elmcroft Road
Stamford, CT 06926
203-356-5000
www.pitneybowes.com

Chairman and CEO: Michael Critelli
President: Marc Breslawsky

Earnings Growth	★
Stock Growth	★ ★ ★
Dividend	★ ★ ★
Consistency	★ ★ ★
Shareholder Perks	★ ★
NYSE: PBI	**12 points**

Through rain, hail, sleet, and snow, Pitney Bowes continues to meter the mail. The Stamford, Connecticut operation is the world's largest maker of postage meters and mailing equipment. It also offers a broad range of fax machines, copiers, and other office equipment.

Postage meters and other mailing equipment account for 64 percent of the company's $4.2 billion in annual revenue. The company typically leases postage metering equipment to its customers and sells supplies. The company also offers related services to its metering customers. In addition to postage meters, Pitney provides mailing machines, address hygiene software, letter and parcel scales, mail openers, mail room furniture, folders, and paper handling and shipping equipment.

Pitney also sells and leases copy machines, facsimile equipment and supplies, and related products. It is the only facsimile systems supplier in the United States that markets exclusively through its own direct sales force. The company concentrates its copier sales on larger corporations with multiunit installations. It endears itself to the large companies with a preventive maintenance program covering all elements of copier performance.

It also offers facilities management services, assisting companies with a variety of support functions such as correspondence mail, copy centers, fax services, electronic printing, reprographics management, high-volume automated mail center management, and related activities. Target customers are large industrial companies, banking and financial institutions, and services organizations such as law firms and accounting firms. The company's office solutions segment accounts for about 28 percent of total revenue.

Pitney also has two other divisions that contribute a small portion to the bottom line. Its mortgage services division provides billing, collecting, and processing services for major investors in residential first mortgages. Mortgage servicing accounts for about 3 percent of total revenue. The company's capital services division provides financing for such large-ticket products as aircraft, over-the-road trucks and trailers, railcars, locomotives, commercial real estate, and high-tech equipment. Capital services accounts for about 4 percent of total revenue.

Pitney has about 30,000 employees and 31,400 shareholders. It has a market capitalization of $18.9 billion.

EARNINGS PER SHARE GROWTH   ★

Past five years: 78 percent (12 percent per year)
Past ten years: 171 percent (10.5 percent per year)

STOCK GROWTH

Past ten years: 458 percent (19 percent per year)
Dollar growth: $10,000 over ten years (including reinvested dividends)
would have grown to $70,000.
Average annual compounded rate of return (including reinvested dividends): 21.5 percent

DIVIDEND

Dividend yield: 1.8 percent
Increased dividend: 16 consecutive years
Past five-year increase: 100 percent (15 percent per year)

CONSISTENCY

Increased earnings per share: nine of the past ten years
Increased sales: nine of the past ten years

SHAREHOLDER PERKS ★ ★

Good dividend reinvestment and stock purchase plan; voluntary stock
purchase plan allows contributions of $100 to $3,000 per quarter.

PITNEY BOWES AT A GLANCE

Fiscal year ended: Dec. 31
Revenue and net income in $ millions

	1993	1994	1995	1996	1997	1998	5-Year Growth Avg. Annual (%)	Total (%)
Revenue ($)	3,543	3,271	3,555	3,859	4,101	4,221	2	19
Net income ($)	369	348	408	469	526	568	9	54
Earnings/share ($)	1.16	1.11	1.34	1.56	1.80	2.07	12	78
Dividends/share ($)	0.45	0.52	0.60	0.69	0.80	0.90	15	100
Dividend yield (%)	2.2	2.7	3.1	2.7	2.2	1.7	—	—
PE ratio range	19–23	13–21	11–18	14–20	15–26	20–32	—	—

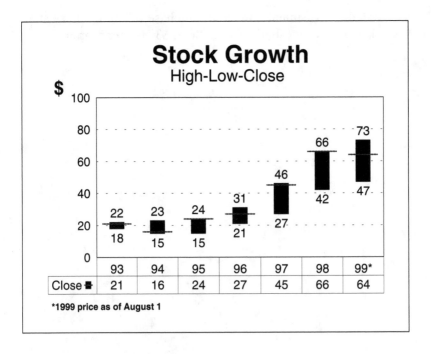

Stock Growth
High-Low-Close

Close ■	93	94	95	96	97	98	99*
	21	16	24	27	45	66	64

*1999 price as of August 1

58

Carlisle Companies, Inc.

250 South Clinton Street, Suite 201
Syracuse, NY 13202
315-474-2500
www.carlisle.com

Chairman and CEO: Stephen P. Munn
President: Dennis J. Hall

Earnings Growth	★ ★ ★ ★
Stock Growth	★ ★
Dividend	★ ★
Consistency	★ ★
Shareholder Perks	★ ★
NYSE: CSL	**12 points**

Carlisle Companies is a diversified manufacturing operation that makes a wide range of commercial and industrial products, from construction materials and auto parts to kitchen equipment and shipping containers.

The company's leading segment is industrial components, which accounts for about 33 percent of its $1.52 billion in annual revenue. The Syracuse-based operation makes small pneumatic tires and wheels for golf carts, trailers, and outdoor power equipment. It also makes heavy duty braking systems and related parts for trucks and heavy equipment, and high performance wire and cable assemblies for aerospace, data processing, and communications equipment.

In addition to its industrial components division, Carlisle operates in three other key segments, including:

1. **Construction materials** (24 percent of revenue). Carlisle makes rubber and plastic membranes for flat roofs and related roofing materials, including flashings, fasteners, sealing tapes, coatings, sealants, and waterproofing materials.
2. **Automotive components** (17 percent of revenue). The firm makes rubber and plastic auto parts for automobiles and light trucks.
3. **General industrial products** (23 percent of revenue). Carlisle makes commercial and institutional plastic food service products such as dishes, cups, tumblers, trays, bowls, catering equipment, dishwashing racks, salad bar equipment, ceramic tableware, and cleaning brushes. It also makes heavy duty truck and trailer dump bodies and low-bed trailers, transportation and storage processing equipment for the food, dairy, and pharmaceutical markets, and refrigerated shipping containers.

The company has begun to expand its sales to overseas markets. European sales account for about 8 percent of Carlisle's total revenue, and Asian sales account for about 2 percent.

Carlisle first opened shop in 1917 as a manufacturer of inner tubes for bicycle and automobile tires. The company has about 7,500 employees and 2,500 shareholders. It has a market capitalization of $1.4 billion.

EARNINGS PER SHARE GROWTH ★ ★ ★ ★

Past five years: 201 percent (25 percent per year)
Past ten years: 269 percent (14 percent per year)

STOCK GROWTH ★ ★

Past ten years: 395 percent (17.5 percent per year)
Dollar growth: $10,000 over ten years (including reinvested dividends) would have grown to $62,000.
Average annual compounded rate of return (including reinvested dividends): 20 percent

DIVIDEND

Dividend yield: 1.5 percent
Increased dividend: 13 consecutive years
Past five-year increase: 71 percent (11.5 percent per year)

CONSISTENCY ★ ★

Increased earnings per share: eight of the past ten years
Increased sales: eight of the past ten years

SHAREHOLDER PERKS ★ ★

Dividend reinvestment and stock purchase plan; voluntary cash contributions of $10 to $3,000 per quarter.

CARLISLE AT A GLANCE

Fiscal year ended: Dec. 31
Revenue and net income in $ millions

	1993	1994	1995	1996	1997	1998	5-Year Growth Avg. Annual (%)	5-Year Growth Total (%)
Revenue ($)	611	693	823	1,018	1,261	1,518	20	148
Net income ($)	28	36	44	56	71	85	24	199
Earnings/share ($)	0.92	1.15	1.41	1.80	2.28	2.77	25	201
Dividends/share ($)	0.35	0.38	0.42	0.47	0.53	0.60	12	71
Dividend yield (%)	2.4	2.3	2.1	1.8	1.4	1.3	—	—
PE ratio range	13–19	13–16	12–15	10–17	12–20	12–19	—	—

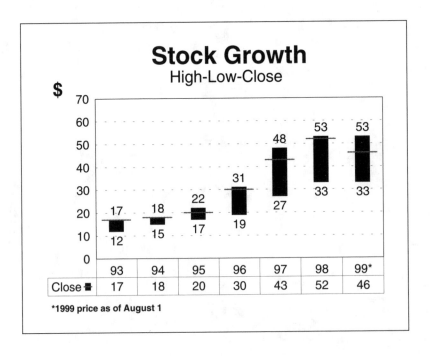

Stock Growth
High-Low-Close

$

	93	94	95	96	97	98	99*
Close ■	17	18	20	30	43	52	46

*1999 price as of August 1

59

The Coca-Cola Company

The Coca-Cola Company

One Coca-Cola Plaza
Atlanta, GA 30313
404-676-2121
www.thecoca-colacompany.com

Chairman and CEO: M. Douglas Ivester

Earnings Growth	★
Stock Growth	★ ★ ★ ★
Dividend	★ ★
Consistency	★ ★ ★
Shareholder Perks	★ ★
NYSE: KO	**12 points**

Either there's no Pepsi machine in Rome, Georgia, or it's a pretty hot place to live. On average, Rome residents drink 821 servings a year of Coca-Cola Company beverages. That's more than two servings a day, 365 days a year, for every man, woman, and child in Rome. Located just up the highway from Coke's Atlanta world headquarters, Rome leads the nation in per capita consumption of Coke products.

Nationwide, Americans drink about 395 8-ounce servings of Coca-Cola Company beverages each year. The company controls a 44.5 percent share of the U.S. soft drink market, compared with PepsiCo's 31 percent share.

In addition to Coke and Diet Coke, the company produces a broad range of other beverages, including Cherry Coke, Fanta, Sprite, Diet Sprite, Mr PiBB, Mellow Yello, TAB, Fresca, Barq's Root Beer, Surge, POWERaDE, Fruitopia, and other products developed for specific countries. In all, Coke sells about 160 different beverage products.

Through Coke's Minute Maid division, the company produces a variety of Minute Maid juices and soft drinks, Five Alive, Bright & Early, Bacardi brand tropical fruit mixers, and Hi-C fruit drinks. It is the world's largest distributor of juices and juice products, with sales of about 10 billion servings per year worldwide.

Coke is by far the company's leading brand, accounting for about 67 percent of all beverage sales by the company. Coca-Cola is the world's most recognized trademark.

The company quenches thirsts in nearly 200 countries around the globe. North American sales account for about 37 percent of Coke's $18.8 billion a year in revenue. Other regions where Coke beverages are sold include Europe, 26 percent of revenue; the Middle East and Far East, 22 percent; Latin America, 12 percent; and Africa, 3 percent.

Mexicans drink the most Coke products, with a per capita consumption rate of 412 servings per year. Other leading markets include Chile, 330 servings per year; Australia, 285; Norway, 277; Israel, 264; Spain, 219; Argentina, 218; and Canada, 212. The company is focusing more effort on China where per capita consumption is just 7 servings per year. But with 1.3 billion people, the Chinese market could become extremely lucrative if Coke could push Chinese consumption rates up to levels similar to Europe and South America.

Founded in 1886, Coca-Cola has about 29,000 employees and 365,000 shareholders. The company has a market capitalization of about $170 billion.

EARNINGS PER SHARE GROWTH   ★

Past five years: 69 percent (11 percent per year)
Past ten years: 294 percent (31 percent per year)

STOCK GROWTH

Past ten years: 816 percent (25 percent per year)
Dollar growth: $10,000 over ten years (including reinvested dividends) would have grown to $101,000.
Average annual compounded rate of return (including reinvested dividends): 26 percent

DIVIDEND

Dividend yield: 0.9 percent
Increased dividend: 37 consecutive years
Past five-year increase: 76 percent (12 percent per year)

CONSISTENCY

Increased earnings per share: nine of the past ten years
Increased sales: nine of the past ten years

SHAREHOLDER PERKS ★ ★

Good dividend reinvestment and stock purchase plan; voluntary stock purchase plan allows contributions of $10 to $125,000 per month.

COCA-COLA AT A GLANCE

Fiscal year ended: Dec. 31
Revenue and net income in $ millions

	1993	1994	1995	1996	1997	1998	5-Year Growth Avg. Annual (%)	Total (%)
Revenue ($)	13,957	16,172	18,018	18,546	18,868	18,813	6	35
Net income ($)	2,188	2,554	2,986	3,492	4,129	3,533	10	61
Earnings/share ($)	0.84	0.99	1.19	1.40	1.64	1.42	11	69
Dividends/share ($)	0.34	0.39	0.44	0.50	0.56	0.60	12	76
Dividend yield (%)	1.6	1.7	1.4	1.1	0.9	0.8	—	—
PE ratio range	22–27	19–27	21–34	26–39	30–44	37–62	—	—

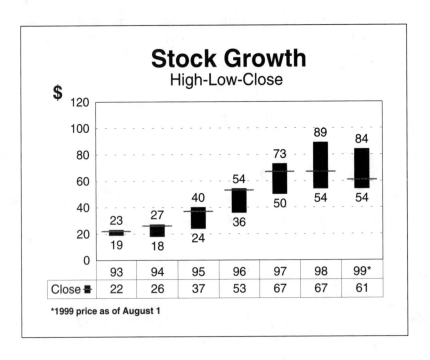

Stock Growth
High-Low-Close

	93	94	95	96	97	98	99*
Close	22	26	37	53	67	67	61

*1999 price as of August 1

Ecolab, Inc.

370 North Wabasha Street
St. Paul, MN 55102
651-293-2233
www.ecolab.com

Chairman: Michael Shannon
President and CEO: Allan Schuman

Earnings Growth	★ ★
Stock Growth	★ ★ ★
Dividend	★ ★ ★
Consistency	★ ★
Shareholder Perks	★ ★
NYSE: ECL	**12 points**

Ecolab helps make the world a cleaner place. The company is the world's leading manufacturer of premium cleaning, sanitizing, and maintenance products and services for the hospitality, institutional, and industrial markets.

The St. Paul operation sells its products to hotels, restaurants, food service operations, laundries, dairy plants and farms, light industry, and health care and educational facilities. Ecolab has operations in 37 countries and sales in more than 150 countries. International sales account for about 23 percent of the company's $1.89 billion in annual revenue.

Ecolab divides its operations into six key segments, including:

1. **Institutional.** The company sells specialized cleaners and sanitizers for washing dishes, laundry, and general housekeeping. The division also provides pool and spa treatment programs for commercial and hospitality customers and products and services for the vehicle wash industry.
2. **Kay line.** The Kay line of products includes chemical cleaning and sanitizing products primarily for the fast-food industry, including fast-food restaurants and other places that prepare and serve fast food such as convenience stores, airports, stadiums, discount stores, and grocery store delis.
3. **Food and beverage.** Ecolab sells detergents, cleaners, sanitizers, lubricants, animal health and water treatment products to dairy plants, livestock farms, breweries, soft-drink bottling plants, pharmaceutical and cosmetic plants, and meat, poultry, and other food processors.
4. **Professional products.** The company produces a line of infection-prevention and janitorial products for the medical and janitorial markets. Products include detergents, general purpose cleaners, carpet care, furniture polishes, disinfectants, floor care products, hand soaps, deodorizers, infection control, and gym floor products.
5. **Water care services.** Ecolab provides water and wastewater treatment products as well as services and systems for commercial and institutional customers.
6. **Pest elimination.** The company provides services for the elimination and prevention of pests to restaurants, food and beverage processors, educational and health care facilities, hotels, and other commercial customers.

Founded in 1923, Ecolab has 12,000 employees and 4,700 shareholders. The company has a market capitalization of about $5.5 billion.

EARNINGS PER SHARE GROWTH ★ ★

Past five years: 92 percent (14 percent per year)
Past ten years: 3,733 percent (43 percent per year)

STOCK GROWTH ★ ★ ★

Past ten years: 417 percent (18 percent per year)
Dollar growth: $10,000 over ten years (including reinvested dividends) would have grown to $62,000.
Average annual compounded rate of return (including reinvested dividends): 20 percent

DIVIDEND ★ ★ ★

Dividend yield: 1.1 percent
Increased dividend: 14 consecutive years
Past five-year increase: 90 percent (14 percent per year)

CONSISTENCY ★ ★

Increased earnings per share: eight of the past ten years
Increased sales: nine of the past ten years

SHAREHOLDER PERKS ★ ★

Good dividend reinvestment and stock purchase plan; voluntary stock purchase plan allows contributions of $10 to $60,000 per year.

ECOLAB AT A GLANCE

Fiscal year ended: Dec. 31
Revenue and net income in $ millions

	1993	1994	1995	1996	1997	1998	5-Year Growth Avg. Annual (%)	Total (%)
Revenue ($)	1,042	1,207	1,341	1,490	1,640	1,888	12	81
Net income ($)	76	92	99	113	134	154	15	103
Earnings/share ($)	0.60	0.67	0.75	0.88	1.00	1.15	14	92
Dividends/share ($)	0.20	0.23	0.26	0.29	0.34	0.38	14	90
Dividend yield (%)	1.9	2.1	2.0	1.8	1.5	1.3	—	—
PE ratio range	15–19	15–19	13–21	17–22	18–27	22–32	—	—

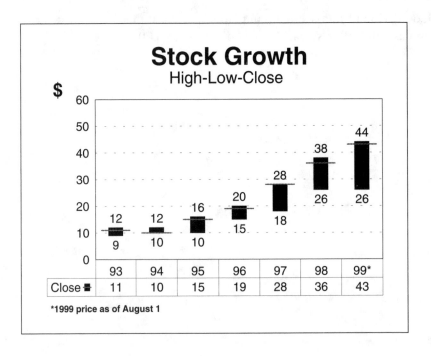

Stock Growth
High-Low-Close

	93	94	95	96	97	98	99*
Close	11	10	15	19	28	36	43

*1999 price as of August 1

The Valspar Corporation

The Valspar Corporation

1101 Third Street South
Minneapolis, MN 55415
612-332-7371
www.valspar.com

Chairman, President, and CEO:
Richard Rompala

Earnings Growth	★
Stock Growth	★ ★
Dividend	★ ★ ★
Consistency	★ ★ ★ ★
Shareholder Perks	★ ★
NYSE: VAL	**12 points**

Valspar has been a mainstay of the American landscape for nearly 200 years. Now the company is splashing its paints and varnishes around the world. The Minneapolis-based operation has sales operations in Europe and Asia, and manufacturing plants in China, Australia, France, Singapore, and Great Britain.

Valspar also has 24 plants throughout North America, including one in Mexico and one in Canada.

The company's largest division is its consumer coatings group, which makes a full line of decorative paints, varnishes, and stains for sale to consumers by home centers, mass merchants, hardware wholesalers, and independent dealers. The consumer group accounts for about 34 percent of the company's $1.16 billion in total revenue.

Among its leading consumer brands are Colony, Valspar, Enterprise, Magicolor, McCloskey, BPS, and Masury.

Valspar's other divisions include:

- **Packaging coatings** (28 percent of revenue). Valspar is the world's largest supplier of coatings for the rigid packaging industry. Its leading segment is the production of coatings for food and beverage cans. It also produces coatings for aerosol cans, bottle crowns, closures for glass bottles, and coatings for flexible packaging—paper, film, and foil substrates.
- **Industrial coatings** (24 percent of revenue). The firm produces decorative and protective coatings for wood, metal, and plastics and is a major supplier to the furniture and wood paneling industry.
- **Special products** (14 percent of revenue). Valspar manufactures coatings and resins for marine applications, automotive and fleet refinish coatings, and heavy-duty maintenance and high-performance floor finishing.

Valspar traces its origins to a Boston paint shop called Color and Paint, which opened in 1806. That business eventually became Valentine & Co., which introduced a line of Valspar quick-drying varnishes and stains in 1906. Valspar was touted as "the varnish that won't turn white." Its claim to fame was a boiling-water test that Valspar-varnished woods could endure with no apparent ill effects.

The company has 3,800 employees and about 1,900 shareholders. Valspar has a market capitalization of about $1.5 billion.

EARNINGS PER SHARE GROWTH ★

Past five years: 75 percent (12 percent per year)
Past ten years: 298 percent (15 percent per year)

STOCK GROWTH ★ ★

Past ten years: 380 percent (17 percent per year)
Dollar growth: $10,000 over ten years (including reinvested dividends) would have grown to about $55,000.
Average annual compounded rate of return (including reinvested dividends): 18.5 percent

DIVIDEND

Dividend yield: 1.4 percent
Increased dividend: 21 consecutive years
Past five-year increase: 91 percent (14 percent per year)

CONSISTENCY

Increased earnings per share: 24 consecutive years
Increased sales: 12 consecutive years

SHAREHOLDER PERKS ★ ★

The company offers a direct stock purchase plan with a minimum initial investment of $1,000. Its dividend reinvestment and stock purchase plan allows contributions of up to $10,000 per year.

VALSPAR AT A GLANCE

Fiscal year ended: Oct. 31
Revenue and net income in $ millions

	1993	1994	1995	1996	1997	1998	5-Year Growth Avg. Annual (%)	5-Year Growth Total (%)
Revenue ($)	694	724	790	860	1,017	1,155	11	67
Net income ($)	40	44	48	56	66	72	12	79
Earnings/share ($)	0.93	1.00	1.08	1.26	1.49	1.63	12	75
Dividends/share ($)	0.22	0.26	0.30	0.33	0.36	0.42	14	91
Dividend yield (%)	1.2	1.5	1.6	1.5	1.2	1.2	—	—
PE ratio range	13–17	13–18	16–21	16–23	18–22	16–21	—	—

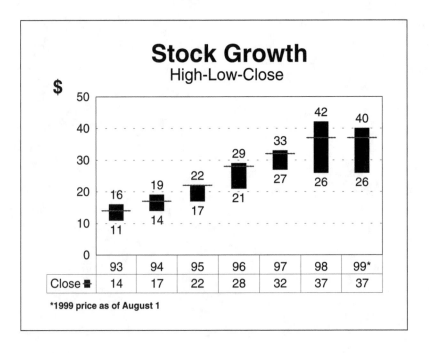

Stock Growth
High-Low-Close

	93	94	95	96	97	98	99*
Close	14	17	22	28	32	37	37

*1999 price as of August 1

Sysco Corporation

1390 Enclave Parkway
Houston, TX 77077
713-584-1390
www.sysco.com

Chairman and CEO: Bill. M. Lindig
President: Charles H. Cotros

Earnings Growth	★
Stock Growth	★ ★
Dividend	★ ★ ★
Consistency	★ ★ ★ ★
Shareholder Perks	★ ★
NYSE: SYY	**12 points**

Sysco delivers the goods. From bread and butter to meat and potatoes, Sysco ships grocery goods to thousands of food service operations around the country. In all, the company distributes about 275,000 food products and related goods.

The Houston-based distributor is the nation's largest marketer of food service products, with operations in the nation's 150 largest cities (plus parts of Canada). In all, Sysco distributes more than 200,000 cases of food a day. Operating from 72 distribution centers, Sysco delivers food and related products to 300,000 restaurants, hotels, schools, hospitals, retirement homes, and other food service operations.

Sysco does not produce its own products but rather procures goods from several thousand independent sources, including both large brand name food producers and independent private label processors and packers.

Sysco's leading product segment is canned and dry products, which account for about 23 percent of the company's $15.3 billion in annual revenue. Other significant contributors are fresh and frozen meats, 15 percent; frozen fruits, vegetables, and bakery goods, 15 percent; dairy products, 9 percent; paper and disposables, 7 percent; and poultry, 10 percent. The company also handles beverages, fresh produce, janitorial products, seafood, and medical supplies.

Restaurant sales account for 62 percent of Sysco's annual revenue, while hospitals and nursing homes account for 11 percent; schools and colleges, 7 percent; hotels and motels, 5 percent; and other sources such as retail groceries, 15 percent.

The company's 10,000 sales and service representatives also help food service clients with menu planning and inventory control, as well as contract services for installing kitchen equipment and beverage dispensers.

Founded in 1969 through the merger of nine small food distributors, Sysco has grown rapidly through a series of acquisitions. In all, the company has acquired more than 50 other food-related businesses.

The company has 33,000 employees and 16,000 shareholders. Sysco has a market capitalization of $9.6 billion.

EARNINGS PER SHARE GROWTH ★

Past five years: 76 percent (12 percent per year)
Past ten years: 296 percent (15 percent per year)

STOCK GROWTH ★★

Past ten years: 392 percent (17 percent per year)
Dollar growth: $10,000 over ten years (including reinvested dividends) would have grown to $53,000.
Average annual compounded rate of return (including reinvested dividends): 18 percent

DIVIDEND

Dividend yield: 1.3 percent
Increased dividend: 28 consecutive years
Past five-year increase: 136 percent (19 percent per year)

CONSISTENCY

Increased earnings per share: 22 consecutive years
Increased sales: 22 consecutive years

SHAREHOLDER PERKS ★ ★

Good dividend reinvestment and stock purchase plan; voluntary stock purchase plan allows contributions of $100 to $10,000 a month.

SYSCO AT A GLANCE

Fiscal year ended: June 30
Revenue and net income in $ millions

	1993	1994	1995	1996	1997	1998	5-Year Growth Avg. Annual (%)	Total (%)
Revenue ($)	10,000	10,900	12,100	13,400	14,500	15,300	9	53
Net income ($)	202	217	252	277	303	325	10	61
Earnings/share ($)	0.54	0.59	0.69	0.76	0.86	0.95	12	76
Dividends/share ($)	0.14	0.16	0.20	0.25	0.29	0.33	19	136
Dividend yield (%)	1.1	1.2	1.5	1.6	1.7	1.5	—	—
PE ratio range	21–29	18–25	18–24	18–23	17–28	21–30	—	—

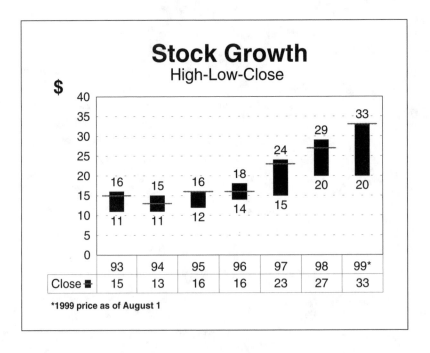

Stock Growth
High-Low-Close

Close ■	93	94	95	96	97	98	99*
	15	13	16	16	23	27	33

*1999 price as of August 1

Hubbell Incorporated

584 Derby Milford Road
Orange, CT 06477-4024
203-799-4100
www.hubbell.com

Chairman, President, and CEO:
G. Jackson Ratcliffe

Earnings Growth	★ ★ ★ ★
Stock Growth	★
Dividend	★ ★ ★
Consistency	★ ★
Shareholder Perks	★ ★
NYSE: HUB.B	**12 points**

Hubbell keeps the current flowing. The company develops and manufactures a broad range of electrical and electronic products, such as lighting fixtures, plugs, switches, cables, adapters, sensors, receptacles, and connectors.

The company's electrical products segment accounts for about 57 percent of its $1.4 billion in annual revenue. The electrical segment includes wiring devices, such as fuses, dimmers, surge suppressors, wall outlets, floor boxes, switches, lampholders, and wallplates; lighting fixtures, such as poles, floodlights, and indoor and outdoor lighting fixtures; and outlet boxes, enclosures, plastic fittings, and electrical cord holding devices.

Based in Orange, Connecticut, the company sells lights and fixtures for athletic fields, service stations, outdoor display signs, parking lots, shopping centers, and roadways. It manufactures indoor lights for gymnasiums, industrial plants, and commercial buildings.

Hubbell's other segments include:

- **Power** (28 percent of sales). Hubbell makes insulated wire and cable, electrical transmission and distribution products, and high-voltage test and measurement equipment, polymer insulators, and high-voltage surge arresters used in the construction of electrical transmission and distribution lines and substations.
- **Telecommunications** (10 percent of sales). Under the Pulsecom trade name, Hubbell manufactures and sells voice and data signal processing equipment used primarily by the telephone and telecommunications industry, Internet and broadcast access equipment, and related products.
- **Other** (5 percent of sales). The company makes test and measurement equipment, high-voltage power supplies, transformers, industrial controls, and electric cable and hose reels.

Hubbell has sales operations in several other countries. Foreign operations account for about 6 percent of total revenue.

Hubbell was founded in 1888 by Harvey Hubbell II, whose first product was a wrapping paper stand and cutter used by retailers to unroll and cut wrapping paper. He later invented, developed, and marketed a number of plugs, cords, and other electrical products.

Hubbell has about 11,000 employees and 5,400 shareholders (class B). The company has a market capitalization of about $3 billion.

EARNINGS PER SHARE GROWTH ★ ★ ★ ★

Past five years: 150 percent (20 percent per year)
Past ten years: 134 percent (9 percent per year)

STOCK GROWTH ★

Past ten years: 150 percent (10 percent per year)
Dollar growth: $10,000 over ten years (including reinvested dividends) would have grown to $35,000.
Average annual compounded rate of return (including reinvested dividends): 13 percent

DIVIDEND ★ ★ ★

Dividend yield: 3.1 percent
Increased dividend: 38 consecutive years
Past five-year increase: 56 percent (9 percent per year)

CONSISTENCY ★ ★

Increased earnings per share: eight of the past ten years
Increased sales: 16 consecutive years

SHAREHOLDER PERKS ★ ★

Good dividend reinvestment and stock purchase plan; voluntary stock
purchase plan allows contributions of $100 to $1,000 per month.

HUBBELL AT A GLANCE

Fiscal year ended: Dec. 31
Revenue and net income in $ millions

	1993	1994	1995	1996	1997	1998	5-Year Growth Avg. Annual (%)	Total (%)
Revenue ($)	832	1,014	1,143	1,297	1,379	1,425	11	71
Net income ($)	66	107	122	142	130	169	21	156
Earnings/share ($)	1.00	1.60	1.83	2.10	1.89	2.50	20	150
Dividends/share ($)	0.78	0.81	0.92	1.02	1.13	1.22	9	56
Dividend yield (%)	3.0	3.0	3.2	2.8	2.5	2.8	—	—
PE ratio range	25–29	16–20	14–18	15–20	21–26	13–21	—	—

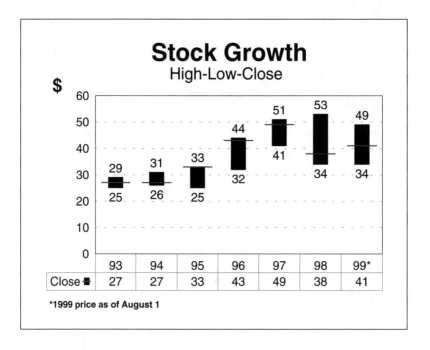

Stock Growth
High-Low-Close

	93	94	95	96	97	98	99*
Close	27	27	33	43	49	38	41

*1999 price as of August 1

Sherwin-Williams Company

101 Prospect Avenue NW
Cleveland, OH 44115
216-566-2000
www.sherwin.com

Chairman and CEO: John G. Breen
President: Thomas A. Commes

Earnings Growth	★
Stock Growth	★ ★
Dividend	★ ★ ★
Consistency	★ ★ ★ ★
Shareholder Perks	★ ★
NYSE: SHW	**12 points**

Sherwin-Williams keeps its paints flowing and its profits rising. The Cleveland-based manufacturer has posted more than 20 consecutive years of record earnings.

The company is the nation's largest producer of paints and varnishes. It has about 2,300 paint stores in the United States and operations in about 30 other countries. The company opens about 50 to 100 new stores each year.

Among its leading brands are Dutch Boy, Kem-Tone, Sherwin-Williams, Martin-Senour, Curinol, Acme, ProMar, Pratt & Lambert, Perma-Clad, Western, Standox, Krylon, Color Works, Rust Tough, Rubberset,

Excelo, Lazzuril, Marson, Globo, Colorgin, White Lightning, Red Devil, Sprayon, Moly-White, and Dupli-Color.

The company's paint stores business segment generates revenue of $2.8 billion a year, which accounts for 56 percent of its $4.93 billion in total annual revenue.

Sherwin-Williams stores offer paints, wallcoverings, floor coverings, window treatments, spray equipment, brushes, scrapers, rollers, and related products. The stores are geared to the do-it-yourself customer, professional painters, industrial and commercial maintenance customers, and small to midsize manufacturers.

The greatest concentration of Sherwin-Williams stores is in the Midwest, with 160 stores in its home state of Ohio, 80 in Illinois, 110 in Pennsylvania, 78 in Michigan, 57 in Indiana, and 55 in Missouri. The company has 90 stores in California, 196 in Texas, and 110 in New York. It also operates about 70 stores in Mexico, 26 in Canada, and 20 in Puerto Rico.

The company continues to upgrade, remodel, and modernize its stores. In 1998, the stores were equipped with satellite dishes that linked all stores with the corporate headquarters.

Sherwin-Williams' other core business is its coatings segment, which accounts for 43 percent of total revenue. The coatings segment manufactures the company's line of paints and related products for homeowners, professional painters, and manufacturers of factory-finished products. It also is responsible for marketing the company's line of consumer paints and private label paints to independent dealers, mass merchandisers, independent dealers, and distributors.

The coatings division also makes auto finishes and refinishing coatings that it markets to body shops and other refinishers. The company operates 119 wholesale automotive paints centers in the United States and about 35 branches outside.

The company also manufactures and markets custom and industrial aerosol paints, paint applicators, retail and wholesale consumer aerosols, and cleaning products.

Sherwin-Williams' paints first adorned homes and barns in northern Ohio shortly after the Civil War in 1866. Sherwin-Williams has about 25,000 employees and 12,000 shareholders. It has a market capitalization of about $5.2 billion.

EARNINGS PER SHARE GROWTH ★

Past five years: 69 percent (11 percent per year)
Past ten years: 171 percent (10.5 percent per year)

STOCK GROWTH ★★

Past ten years: 290 percent (14.5 percent per year)
Dollar growth: $10,000 over ten years (including reinvested dividends) would have grown to about $44,000.
Average annual compounded rate of return (including reinvested dividends): 16 percent

DIVIDEND ★★★

Dividend yield: 1.9 percent
Increased dividend: 21 consecutive years
Past five-year increase: 80 percent (13 percent per year)

CONSISTENCY ★★★★

Increased earnings per share: 21 consecutive years
Increased sales: 21 consecutive years

SHAREHOLDER PERKS ★★

Good dividend reinvestment and stock purchase plan; voluntary stock purchase plan allows contributions of $10 to $2,000 per month.

SHERWIN-WILLIAMS AT A GLANCE

Fiscal year ended: Dec. 31
Revenue and net income in $ millions

	1993	1994	1995	1996	1997	1998	5-Year Growth Avg. Annual (%)	Total (%)
Revenue ($)	2,949	3,100	3,274	4,133	4,881	4,934	11	67
Net income ($)	165	187	201	229	261	273	10	65
Earnings/share ($)	0.93	1.08	1.17	1.33	1.50	1.57	11	69
Dividends/share ($)	0.25	0.28	0.32	0.35	0.40	0.45	13	80
Dividend yield (%)	1.5	1.7	1.8	1.5	1.4	1.5	—	—
PE ratio range	16–20	14–17	14–18	15–22	16–22	12–24	—	—

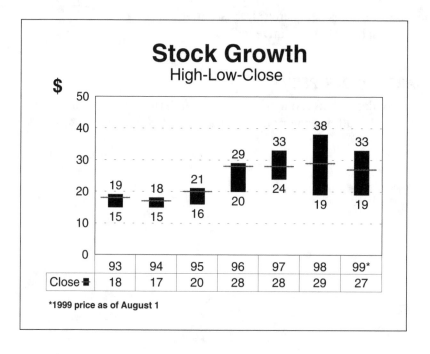

Stock Growth
High-Low-Close

	93	94	95	96	97	98	99*
Close	18	17	20	28	28	29	27

*1999 price as of August 1

ConAgra, Inc.

One ConAgra Drive
Omaha, NE 68102
402-595-4000
www.conagra.com

Chairman, President, and CEO:
Bruce Rohde

Earnings Growth	★
Stock Growth	★
Dividend	★ ★ ★ ★
Consistency	★ ★ ★ ★
Shareholder Perks	★ ★
NYSE: CAG	**12 points**

ConAgra puts food on a lot of tables. The Omaha operation sells $24 billion worth of food and related products each year. It is the world's second largest food processor.

From feeds and fertilizer to Banquet chickens and Peter Pan peanut butter, ConAgra covers nearly every furrow and fowl of the agricultural industry. The company is involved in a wide range of ventures, including grain merchandising, crop inputs (fertilizers, seeds, insecticides, and other crop protection chemicals), and commodity services.

But ConAgra's bread and butter is its grocery and refrigerated foods divisions. Among the company's most recognized brands are Hunt's, Peter Pan, Orville Redenbacher's popcorn, Act II popcorn, Wesson, Morton, Chun King, Banquet, Armour, Country Pride, Eckrich, and Healthy Choice.

Other well-known ConAgra brands include Swift, Reddi Wip, Swiss Miss, Knott's, Manwich, La Choy, Patio, Decker, Butterball turkey, and Country Skillet. The company also produces frozen potato products, delicatessen and food service products, and pet accessories.

ConAgra recently acquired Nabisco's margarine business, including Parkay, Blue Bonnet, and Fleishmann's brands, and it acquired GoodMark Foods, maker of Slim Jim meat snacks.

Grocery products account for about 24 percent of the company's total revenue, and refrigerated foods make up 52 percent.

ConAgra also operates a North American network of grain merchandising offices and more than 90 grain elevators, river loading facilities, export elevators, and barges.

It also operates 24 flour mills in 14 states and a commodity trading business with offices in 15 nations that trade agricultural commodities and foodstuffs on the world market. ConAgra's food inputs and ingredients division accounts for 25 percent of total revenue.

The 79-year-old company has operations in 35 countries. International sales account for about 7 percent of ConAgra's pre-tax income.

ConAgra has 83,000 employees and 165,000 shareholders. The company has a market capitalization of $13.5 billion.

EARNINGS PER SHARE GROWTH ★

Past five years: 72 percent (11.5 percent per year)
Past ten years: 216 percent (12 percent per year)

STOCK GROWTH ★

Past ten years: 203 percent (11.5 percent per year)
Dollar growth: $10,000 over ten years (including reinvested dividends) would have grown to $35,000.
Average annual compounded rate of return (including reinvested dividends): 13.5 percent

DIVIDEND ★ ★ ★ ★

Dividend yield: 3.0 percent
Increased dividend: 23 consecutive years
Past five-year increase: 91 percent (14 percent per year)

CONSISTENCY ★ ★ ★ ★

Increased earnings per share: 18 consecutive years
Increased sales: eight of the past ten years

SHAREHOLDER PERKS ★ ★

Good dividend reinvestment and stock purchase plan; voluntary stock purchase plan allows contributions of $50 to $50,000 per year. About 60 percent of shareholders participate.

At its annual meetings, the company passes out a gift pack of some of its foods to shareholders, and it sometimes sends out discount offers along with its quarterly earnings reports.

CONAGRA AT A GLANCE

Fiscal year ended: May 31
Revenue and net income in $ millions

	1993	1994	1995	1996	1997	1998	5-Year Growth Avg. Annual (%)	5-Year Growth Total (%)
Revenue ($)	21,519	23,512	24,109	24,822	24,002	23,841	3	11
Net income ($)	392	437	496	545	615	628	10	60
Earnings/share ($)	0.79	0.91	1.03	1.17	1.34	1.36	12	72
Dividends/share ($)	0.32	0.35	0.42	0.46	0.53	0.61	14	91
Dividend yield (%)	2.3	2.7	2.6	2.3	2.1	1.9	—	—
PE ratio range	12–18	12–16	37–52	14–20	18–28	18–22	—	—

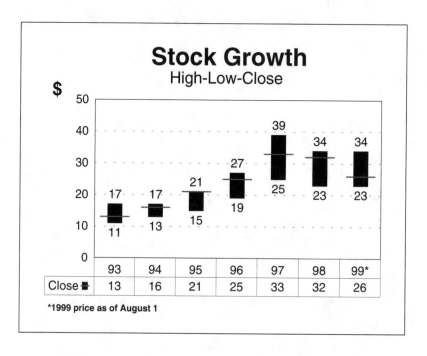

Stock Growth
High-Low-Close

	93	94	95	96	97	98	99*
Close ■	13	16	21	25	33	32	26

*1999 price as of August 1

Bemis Company, Inc.

222 South Ninth Street
Minneapolis, MN 55402-4099
612-376-3000
www.bemis.com

Chairman and CEO: John H. Roe
President: Jeffrey Curler

Earnings Growth	★ ★
Stock Growth	
Dividend	★ ★ ★ ★
Consistency	★ ★ ★ ★
Shareholder Perks	★ ★
NYSE: BMS	**12 points**

Bemis makes the wrappers and packages for hundreds of foods, candies, medical products, and household goods. The 141-year-old Minneapolis operation is North America's largest manufacturer of flexible packaging.

Flexible packaging includes plastic, polyethylene, and paper packaging used for a wide variety of foods and other products.

Flexible packaging accounts for about 74 percent of the company's $1.85 billion in total annual revenue. Its flexible packaging includes:

- **Coated and laminated film packaging (plastics).** The company does resin manufacturing, extruding, coating, laminating, metallizing, printing, and converting for packaging for products such as meats, cheese, coffee, condiments, potato chips, candy, and medical products.

- **Polyethylene packaging products.** Bemis makes preformed bags, extruded products, and printed roll packaging for items such as bread, bakery goods, seeds, lawn and garden products, ice, and fresh and frozen vegetables.
- **Industrial and consumer paper bags.** The firm makes multiwall and small paper bags, balers, printed paper roll stock, and bag closing materials for industrial and consumer packaging products such as pet foods, chemicals, dairy products, fertilizers, feed, minerals, flour, and sugar.

Bemis also manufactures packaging systems that provide automated bag handling, weighing, filling, closing, and sealing.

The company's other leading segment is its specialty coated and graphics products, which account for 26 percent of total sales. Products include industrial adhesives for mounting and bonding, quality roll label and sheet print stock for packaging labels, and a line of specialized laminates for graphics and photography.

Founded in 1858 as a grain bag manufacturer, Bemis has sales offices and plants throughout the United States, Canada, Great Britain, Europe, Scandinavia, Australia, and South Central America. About 9 percent of the company's annual revenue comes from its foreign operations.

Bemis has about 9,500 employees and 6,000 shareholders. It has a market capitalization of $2.1 billion.

EARNINGS PER SHARE GROWTH   ★ ★

Past five years: 83 percent (13 percent per year)
Past ten years: 182 percent (11 percent per year)

STOCK GROWTH

Past ten years: 107 percent (7.5 percent per year)
Dollar growth: $10,000 over ten years (including reinvested dividends) would have grown to $26,000.
Average annual compounded rate of return (including reinvested dividends): 10 percent

DIVIDEND

Dividend yield: 3.0 percent
Increased dividend: 15 consecutive years
Past five-year increase: 76 percent (12 percent per year)

CONSISTENCY

Increased earnings per share: 14 consecutive years
Increased sales: nine of the past ten years

SHAREHOLDER PERKS ★ ★

Good dividend reinvestment and stock purchase plan; voluntary stock
purchase plan allows contributions of $25 to $10,000 per quarter.

BEMIS AT A GLANCE

Fiscal year ended: Dec. 31
Revenue and net income in $ millions

	1993	1994	1995	1996	1997	1998	5-Year Growth Avg. Annual (%)	5-Year Growth Total (%)
Revenue ($)	1,204	1,391	1,523	1,655	1,877	1,848	9	54
Net income ($)	59	73	85	101	108	111	13	88
Earnings/share ($)	1.14	1.40	1.63	1.90	2.00	2.09	13	83
Dividends/share ($)	0.50	0.54	0.64	0.72	0.80	0.88	12	76
Dividend yield (%)	2.2	2.3	2.4	2.2	1.9	2.2	—	—
PE ratio range	22–31	15–18	14–18	13–20	17–24	16–22	—	—

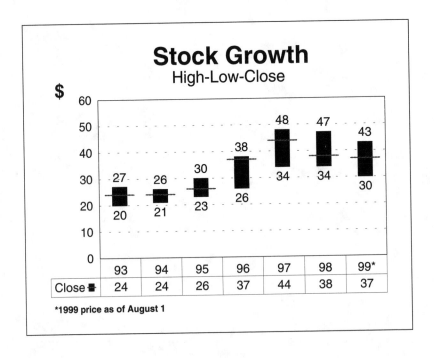

Stock Growth
High-Low-Close

	93	94	95	96	97	98	99*
Close	24	24	26	37	44	38	37

*1999 price as of August 1

Dell Computer Corporation

One Dell Way
Round Rock, TX 78682
512-338-4400
www.dell.com

Chairman and CEO: Michael S. Dell

Earnings Growth	★ ★ ★ ★
Stock Growth	★ ★ ★ ★
Dividend	
Consistency	★ ★ ★
Shareholder Perks	
Nasdaq: DELL	**11 points**

Dell Computer founder Michael Dell has made billions of dollars by selling computers directly to consumers. The Dell direct approach cuts costs by eliminating the markups that would otherwise go to the wholesale and retail dealers. It also avoids the higher inventory costs associated with the traditional distribution channels and reduces the high risk of product obsolescence in the rapidly changing computer market.

The direct sales strategy also gives the company a better opportunity to maintain, monitor, and update its customer database, so that it can be used for future product offerings and post-sale service and support programs.

Founded in 1984, Dell is the world's largest direct seller of computer systems. The Round Rock, Texas operation sells a wide range of computer systems, including desktop computers, notebook computers, workstations and network server and storage products, and an extended selection of peripheral hardware and computing software.

Dell offers two lines of desktop computers: the OptiPlex line for corporate and institutional customers using a network and the Dimension line for small businesses, workgroups, and individuals.

The company also offers a number of specialized services, including custom hardware and software integration, leasing and asset management, and network installation and support. The firm also offers next-business-day delivery and extended training and support programs for many of its software offerings.

Dell's customers range from large corporations, government agencies, and medical and educational institutions to small businesses and individuals. The company markets its products to the business sector through sales teams and to consumers through direct marketing advertising and through the Internet.

The company sells its products worldwide. Foreign sales account for about 32 percent of Dell's $18 billion in annual revenue.

The firm has manufacturing facilities in Texas, Ireland, Malaysia, and China, with plans to open a new facility soon in Brazil.

Dell has 16,000 employees and 9,000 shareholders. It has a market capitalization of $104 billion.

EARNINGS PER SHARE GROWTH   ★ ★ ★ ★

Past four years: 960 percent (81 percent per year)
Past ten years: 6,695 percent (52 percent per year)

STOCK GROWTH   ★ ★ ★ ★

Past ten years: 38,100 percent (81 percent per year)
Dollar growth: $10,000 over ten years would have grown to $3.9 million.
Average annual compounded rate of return: 81 percent

DIVIDEND

Dell pays no dividends.

CONSISTENCY

Increased earnings per share: nine of the past ten years
Increased sales: ten consecutive years

SHAREHOLDER PERKS

Dell does not offer a dividend reinvestment plan, nor does it offer other shareholder perks.

DELL COMPUTER AT A GLANCE

Fiscal year ended: Jan. 31
Revenue and net income in $ millions

	1994	1995	1996	1997	1998	1999	4-Year Growth Avg. Annual (%)	Total (%)
Revenue ($)	2,873	3,475	5,296	7,759	12,327	18,243	44	535
Net income ($)	–36	149	272	531	944	1,460	77	880
Earnings/share ($)	–0.02	0.05	0.09	0.17	0.32	0.53	81	960
Dividends/share ($)	—	—	—	—	—	—	—	—
Dividend yield (%)	—	—	—	—	—	—	—	—
PE ratio range	—	5–13	7–17	4–22	9–36	17–66	—	—

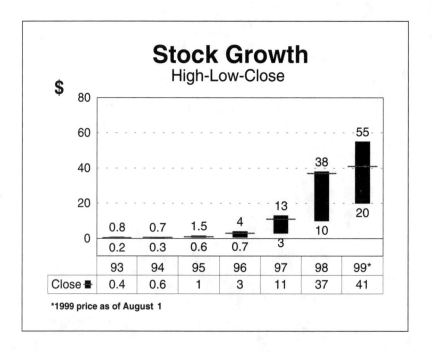

Stock Growth
High-Low-Close

	93	94	95	96	97	98	99*
Close ■	0.4	0.6	1	3	11	37	41

*1999 price as of August 1

Kohl's Corporation

N56 W17000 Ridgewood Drive
Menomonee Falls, WI 53051
414-703-7000
www.kohls.com

Chairman: William S. Kellogg
CEO: R. Lawrence Montgomery
President: Kevin Mansell

Earnings Growth	★ ★ ★ ★
Stock Growth	★ ★ ★ ★
Dividend	
Consistency	★ ★ ★
Shareholder Perks	
NYSE: KSS	**11 points**

Kohl's is a rapidly growing department store chain that has become popular with consumers who are attracted to its wide range of name brand merchandise and modest prices.

The Menomonee Falls, Wisconsin retailer has grown from 40 stores in 1986 to more than 225 stores today. Part of that growth has been through acquisitions of existing stores, and part has come through new store openings. Kohl's opens about 30 new stores each year.

Its stores are located in 24 eastern and midwestern states. Kohl's has 27 stores in its home state of Wisconsin, 33 in Illinois, 31 in Ohio, and 17 in Pennsylvania.

The stores sell moderately priced apparel; shoes; accessories; soft home products such as towels, sheets, and pillows; housewares; and a variety of other goods. It gears its merchandise to middle-income customers shopping for their families.

Kohl's stores have fewer departments than traditional department stores, but they offer customers a broad assortment of merchandise displayed in complete selections of styles, colors, and sizes.

The company focuses strongly on cost controls, with lean staffing levels, sophisticated management information systems, and operating efficiencies resulting from centralized buying, advertising, and distribution. The strategy has worked extremely well for Kohl's, which has posted record earnings and revenue all eight years since it began reporting its financial results. The company went public with its initial stock offering in 1992.

Apparel products account for about 61 percent of Kohl's $3.7 billion in annual revenue. Shoes and accessories account for about 19 percent, soft home products and housewares make up 12 percent, and hard goods account for 8 percent.

Most of Kohl's stores are located in shopping centers. The company supplies its stores through its three distribution centers in Wisconsin, Virginia, and Ohio.

Kohl's has 11,000 full-time employees and 23,000 part-time employees, and 5,600 shareholders. The company has a market capitalization of $11.4 billion.

EARNINGS PER SHARE GROWTH ★ ★ ★ ★

Past five years: 216 percent (26 percent per year)
Past eight years: 3,833 percent (44 percent per year)

STOCK GROWTH ★ ★ ★ ★

Past six years: 1,210 percent (54 percent per year)
Dollar growth: $10,000 over six years would have grown to $130,000.
Average annual compounded rate of return: 54 percent

DIVIDEND

The company pays no dividends.

CONSISTENCY   ★ ★ ★

Increased earnings per share: eight consecutive years
Increased sales: eight consecutive years

SHAREHOLDER PERKS

The company does not offer a dividend reinvestment and stock purchase plan, nor does it offer other perks.

KOHL'S AT A GLANCE

Fiscal year ended: Jan. 31
Revenue and net income in $ millions

	1993	1994	1995	1996	1997	1998	5-Year Growth Avg. Annual (%)	5-Year Growth Total (%)
Revenue ($)	1,306	1,554	1,926	2,388	3,060	3,682	23	182
Net income ($)	56	69	81	103	141	192	28	243
Earnings/share ($)	0.38	0.47	0.55	0.70	0.91	1.20	26	216
Dividends/share ($)	—	—	—	—	—	—	—	—
Dividend yield (%)	—	—	—	—	—	—	—	—
PE ratio range	17–34	21–30	19–28	18–30	20–41	27–51	—	—

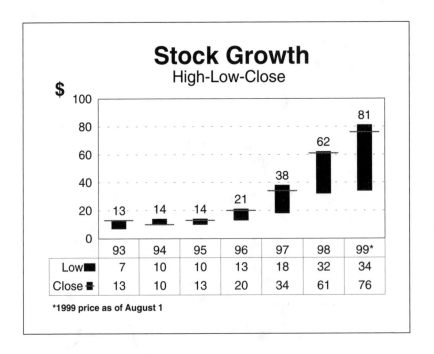

Stock Growth
High-Low-Close

	93	94	95	96	97	98	99*
Low	7	10	10	13	18	32	34
Close	13	10	13	20	34	61	76

*1999 price as of August 1

The Gap, Inc.

Gap Inc.

One Harrison Street
San Francisco, CA 94105
415-427-2000
www.gap.com

President and CEO: Millard S. Drexler
Chairman: Donald G. Fisher

Earnings Growth	★ ★ ★ ★
Stock Growth	★ ★ ★ ★
Dividend	
Consistency	★ ★ ★
Shareholder Perks	
NYSE: GPS	**11 points**

What do The Gap, Banana Republic, and Old Navy have in common? They are all owned and operated by The Gap, Inc. After a stagnant period in the mid-1990s, The Gap has reemerged as one of the fastest-growing retailers in America. In all, the company operates about 2,500 stores throughout the United States, Canada, Japan, Germany, France, and the United Kingdom.

One distinction that sets the The Gap apart from its competition is that the company designs nearly all of the clothing items featured in its stores, rather than relying on outside clothing manufacturers.

The company's biggest chain is its flagship Gap stores, with about 1,100 outlets, including 165 stores outside the United States. The Gap features casual attire at moderate prices, including denim, khakis, and

T-shirts. The stores also sell accessories and personal care products for men, women, and teenagers.

The San Francisco–based retailer opened its first GapKids store in 1986 and its first babyGap in 1989. The stores sell casual basics, outerwear, shoes, and other accessories for children and babies. The company operates about 640 GapKids and babyGap stores, including 133 stores outside the United States.

The Gap acquired Banana Republic in 1983 when it operated just two stores. Now the chain includes about 300 stores throughout the United States and Canada. Banana Republic stores feature more expensive apparel than The Gap, with fashionable dress, casual, and tailored clothing for men and women. The stores also sell some accessories, personal care products, and home products.

Old Navy stores were first launched by The Gap in 1994 to appeal to value-oriented families. The stores offer a broad selection of apparel, shoes, and accessories for adults, children, and babies at relatively low prices. It also sells some personal care products. The company operates more than 400 Old Navy stores throughout the United States.

The company established Gap Online in 1997 to sell products over the Internet.

The Gap purchases merchandise from about 1,200 suppliers, including 20 percent in the United States and 80 percent abroad. In all, it buys merchandise from producers in 55 countries.

The company opens more than 300 new stores each year.

The Gap opened its first store on Ocean Avenue in San Francisco in 1969 and went public with its initial stock offering in 1976. The firm has about 110,000 employees and 7,000 shareholders. It has a market capitalization of about $36 billion.

EARNINGS PER SHARE GROWTH   ★ ★ ★ ★

Past five years: 243 percent (28 percent per year)
Past ten years: 1,145 percent (28.5 percent per year)

STOCK GROWTH ★ ★ ★ ★

Past ten years: 2,196 percent (36 percent per year)
Dollar growth: $10,000 over ten years (including reinvested dividends) would have grown to $220,000.
Average annual compounded rate of return (including reinvested dividends): 37 percent

DIVIDEND

Dividend yield: 0.2 percent
Increased dividend: The company has not raised its dividend since 1996.
Past five-year increase: 63 percent (10 percent per year)

CONSISTENCY ★ ★ ★

Increased earnings per share: nine of the past ten years
Increased sales: 15 consecutive years

SHAREHOLDER PERKS

The company does not offer a dividend reinvestment plan, nor does it provide other shareholder perks.

THE GAP AT A GLANCE

Fiscal year ended: Jan. 31
Revenue and net income in $ millions

	1993	1994	1995	1996	1997	1998	5-Year Growth Avg. Annual (%)	Total (%)
Revenue ($)	3,296	3,723	4,395	5,284	6,508	9,054	22	175
Net income ($)	258	320	354	453	534	825	26	220
Earnings/share ($)	0.40	0.49	0.55	0.71	0.87	1.37	28	243
Dividends/share ($)	0.08	0.10	0.11	0.13	0.13	0.13	10	63
Dividend yield (%)	1.1	1.2	1.3	1.0	0.7	0.3	—	—
PE ratio range	14–23	13–22	12–20	13–22	14–29	16–43	—	—

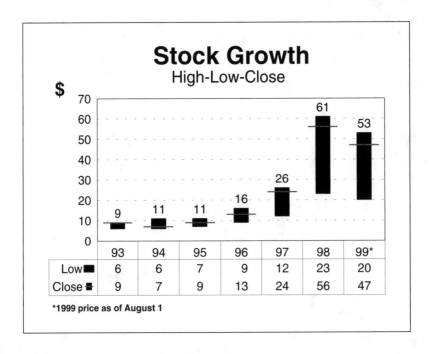

Stock Growth
High-Low-Close

	93	94	95	96	97	98	99*
Low	6	6	7	9	12	23	20
Close	9	7	9	13	24	56	47

*1999 price as of August 1

Oracle Corporation

500 Oracle Parkway
Redwood Shores, CA 94065
650-506-7000
www.oracle.com

Chairman and CEO: Lawrence J. Ellison
President: Raymond L. Lane

Earnings Growth	★ ★ ★ ★
Stock Growth	★ ★ ★ ★
Dividend	
Consistency	★ ★ ★
Shareholder Perks	
Nasdaq: ORCL	**11 points**

Oracle Corporation is the world's second largest software manufacturer—but it's a long way from number one. The company's annual revenue is about half that of industry leader Microsoft. But even at number two, Oracle still puts up some impressive numbers. The Redwood Shores, California operation has seen its revenue triple in just four years.

Oracle specializes in database and development software, business applications for sales and service, manufacturing and supply chain, and finance and human resources.

Oracle software gives computer users the ability to tap into computer resources anywhere, anytime. Its Oracle relational database management systems enable users to define, retrieve, manipulate, and control data stored on multiple computers, and to manage video, audio, text, messaging, and spatial data.

Even laptop users can tap into other computers with the Oracle Mobile Agents product, which uses digital radio networks to link up with other computers. Oracle also makes a WebSystem software program that helps companies create and manage Web applications.

Oracle is the world's leading supplier of database software and information management services. It makes software products that fit into three different categories: (1) server technologies, (2) application development and business intelligence tools, and (3) business applications.

The company's server technologies products include database servers, connectivity products, and gateways. Its Oracle8 relational database management system is the key component of its server technologies database for storing, manipulating, and retrieving relational, object-relational, multidimensional text, spatial, video, and other types of data.

Its application development tools consist of a set of software products used to build database applications for both client server and Web environments.

Oracle's business application products consist of more than 45 integrated software modules for financial management, supply chain management, manufacturing, project systems, human resources, and front office applications.

The company's principal products run on a broad range of computers, including mainframes, minicomputers, workstations, personal computers, and laptops. Oracle software can function on 85 different operating systems, including UNIX, Windows, and Windows NT.

Oracle markets its products in 140 countries around the world. About 50 percent of its $9 billion in annual revenue comes from foreign sales.

Founded in 1977, the company has about 37,000 employees and 14,500 shareholders. It has a market capitalization of $37 billion.

EARNINGS PER SHARE GROWTH   ★ ★ ★ ★

Past five years: 482 percent (42 percent per year)
Past ten years: 2,030 percent (36 percent per year)

STOCK GROWTH   ★ ★ ★ ★

Past ten years: 1,214 percent (29.5 percent per year)
Dollar growth: $10,000 over ten years would have grown to $131,000.
Average annual compounded rate of return: 29.5 percent

DIVIDEND
Oracle pays no dividends.

CONSISTENCY
Increased earnings per share: nine of the past ten years
Increased sales: 12 consecutive years

SHAREHOLDER PERKS
The company does not offer a stock purchase plan, nor does it offer other shareholder perks.

ORACLE AT A GLANCE

Fiscal year ended: May 31
Revenue and net income in $ millions

	1993	1994	1995	1996	1997	1998	5-Year Growth Avg. Annual (%)	Total (%)
Revenue ($)	1,503	2,001	2,967	4,223	5,684	7,144	36	375
Net income ($)	156	284	442	637	846	955	43	512
Earnings/share ($)	0.11	0.19	0.30	0.42	0.56	0.64	42	482
Dividends/share ($)	—	—	—	—	—	—	—	—
Dividend yield (%)	—	—	—	—	—	—	—	—
PE ratio range	14–39	18–31	19–35	21–41	25–51	28–50	—	—

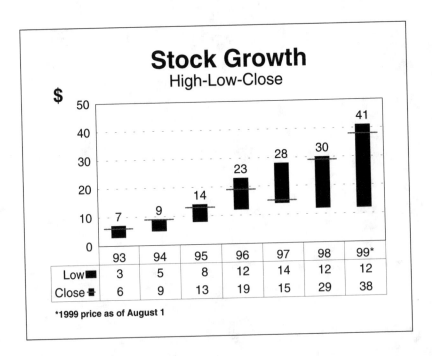

Stock Growth
High-Low-Close

$	93	94	95	96	97	98	99*
Low	3	5	8	12	14	12	12
Close	6	9	13	19	15	29	38

*1999 price as of August 1

American International Group, Inc.

70 Pine Street
New York, NY 10270
212-770-6293
www.aig.com

Chairman and CEO: Maurice R. Greenberg
President: Evan G. Greenberg

Earnings Growth	★ ★
Stock Growth	★ ★ ★ ★
Dividend	★
Consistency	★ ★ ★ ★
Shareholder Perks	
NYSE: AIG	**11 points**

American International Group (AIG) offers insurance and related financial services to customers in 130 countries around the world. The New York–based operation is the nation's leading international insurance organization and one of the largest underwriters of commercial and industrial coverage in the United States.

AIG's mainstay is property and casualty insurance, which accounts for about 50 percent of its annual revenue. Life insurance accounts for 33 percent of revenue and financial services account for 17 percent.

The company was founded in China in 1919 by C.V. Starr, who opened a small insurance agency in Shanghai. At the time, Shanghai was the bustling commercial center of China and East Asia. Because of political unrest, Starr had to move his agency to New York in 1939, where it adopted its current name. As a sign of the times, AIG reestablished a presence in Shanghai in 1992. The same year, AIG opened an office in Moscow, the first American insurance company to do so.

AIG continues to rely on its overseas operations for a substantial share of its income. Overseas operations account for about 35 percent of net premiums written and 50 percent of total revenue. In the U.S. market, AIG is one of the largest underwriters of commercial and industrial insurance policies.

The company has been growing steadily in recent years, with 14 consecutive years of record earnings. That steady pace should continue as AIG aggressively pursues opportunities in largely underinsured foreign markets. The recent ratification of the NAFTA and GATT treaties will help spur international growth.

Underlying AIG's financial success is its commitment to efficiency, which has resulted in one of the lowest expense ratios in the industry.

The company has about 40,000 employees and 10,000 shareholders. It has a market capitalization of about $147 billion.

EARNINGS PER SHARE GROWTH   ★ ★

Past five years: 100 percent (15 percent per year)
Past ten years: 249 percent (13.5 percent per year)

STOCK GROWTH   ★ ★ ★ ★

Past ten years: 1115 percent (28.5 percent per year)
Dollar growth: $10,000 over ten years (including reinvested dividends) would have grown to $128,000.
Average annual compounded rate of return (including reinvested dividends): 29 percent

DIVIDEND   ★

Dividend yield: 0.3
Increased dividend: 14 consecutive years
Past five-year increase: 92 percent (14 percent per year)

CONSISTENCY

Increased earnings per share: 14 consecutive years

SHAREHOLDER PERKS

The company does not offer a dividend reinvestment and stock purchase plan, nor does it provide other shareholder perks.

AIG AT A GLANCE

Fiscal year ended: Dec. 31
Total assets and net income in $ millions

	1993	1994	1995	1996	1997	1998	5-Year Growth Avg. Annual (%)	Total (%)
Total assets ($)	101,015	114,346	134,136	148,431	163,971	194,398	14	92
Net income ($)	1,939	2,176	2,510	2,897	3,332	3,766	14	94
Earnings/share ($)	1.79	2.04	2.36	2.73	3.17	3.59	15	100
Dividends/share ($)	0.12	0.13	0.14	0.17	0.19	0.23	14	92
Dividend yield (%)	0.4	0.5	0.4	0.4	0.3	0.2	—	—
PE ratio range	12–17	12–15	12–18	14–19	15–24	18–29	—	—

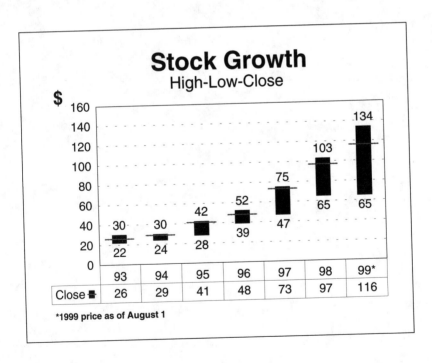

Stock Growth
High-Low-Close

	93	94	95	96	97	98	99*
High	30	30	42	52	75	103	134
Low	22	24	28	39	47	65	65
Close	26	29	41	48	73	97	116

*1999 price as of August 1

Colgate-Palmolive Company

300 Park Avenue
New York, NY 10022
212-310-2000
www.colgate.com

Chairman and CEO: Reuben Mark
President: William Shanahan

Earnings Growth	★
Stock Growth	★ ★ ★
Dividend	★ ★
Consistency	★ ★ ★
Shareholder Perks	★ ★
NYSE: CL	**11 points**

Colgate-Palmolive products help keep teeth whiter, floors brighter, clothes cleaner, and pets healthier. The company makes a veritable grocery cart full of household products that it markets to every corner of the globe.

Colgate commands half of the world's market share of toothpaste and about one-quarter of the soap and all-purpose cleaner markets. Its products are sold in more than 200 countries. Foreign sales account for about 67 percent of the company's $8.97 billion in annual revenue.

In addition to its Colgate and Ultra Brite toothpastes, the company makes a line of toothbrushes, dental floss, mouthwash, and professional dental products. Oral care products account for about 32 percent of total sales.

Colgate's other four major product segments include:

1. **Personal care products** (24 percent of revenue). The company makes a variety of soaps and related products, such as Irish Spring and Palmolive bar soap, Softsoap liquid soap, Wash n' Dri disposable towelettes, Speedstick and Irish Spring deodorants, Baby Magic baby care products, Colgate and Palmolive shave cream, and Skin Bracer and Afta aftershave.
2. **Household surface care** (16 percent of revenue). Its leading brands include Ajax cleaners, Palmolive cleaners and detergents, and Murphy Oil Soap cleaner.
3. **Fabric care** (15 percent of revenue). The company makes Fab and Dynamo, Ajax Ultra, and Fresh Start laundry detergents.
4. **Pet nutrition** (11 percent of revenue). Its Science Diet line of pet foods is one of the fastest growing brands in the business.

One of the keys to Colgate's international success has been the development of new products that can work in multiple markets. The company has been generating more than half its sales in foreign markets since 1960 and has been selling toothpaste in Latin America since 1925.

The company's new product development process begins by analyzing consumer insights from targeted countries to create universal products. To improve the odds of success, potential new products are test-marketed in lead countries that represent both developing and mature economies.

Colgate has about 38,000 employees and 46,000 shareholders. It has a market capitalization of $27.7 billion.

EARNINGS PER SHARE GROWTH ★

Past five years: 54 percent (9 percent per year)
Past ten years: 203 percent (11.5 percent per year)

STOCK GROWTH ★ ★ ★

Past ten years: 591 percent (21.5 percent per year)
Dollar growth: $10,000 over 10 years (including reinvested dividends) would have grown to $86,000.
Average annual compounded rate of return (including reinvested dividends): 24 percent

DIVIDEND

Dividend yield: 1.2 percent
Increased dividend: More than 21 consecutive years
Past five-year increase: 64 percent (10.5 percent per year)

CONSISTENCY

Increased earnings per share: nine of the past ten years
Increased sales: nine of the past ten years

SHAREHOLDER PERKS ★★

Good dividend reinvestment and stock purchase plan; voluntary stock purchase plan allows contributions of $20 per month up to $60,000 per year. (Nominal cash-in fee of $10 plus 12 cents per share.)

COLGATE-PALMOLIVE AT A GLANCE

Fiscal year ended: Dec. 31
Revenue and net income in $ millions

	1993	1994	1995	1996	1997	1998	5-Year Growth Avg. Annual (%)	5-Year Growth Total (%)
Revenue ($)	7,141	7,588	8,358	8,749	9,057	8,972	5	26
Net income ($)	548	580	541	635	740	849	9	55
Earnings/share ($)	1.69	1.91	1.79	2.10	2.27	2.61	9	54
Dividends/share ($)	0.67	0.77	0.88	0. 94	1.06	1.10	10	64
Dividend yield (%)	2.3	2.6	2.6	2.3	1.7	1.3	—	—
PE ratio range	14–20	13–18	56–75	16–23	18–32	23–35	—	—

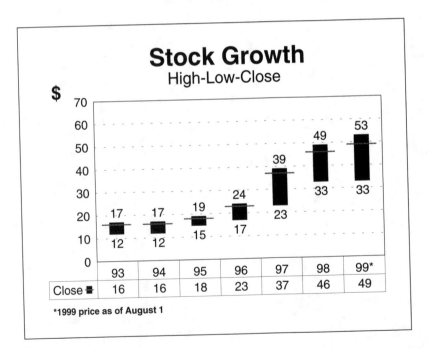

Stock Growth
High-Low-Close

*1999 price as of August 1

73

Dionex Corporation

1228 Titan Way
P.O. Box 3603
Sunnyvale, CA 94088
408-737-0700
www.dionex.com

President and CEO: A. Blaine Bowman

Earnings Growth	★ ★ ★
Stock Growth	★ ★ ★ ★
Dividend	
Consistency	★ ★ ★ ★
Shareholder Perks	
Nasdaq: DNEX	**11 points**

Dionex equipment helps researchers analyze product ingredients, monitor pollutants and impurities, and identify the molecular components of a wide range of solutions and materials.

The tartar control impact of the toothpaste you use, the level of nitrates in the hot dogs you eat, the trace amounts of zinc or iron in the beer you drink, the measure of phosphates in your rain water can all be determined through Dionex equipment.

The Sunnyvale, California operation manufactures a range of chromatography systems, sample preparation devices, and related products that are used by chemists to separate and quantify the individual components of complex chemical mixtures. The systems are used by many of the largest industrial companies in the world, as well as government agencies, researchers, and universities.

The advanced technology has helped Dionex grow rapidly, posting 18 consecutive years of record sales and earnings.

The company's top-selling product is the Dionex Ion Chromatography system, which separates and analyzes charged (ionic) molecules in water-based solutions. The systems are used for such applications as environmental monitoring, corrosion monitoring, evaluation of raw materials, quality control of industrial processes and pharmaceutical and industrial products, research and development, and regulation of the chemical composition of foods, beverages, and cosmetics.

The Ion Chromatography systems are used by environmental testing laboratories, food companies, chemical and petrochemical firms, power generating facilities, electronics manufacturers, government agencies, and academic institutions.

Dionex's other leading system is the high-performance liquid chromatography system used to separate and identify molecules such as proteins, carbohydrates, amino acids, pharmaceuticals, and chemicals. The system identifies the molecules by measuring the amount of light that the molecules absorb or emit when exposed to a light source.

Dionex markets its instruments worldwide. It has sales offices in the United States, Canada, Japan, and throughout Europe. About 57 percent of the company's $175 million in annual sales comes from its overseas operations.

Dionex has 715 employees and 1,600 shareholders. It has a market capitalization of about $950 million.

EARNINGS PER SHARE GROWTH ★ ★ ★

Past five years: 131 percent (18 percent per year)
Past ten years: 281 percent (14 percent per year)

STOCK GROWTH ★ ★ ★ ★

Past ten years: 650 percent (22 percent per year)
Dollar growth: $10,000 over ten years would have grown to $73,000.
Average annual compounded rate of return: 22 percent

DIVIDEND

Dionex pays no dividends.

CONSISTENCY

Increased earnings per share: 18 consecutive years
Increased sales: 18 consecutive years

SHAREHOLDER PERKS

The company offers no dividend reinvestment and stock purchase plan, nor does it provide other shareholder perks.

DIONEX AT A GLANCE

Fiscal year ended: June 30
Revenue and net income in $ millions

	1993	1994	1995	1996	1997	1998	5-Year Growth Avg. Annual (%)	5-Year Growth Total (%)
Revenue ($)	106	110	120	133	142	151	7	42
Net income ($)	16	17	19	23	26	29	13	81
Earnings/share ($)	0.51	0.55	0.66	0.85	1.03	1.18	18	131
Dividends/share ($)	—	—	—	—	—	—	—	—
Dividend yield (%)	—	—	—	—	—	—	—	—
PE ratio range	15–22	14–17	13–21	15–22	16–25	15–32	—	—

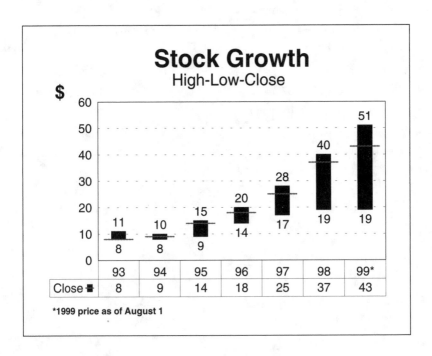

Stock Growth
High-Low-Close

	93	94	95	96	97	98	99*
Close ■	8	9	14	18	25	37	43

*1999 price as of August 1

Computer Sciences Corporation

2100 East Grand Avenue
El Segundo, CA 90245
310-615-0311
www.csc.com

Chairman, President, and CEO: Van B. Honeycutt

Earnings Growth	★ ★ ★
Stock Growth	★ ★ ★ ★
Dividend	
Consistency	★ ★ ★ ★
Shareholder Perks	
NYSE: CSC	**11 points**

Corporate managers tired of pulling their hair out dealing with the complex and often irritating world of corporate computer systems can turn to Computer Sciences Corporation (CSC) for a helping hand. CSC offers a broad array of information-technology-related services, including designing and developing complete information systems and, in some cases, operating all or a portion of a customer's technology infrastructure.

The El Segundo, California operation offers services in three broad areas: outsourcing (managing a company's technology infrastructure), systems integration (designing, developing, implementing, and integrating complete information systems), and information technology management consulting (helping clients purchase and operate their computer systems).

Founded in 1959, CSC originally did most of its business designing, installing, and servicing computer and communications systems for the U.S. government. The company has been steadily pushing into both the private sector and the international arena. As recently as 1992, some 57 percent of its revenue came from U.S. government contracts. By 1998, that figure had slipped to just 25 percent. U.S. commercial customers account for 42 percent of revenue, and international commercial accounts make up the other 33 percent of revenue.

The company has offices in the United Kingdom, France, Germany, Belgium, the Netherlands, Denmark, Australia, and Singapore.

For many of its customers, CSC designs, engineers, and integrates computer-based systems and communications systems, providing all the necessary hardware, software, training, and related elements. The company has special expertise in the development of software for aerospace and defense systems. It also provides engineering and technical assistance in satellite communications, intelligence, aerospace, logistics, and related high-technology fields.

Among its clients are CNA Financial, DuPont, General Dynamics, and Managed Care Assistance Corp. CSC also has been working on a system for the U.S. Department of Defense designed to automate the way the government manages weapons systems information.

Among its other specialties are electronic commerce, data warehousing, enterprise resource planning, information security, supply chain management, and Y2K compliance.

Computer Sciences has about 44,000 employees and 8,000 shareholders. It has a market capitalization of $10 billion.

EARNINGS PER SHARE GROWTH ★ ★ ★

Past five years: 137 percent (19 percent per year)
Past ten years: 284 percent (14.5 percent per year)

STOCK GROWTH ★ ★ ★ ★

Past ten years: 608 percent (21.5 percent per year)
Dollar growth: $10,000 over ten years would have grown to $70,000.
Average annual compounded rate of return: 21.5 percent

DIVIDEND

Computer Sciences pays no dividends.

CONSISTENCY

Increased earnings per share: 15 consecutive years
Increased sales: 17 consecutive years

SHAREHOLDER PERKS

The company offers no dividend reinvestment and stock purchase plan, nor does it provide other shareholder perks.

COMPUTER SCIENCES AT A GLANCE

Fiscal year ended: March 31
Revenue and net income in $ millions

	1993	1994	1995	1996	1997	1998	5-Year Growth Avg. Annual (%)	Total (%)
Revenue ($)	2,583	3,373	4,242	5,616	6,601	7,660	24	197
Net income ($)	91	111	142	228	273	341	30	275
Earnings/share ($)	0.89	1.05	1.24	1.46	1.72	2.11	19	137
Dividends/share ($)	—	—	—	—	—	—	—	—
Dividend yield (%)	—	—	—	—	—	—	—	—
PE ratio range	8–11	5–26	32–51	25–34	17–26	19–36	—	—

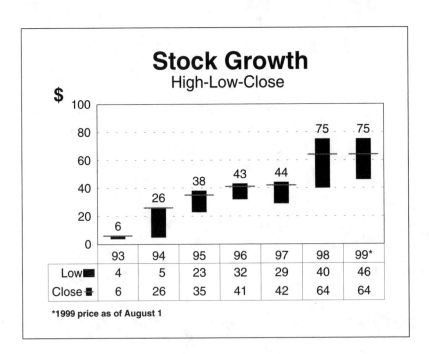

Stock Growth
High-Low-Close

$	93	94	95	96	97	98	99*
Low	4	5	23	32	29	40	46
Close	6	26	35	41	42	64	64

*1999 price as of August 1

SunTrust Banks, Inc.

SUNTRUST

303 Peachtree Street NE
Atlanta, GA 30308
404-588-7711
www.suntrust.com

Chairman, President, and CEO: L. Phillip Humann

Earnings Growth	★
Stock Growth	★ ★ ★
Dividend	★ ★
Consistency	★ ★ ★
Shareholder Perks	★ ★
NYSE: STI	**11 points**

SunTrust's recent acquisition of Crestar Financial Corp. puts the Atlanta institution in the major leagues. In terms of assets, it is now the nation's tenth largest banking organization.

The company provides a wide range of personal, corporate, and institutional banking services; trust and investment management; investment banking; factoring; mortgage banking; credit cards; discount brokerage; credit-related insurance; and data processing and information services.

The company has more than 1,000 branches in the southeastern United States. Its highest concentration of branches is in Florida, with 377 branch offices and 580 automatic teller machines (ATMs), followed by Georgia, with 218 branches and 380 ATMs, and Tennessee, with 120 branches and

175 ATMs. With the addition of Crestar, the company added 370 branches and 709 ATMs in Virginia, Maryland, and Washington, D.C.

SunTrust was one of the first banks to offer PC banking, a home banking service using personal computers. It was the first bank to offer corporate customers information access through both CD-ROM and an online network. The company also is developing other online banking services through the Internet. SunTrust's new innovations are part of a trend the company has established to be among the industry leaders in the introduction of new services.

Commercial loans account for about 36 percent of the company's outstanding loans, followed by mortgages, 32 percent; consumer loans, 16 percent; construction, 4 percent; and other real-estate-related loans, 12 percent.

The company took on its present identity as SunTrust Banks in 1985 with the merger of Sun Banks of Florida and Trust Company of Georgia. It has grown rapidly through a series of acquisitions throughout its four-state operating area.

The Atlanta-based institution must credit part of its strong recent growth to an investment it picked up in 1919 as the Trust Company of Georgia.

When the Coca-Cola Company went public in 1919, it gave 5,000 shares (worth $110,000) of its stock as part of the underwriting fee to the two underwriters, JP Morgan Bank and the Trust Company of Georgia (now SunTrust Banks). JP Morgan sold its stock, but Trust Company held onto its original shares.

After years of stock splits, that original $110,000 investment is now worth more than $3 billion. Even when the banking business is in a funk, SunTrust continues to ride high on the strength of its Coca-Cola stock.

SunTrust has about 31,000 employees. The company has a market capitalization of about $23 billion.

EARNINGS PER SHARE GROWTH

Past five years: 60 percent (10 percent per year)
Past ten years: 155 percent (10 percent per year)

STOCK GROWTH   ★ ★ ★

Past ten years: 518 percent (20 percent per year)
Dollar growth: $10,000 over ten years (including reinvested dividends)
would have grown to $77,000.
Average annual compounded rate of return (including reinvested dividends): 23 percent

DIVIDEND   ★ ★

Dividend yield: 2.0
Increased dividend: 21 consecutive years
Past five-year increase: 72 percent (12 percent per year)

CONSISTENCY   ★ ★ ★

Increased earnings per share: nine of the past ten years

SHAREHOLDER PERKS   ★ ★

Good dividend reinvestment and stock purchase plan; voluntary stock
purchase plan allows contributions of $10 to $60,000 per year.

SUNTRUST BANKS AT A GLANCE

Fiscal year ended: Dec. 31
Total assets and net income in $ millions

	1993	1994	1995	1996	1997	1998	5-Year Growth Avg. Annual (%)	Total (%)
Total assets ($)	40,728	42,709	46,471	52,468	57,983	93,170	18	129
Net income ($)	474	523	566	617	667	971	15	105
Earnings/share ($)	1.90	2.22	2.38	2.59	3.04	3.04	10	60
Dividends/share ($)	0.58	0.65	0.74	0.83	0.93	1.00	12	72
Dividend yield (%)	2.6	2.8	2.5	2.1	1.6	1.4	—	—
PE ratio range	11–13	10–12	9–14	12–20	14–24	18–28	—	—

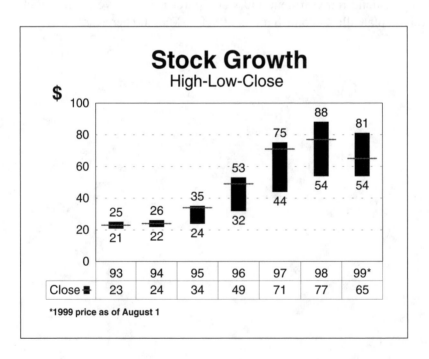

Stock Growth
High-Low-Close

	93	94	95	96	97	98	99*
Close ■	23	24	34	49	71	77	65

*1999 price as of August 1

Mcdonald's Corporation

Mcdonald's Plaza
Oak Brook, IL 60523
630-623-3000
www.mcdonalds.com

Chairman and CEO: Jack M. Greenberg
President: James R. Cantalupo

Earnings Growth	★
Stock Growth	★ ★ ★
Dividend	★
Consistency	★ ★ ★ ★
Shareholder Perks	★ ★
NYSE: MCD	**11 points**

It may be hard to think of McDonald's fare as French cuisine, but the Big Mac is sweeping through France like a Jerry Lewis film festival. There are more than 700 McDonald's restaurants in France—a figure that has more than doubled in the past five years. Throughout Europe there are more than 4,500 McDonald's restaurants, including 810 in England and 940 in Germany.

But it is in Japan where McDonald's is growing the fastest. There are more than 3,000 McD's in Japan—nearly triple the figure of five years ago. Throughout Asia there are more than 5,000 McD's, and worldwide McDonald's operates about 25,000 restaurants—half in the United States and half outside.

In all, the Chicago-based business has restaurants in nearly 115 countries. With same store sales flattening out in the U.S. market, McDonald's is relying more heavily than ever on its overseas franchises.

In recent years, McDonald's has been opening about twice as many restaurants in foreign markets as in the United States. The fast-food chain is now well entrenched in the former Eastern Bloc and also has opened restaurants in Russia and China.

In addition to its foreign expansion, McDonald's has tried to keep its earnings growing by introducing a continuing line of new selections, such as ice cream, chicken, salads, breakfast products, and other specialties. McDonald's also maintains its marketing edge by keeping prices as low as any restaurant in the fast-food business.

The company is very careful to shape its foreign offerings to the tastes of the local culture. In Norway, McDonald's serves a grilled salmon sandwich with dill sauce; in Japan, it serves Chicken Tatsuta, a fried chicken sandwich spiced with soy sauce and ginger; in Germany, the restaurants serve frankfurters, beer, and a cold four-course meal; and in India, where the cow is sacred, McDonald's features chicken and fish sandwiches along with some special veggie nuggets and a veggie burger. No beef is served.

Most McDonald's restaurants are owned by independent business-people who operate them through a franchise agreement. Typically, the company tries to recruit investors who will be active, on-premises owners rather than outside investors. The conventional franchise arrangement is for a term of 20 years and requires an investment of about $600,000, 60 percent of which may be financed. Each outlet also is subject to franchise fees based on a percentage of sales. With few exceptions, McDonald's does not supply food, paper, or equipment to any restaurants, but approves suppliers from which those items can be purchased.

Restaurant managers receive training at the company's Hamburger University at the McDonald's corporate headquarters in Oak Brook, Illinois. Outside the United States, there are Hamburger University training centers in Germany, England, Japan, Brazil, and Australia.

The typical new restaurant generates revenues of about $1.3 million the first year.

McDonald's was founded in 1955 by the late Ray Kroc. Now, more than 40 million customers a day dine beneath the golden arches.

McDonald's has 284,000 employees and about 980,000 shareholders. The company has a market capitalization of $54 billion.

EARNINGS PER SHARE GROWTH ★

Past five years: 73 percent (12 percent per year)
Past ten years: 193 percent (11 percent per year)

STOCK GROWTH ★ ★ ★

Past ten years: 507 percent (20 percent per year)
Dollar growth: $10,000 over ten years (including reinvested dividends) would have grown to $67,000.
Average annual compounded rate of return (including reinvested dividends): 21 percent

DIVIDEND ★

Dividend yield: 0.5 percent
Increased dividend: Every year since the company went public in 1966
Past five-year increase: 64 percent (10.5 percent per year)

CONSISTENCY ★ ★ ★ ★

Increased earnings per share: 32 consecutive years (dating back to the year the company went public)
Increased sales: 32 consecutive years

SHAREHOLDER PERKS ★ ★

McDonald's has a direct purchase plan with a minimum initial investment of $1,000 (or a $100 per month automatic deduction). Shareholders may have dividends automatically reinvested and may make voluntary stock purchase payments of $100 per payment to a maximum of $250,000 per year.

A wealth of literature on McDonald's and its locations and product ingredients is available to shareholders (or anyone else requesting it). The company also provides an investor hotline (not toll-free) that gives company news.

McDONALD'S AT A GLANCE

Fiscal year ended: Dec. 31
Revenue and net income in $ millions

	1993	1994	1995	1996	1997	1998	5-Year Growth Avg. Annual (%)	Total (%)
Revenue ($)	7,408	8,321	9,795	10,687	11,409	12,421	11	68
Net income ($)	1,083	1,224	1,427	1,573	1,643	1,769	10	63
Earnings/share ($)	0.73	0.84	0.99	1.11	1.15	1.26	12	73
Dividends/share ($)	0.11	0.12	0.13	0.15	0.16	0.18	10	64
Dividend yield (%)	0.8	0.8	0.7	0.6	0.7	0.6	—	—
PE ratio range	16–20	15–19	14–24	19–25	18–23	20–35	—	—

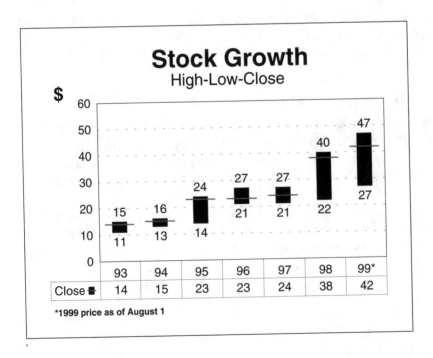

Stock Growth
High-Low-Close

Close ▪	93	94	95	96	97	98	99*
	14	15	23	23	24	38	42

*1999 price as of August 1

77

RPM, Inc.

P.O. Box 777
Medina, OH 44258
330-273-5090
www.rpmcorp.com

Chairman and CEO: Thomas C. Sullivan
President: James A. Karman

Earnings Growth	★
Stock Growth	
Dividend	★ ★ ★ ★
Consistency	★ ★ ★ ★
Shareholder Perks	★ ★
NYSE: RPM	**11 points**

RPM has upped its revenue and earnings every year for more than half a century. In all, the Medina, Ohio paints and coatings manufacturer has posted 51 straight years of record revenue and earnings per share—making it America's most consistent company.

RPM has grown through a long-term, persistent strategy of acquiring smaller companies in the paints and coatings business and merging them into its overall operation. RPM, which has acquired nearly 50 companies in recent years, looks for firms that are already profitable and are run by experienced managers. RPM generally keeps the management of its acquired companies in tact but attains cost efficiency by assuming control of other aspects of the operations.

RPM was founded in 1947 by Frank C. Sullivan who invented the "Alumanation" process for coating outdoor metal structures. While Alumanation continues to be the world's leading liquid aluminum coating solution, the process is now just a small part of RPM's total business.

The company has about 31 operating companies, all of which are involved in the manufacture of coatings, sealants, and specialty chemicals (including corrosion protection, waterproofing and maintenance products, roofing materials, touch-up products for autos and furniture, and fabrics and wallcoverings).

RPM has sales in more than 100 countries. Foreign sales account for about 19 percent of the company's $1.62 billion in annual revenue. The firm has manufacturing plants in 13 foreign countries.

About 62 percent of the company's sales comes from the industrial market, while the other 38 percent comes from its line of consumer products.

In the industrial market, RPM produces a wide range of coatings and chemicals for power plants, oil rigs, railcars, tankers, smoke stacks, and other structures that are subject to harsh environments. Leading brands include Carboline, Plasite, and Bitumastic. The firm also makes a wide range of specialty chemicals, such as fluorescent colorants and pigments; concrete additives that provide corrosion resistance and add strength to cement used in construction; additives for coatings and dyes; and coatings and cleaners for the textile trade. It produces furniture stains, fillers and polishes, auto refinishing products, and auto corrosion control additives. Its leading lines include Day-Glo Color, Alox, Mohawk, and American Emulsions.

RPM also produces coatings and waterproofing products for metal structures such as buildings, bridges, and industrial facilities; it also produces sheet roofing, sealants, and deck coatings. Its leading lines include RPM Alumanation coating, Mameco sealants and Martin Mathys water-based coatings, and Stonhard polymer floors, linings, and wall systems.

In the consumer market, RPM's Testor subsidiary is America's leading producer of models, paints, and accessory items for the model and hobby market. RPM's Craft House subsidiary markets a variety of crafts including paint-by-numbers sets.

The company sells a wide range of paints and coatings for the consumer do-it-yourself market, including Zinsser shellac-based coatings, Bondax patch and repair products, Dynatron/Bondo, Talsol, and Rust-Oleum.

RPM's coatings cover the Statue of Liberty, the Eiffel Tower, and hundreds of bridges, ships, highways, factories, office towers, warehouses, and other structures around the world.

RPM has about 6,800 employees and 80,000 shareholders. It has a market capitalization of about $1.43 billion.

EARNINGS PER SHARE GROWTH ★

Past five years: 65 percent (10 percent per year)
Past ten years: 165 percent (10 percent per year)

STOCK GROWTH

Past ten years: 133 percent (9 percent per year)
Dollar growth: $10,000 over ten years (including reinvested dividends) would have grown to about $31,000.
Average annual compounded rate of return (including reinvested dividends): 12 percent

DIVIDEND

Dividend yield: 3.5 percent
Increased dividend: 22 consecutive years
Past five-year increase: 47 percent (8 percent per year)

CONSISTENCY ★ ★ ★ ★

Increased earnings per share: 51 consecutive years
Increased sales: 51 consecutive years

SHAREHOLDER PERKS

Good dividend reinvestment and stock purchase plan; voluntary stock purchase plan allows contributions of up to $5,000 per month.

RPM AT A GLANCE

Fiscal year ended: May 31
Revenue and net income in $ millions

	1993	1994	1995	1996	1997	1998	5-Year Growth Avg. Annual (%)	Total (%)
Revenue ($)	626	816	1,017	1,136	1,351	1,615	21	158
Net income ($)	39	53	61	69	78	88	17	123
Earnings/share ($)	0.51	0.57	0.65	0.69	0.76	0.84	10	65
Dividends/share ($)	0.30	0.33	0.35	0.38	0.41	0.44	8	47
Dividend yield (%)	2.8	2.9	3.0	3.0	3.0	2.7	—	—
PE ratio range	18–21	15–18	16–19	14–19	14–19	16–21	—	—

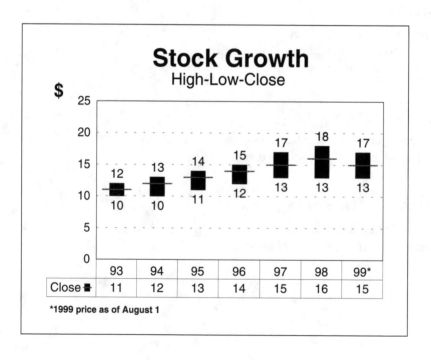

Stock Growth
High-Low-Close

	93	94	95	96	97	98	99*
Close	11	12	13	14	15	16	15

*1999 price as of August 1

Emerson Electric Company

8000 West Florissant Avenue
P.O. Box 4100
Saint Louis, MO 63136
314-553-2000
www.emersonelectric.com

Chairman and CEO: Charles F. Knight
President: G. W. Tamke

Earnings Growth	★
Stock Growth	★ ★
Dividend	★ ★
Consistency	★ ★ ★ ★
Shareholder Perks	★ ★
NYSE: EMR	**11 points**

Like its broad line of fans, motors, and compressors, Emerson Electric continues to purr smoothly along, posting increased earnings and dividends for more than 40 consecutive years.

The 109-year-old operation manufactures a wide range of electrical equipment, including motors for industrial and heavy commercial applications, industrial automation equipment, gear drives, power distribution equipment, and temperature and environmental control systems.

Emerson divides its operations into two key segments:

1. **Commercial and industrial components and systems** (60 percent of revenue). The company manufactures process control instruments and

systems, industrial motors and drives, industrial machinery, and computer support products.

2. **Appliance and construction-related components** (40 percent of revenue). Emerson manufactures a wide range of small motors, appliance components, heating, ventilating and air-conditioning components, refrigeration and comfort control components, timers, switches, humidifiers, exhaust fans, wrenches, pipe cutters, and related equipment. Among its consumer products are portable and stationary power tools, hobby tools, hand tools, garbage disposers, hot water dispensers, dishwashers, ladders, scaffolding, and shop vacuums.

Emerson makes Sears Craftsman hand tools, Fisher Controls, and Louisville ladders.

Much of the company's success can be traced to its ability to continue to fill the product pipeline with innovative new offerings. About 33 percent of its revenue comes from products introduced in the previous five years, and the company introduces about 500 new products each year.

The St. Louis–based operation sells its products worldwide. About a third of its revenue comes from foreign sales, including 24 percent from Europe.

The company was founded by John Wesley Emerson in 1890—shortly after Thomas A. Edison installed his first electrical generators. In his small St. Louis shop, Emerson manufactured room fans, ceiling fans, and electrical motors.

Emerson has grown to about 112,000 employees and 36,000 shareholders. The company has a market capitalization of about $29 billion.

EARNINGS PER SHARE GROWTH   ★

Past five years: 75 percent (12 percent per year)
Past ten years: 139 percent (9 percent per year)

STOCK GROWTH   ★ ★

Past ten years: 252 percent (13 percent per year)
Dollar growth: $10,000 over ten years (including reinvested dividends) would have grown to $42,000.
Average annual compounded rate of return (including reinvested dividends): 15.5 percent

DIVIDEND

Dividend yield: 2.2 percent
Increased dividend: 42 consecutive years
Past five-year increase: 64 percent (10 percent per year)

CONSISTENCY ★ ★ ★ ★

Increased earnings per share: 41 consecutive years
Increased sales: nine of the past ten years

SHAREHOLDER PERKS ★ ★

Good dividend reinvestment and stock purchase plan; voluntary stock purchase plan allows contributions of $50 to $120,000 per year.

EMERSON AT A GLANCE

Fiscal year ended: Sept. 30
Revenue and net income in $ millions

	1993	1994	1995	1996	1997	1998	5-Year Growth Avg. Annual (%)	Total (%)
Revenue ($)	8,174	8,607	10,013	11,149	12,298	13,447	11	65
Net income ($)	708	789	908	1,019	1,122	1,229	12	74
Earnings/share ($)	1.58	1.76	2.03	2.28	2.52	2.77	12	75
Dividends/share ($)	0.72	0.78	0.89	0.98	1.08	1.18	10	64
Dividend yield (%)	2.5	2.6	2.7	2.4	2.1	2.0	—	—
PE ratio range	17–20	14–16	15–20	17–23	18–24	19–24	—	—

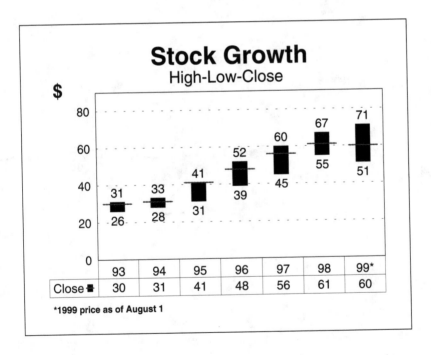

Stock Growth
High-Low-Close

	93	94	95	96	97	98	99*
Close	30	31	41	48	56	61	60

*1999 price as of August 1

Sara Lee Corporation

Three First National Plaza
Chicago, IL 60602
312-726-2600
www.saralee.com

Chairman and CEO: John H. Bryan
President: C. Steven McMillan

Earnings Growth	★
Stock Growth	★
Dividend	★ ★ ★
Consistency	★ ★ ★ ★
Shareholder Perks	★ ★
NYSE: SLE	**11 points**

Sara Lee management has coined a new term to describe its latest business strategy: "de-verticalization." What that means is that the company will no longer be developing, producing, and distributing its products through its own in-house resources. In other words, it will no longer be vertically integrated.

Under its new strategy, the company has been selling its manufacturing and production plants around the world and has begun to outsource the production of its products to independent manufacturers. "We will now concentrate our abilities in the areas of sourcing, product design, and development, as well as merchandising and marketing," explained Sara

Lee Chairman and CEO John H. Bryan. "Unconstrained by owning and maintaining a network of factories, we can be quicker to the market and undertake more growth initiatives with greater speed and lower risk than ever before."

The Chicago-based operation sells a broad range of foods and consumer products. It is the nation's leading marketer of packaged meats, including Ball Park, Best's Kosher, Hillshire Farms, Mr. Turkey, State Fair, Argal, Hygrade, Imperial, and Jimmy Dean.

Sara Lee is also the leader in frozen desserts, including cheese cake, pound cake, pies, and other desserts. In all, the foods division accounts for 27 percent of Sara Lee's $20 billion in annual sales.

But despite its dominant position in packaged meats and frozen desserts, Sara Lee's leading product segment in terms of total revenue is branded apparel. With its Hanes, Playtex, L'eggs, Isotoner, Sheer Energy, Wonderbra, Champion, and other lines of hosiery, knits, and intimate apparel, Sara Lee's branded apparel segment accounts for about 30 percent of total revenue.

Sara Lee is the leading manufacturer of women's hosiery, brassiers, and other intimate apparel, and the second leading manufacturer of mens and boys underwear and printed T-shirts.

Sara Lee's other segments include:

- **Household and body care products** (10 percent of revenue). Sara Lee's household goods and personal care products division generates 90 percent of its sales revenue outside the United States. The company makes shoe care products (Kiwi, Esquire, and Meltonian shoe polish), toiletries, over-the-counter medications, specialty detergents, and insecticides.
- **Coffee and tea** (14 percent of revenue). Sara Lee holds leading positions in coffee sales in several Scandanavian countries. Its brands include Chat Noir, Douwe Egbert, Maison du Cafe, Merrild and several others. More than 80 percent of the company's coffee and grocery products revenue is generated outside the United States.

Sara Lee has operations in more than 40 countries and sales in about 140 countries. Foreign sales account for about 41 percent of total revenue.

The company was founded in 1939 when Nathan Cummings acquired the C.D. Kenny Company, a small Baltimore sugar, tea, and coffee distributor. The company changed its named to Consolidated Grocers Corp. in

1945—a name that stuck until 1985 when the firm changed names again, this time to Sara Lee.

Sara Lee has about 140,000 employees and 85,000 shareholders. It has a market capitalization of about $21 billion.

EARNINGS PER SHARE GROWTH ★

Past five years: 59 percent (10 percent per year)
Past ten years: 217 percent (12 percent per year)

STOCK GROWTH ★

Past ten years: 228 percent (13 percent per year)
Dollar growth: $10,000 over ten years (including reinvested dividends) would have grown to $42,000.
Average annual compounded rate of return (including reinvested dividends): 15 percent

DIVIDEND ★ ★ ★

Dividend yield: 2.5 percent
Increased dividend: 21 consecutive years
Past five-year increase: 61 percent (10 percent per year)

CONSISTENCY ★ ★ ★ ★

Increased earnings per share: 23 consecutive years
Increased sales: eight consecutive years

SHAREHOLDER PERKS ★ ★

Good dividend reinvestment and stock purchase plan; voluntary stock purchase plan allows contributions of $10 to $5,000 per quarter.

Each year at the annual meeting, Sara Lee shareholders receive a gift box of Sara Lee products, including such items as coupons, foods, soaps, and other product samples.

SARA LEE AT A GLANCE

Fiscal year ended: Dec. 31
Revenue and net income in $ millions

	1993	1994	1995	1996	1997	1998	5-Year Growth Avg. Annual (%)	Total (%)
Revenue ($)	14,580	15,536	17,719	18,624	19,734	20,011	6	37
Net income ($)	704	729	804	916	1,009	1,102	9	57
Earnings/share ($)	0.70	0.74	0.81	0.92	1.02	1.11	10	59
Dividends/share ($)	0.28	0.31	0.34	0.37	0.41	0.45	10	61
Dividend yield (%)	2.0	2.6	2.7	2.4	2.2	1.7	—	—
PE ratio range	15–22	44–59	15–21	16–22	18–28	17–19	—	—

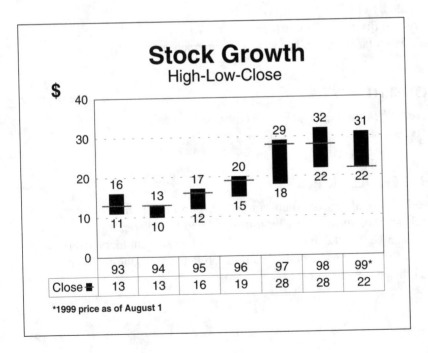

Stock Growth
High-Low-Close

$	93	94	95	96	97	98	99*
Close	13	13	16	19	28	28	22

*1999 price as of August 1

May Department Stores Company

611 Olive Street
St. Louis, MO 63101
314-342-6300
www.maycompany.com

Chairman: Jerome T. Loeb
President and CEO: Eugene S. Kahn

Earnings Growth	★
Stock Growth	★
Dividend	★ ★ ★
Consistency	★ ★ ★ ★
Shareholder Perks	★ ★
NYSE: MAY	**11 points**

Founded more than 120 years ago, May Department Stores operates clothing and department stores across the country, although most don't carry the name May. In all, the company operates about 400 stores in 32 states with 11 different names.

May, which has posted 24 consecutive years of record earnings, has grown steadily through acquisitions and new store openings.

Its stores include:

- Lord & Taylor—63 stores primarily in the East and South (15 percent of revenue)
- Hecht's and Strawbridge's—71 stores in the East (19 percent of revenue)

- Foley's—55 stores in Texas, Colorado, and Oklahoma (15 percent of revenue)
- Robinsons-May—55 stores in California and Arizona (15 percent of revenue)
- Famous-Barr, L.S. Ayers, and The Jones Store—30 stores in St. Louis and Indiana (9 percent of revenue)
- Kaufmann's, Pittsburgh—47 stores primarily in New York, Ohio, and Pennsylvania (12 percent of revenue)
- Filene's, Boston—40 stores primarily in the East (12 percent of revenue)
- Meier & Frank—8 stores in Oregon (3 percent of revenue)

May also acquired 11 former Mercantile stores in 1998. The company adds about 20 new stores each year. The St. Louis–based retailer spun off its Payless Shoe Stores subsidiary in 1996 in order to concentrate more on its department store business.

The firm was founded in 1877 by David May, who opened his first store in Leadville, Colorado, during the silver mining boom. May later purchased stores in St. Louis and Cleveland, moving the headquarters from Colorado to St. Louis in 1905. The company was listed on the New York Stock Exchange in 1911. The retailer has continued to acquire individual stores and small chains throughout this century.

May now has about 60,000 full-time employees and 67,000 part-time employees, and 47,000 shareholders. It has a market capitalization of $15 billion.

EARNINGS PER SHARE GROWTH ★

Past five years: 63 percent (10 percent per year)
Past ten years: 102 percent (7 percent per year)

STOCK GROWTH ★

Past ten years: 210 percent (12 percent per year)
Dollar growth: $10,000 over ten years (including reinvested dividends) would have grown to $38,500.
Average annual compounded rate of return (including reinvested dividends): 14.5 percent

DIVIDEND

Dividend yield: 2.0 percent
Increased dividend: 24 consecutive years
Past five-year increase: 41 percent (7 percent per year)

CONSISTENCY

Increased earnings per share: 24 consecutive years
Increased sales: 24 consecutive years

SHAREHOLDER PERKS ★ ★

Outstanding dividend reinvestment and stock purchase plan; voluntary stock purchase plan allows contributions of $25 and up (with no upper limit) per month.

MAY DEPARTMENT STORES AT A GLANCE

Fiscal year ended: Jan. 31
Revenue and net income in $ millions

	1993	1994	1995	1996	1997	1998	5-Year Growth Avg. Annual (%)	Total (%)
Revenue ($)	8,945	9,688	10,402	11,546	12,352	13,413	9	50
Net income ($)	578	650	700	749	779	849	8	47
Earnings/share ($)	1.49	1.69	1.83	1.97	2.18	2.43	10	63
Dividends/share ($)	0.60	0.67	0.74	0.77	0.80	0.85	7	41
Dividend yield (%)	2.3	2.6	2.7	2.5	2.4	2.1	—	—
PE ratio range	15–21	12–18	12–17	14–18	13–17	14–19	—	—

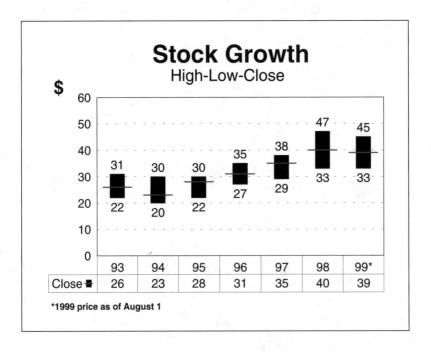

Stock Growth
High-Low-Close

	93	94	95	96	97	98	99*
Close	26	23	28	31	35	40	39

*1999 price as of August 1

81

Newell Rubbermaid, Inc.

Newell Rubbermaid.

29 East Stephenson Street
Freeport, IL 61032
815-235-4171
www.newellco.com

Chairman: William P. Sovey
President: Thomas A. Ferguson

Earnings Growth	★ ★
Stock Growth	★ ★
Dividend	★ ★
Consistency	★ ★ ★
Shareholder Perks	★ ★
NYSE: NWL	**11 points**

Acquisitions have always been a part of Newell's growth strategy, but its 1999 buyout of Rubbermaid was its biggest yet.

With such other recent acquisitions as Rolodex and Eldon (office storage and organization products), and Kirch (shades, blinds, and other window treatments), Newell has become one of the nation's largest consumer products companies. In all, Newell has acquired more than 18 other companies in the past decade.

In fact, acquisitions are so much a part of the company's strategy that Newell management coined the term "Newellization" to describe its system of acquiring other companies, streamlining them, and assimilating them into the Newell operation.

The Freeport, Illinois manufacturer is a leading maker of hardware and home furnishings, including Amerock cabinet hardware; Bulldog home hardware; EZ Paintr paint applicators; BernzOmatic torches; Levolor and Newell window treatments (blinds, shades, and rods); and Intercraft, Decorel, and Holson Burnes picture frames. It also makes home storage products, pens, office storage products, and other office products. And, it makes Anchor Hocking glassware.

Prior its acquisition, Rubbermaid was a leading worldwide manufacturer of houseware products with more than 1,000 products in all, including dustpans, soap dishes, plastic food containers, mops, brooms, buckets, wastebaskets, lawn furniture, infant furnishings, and Little Tikes toys.

Newell Rubbermaid is a leading supplier for Wal-Mart, Kmart, Home Depot, Target, Office Depot, JC Penney, and other leading discount and department stores.

Newell's success has come with little consumer awareness. Although its goods are sold in hundreds of stores from coast to coast, you rarely see the Newell brand name on the shelves. Many of its goods are custom labeled for its clients (such as True Value paint brushes or Target cookware) or are manufactured under other brand names.

Newell's leading product segment is housewares and home furnishings, which accounts for about 46 percent of the company's $3.7 billion in annual revenue. (With the addition of Rubbermaid, annual revenue would be about $6.5 billion.) Its other two segments are office furniture, 28 percent of revenue, and housewares, 26 percent.

Newell's primary customer base includes office suppliers (18 percent of revenue), home centers and hardware stores (17 percent), department stores and specialty stores (38 percent), and discount stores and warehouse clubs (27 percent).

Newell was founded in 1902 as a manufacturer of curtain rods. Today the company has about 32,000 employees and 16,000 shareholders. Newell Rubbermaid has a market capitalization of about $13 billion.

EARNINGS PER SHARE GROWTH ★ ★

Past five years: 76 percent (12 percent per year)
Past ten years: 263 percent (14 percent per year)

STOCK GROWTH

Past ten years: 395 percent (17 percent per year)
Dollar growth: $10,000 over ten years (including reinvested dividends)
would have grown to $54,000.
Average annual compounded rate of return (including reinvested dividends): 18.5 percent

DIVIDEND

Dividend yield: 1.7 percent
Increased dividend: six consecutive years
Past five-year increase: 106 percent (16.5 percent per year)

CONSISTENCY ★ ★ ★

Increased earnings per share: nine of the past ten years
Increased sales: eight consecutive years

SHAREHOLDER PERKS ★ ★

Good dividend reinvestment and stock purchase plan; voluntary stock
purchase plan allows contributions of $10 to $30,000 per year.

The company often hands out product samples or special gifts to
shareholders at the annual meeting.

NEWELL RUBBERMAID AT A GLANCE

Fiscal year ended: Dec. 31
Revenue and net income in $ millions

	1993	1994	1995	1996	1997	1998	5-Year Growth Avg. Annual (%)	Total (%)
Revenue ($)	1,645	2,075	2,498	2,873	3,234	3,720	18	126
Net income ($)	165	196	223	257	290	320	14	94
Earnings/share ($)	1.05	1.24	1.41	1.62	1.82	1.85	12	76
Dividends/share ($)	0.35	0.39	0.46	0.56	0.64	0.72	16	106
Dividend yield (%)	1.8	1.8	1.9	1.9	1.7	1.6	—	—
PE ratio range	15–20	15–19	14–19	16–21	17–24	15–23	—	—

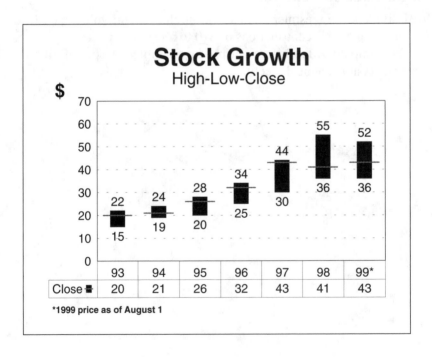

Stock Growth
High-Low-Close

	93	94	95	96	97	98	99*
Close	20	21	26	32	43	41	43

*1999 price as of August 1

Hershey Foods Corporation

100 Crystal A Drive
Hershey, PA 17033
717-534-6799
www.hersheys.com

Chairman and CEO: Kenneth L. Wolfe
President: Joseph P. Viviano

Earnings Growth	★
Stock Growth	★ ★
Dividend	★ ★
Consistency	★ ★ ★ ★
Shareholder Perks	★ ★
NYSE: HSY	**11 points**

In Hershey, Pennsylvania, the street lamps are shaped like Hershey's Kisses and the sweet smell of chocolate wafts across the town square with every passing breeze. Hershey is the chocolate lover's mecca.

Founded by Milton Hershey in 1893, Hershey Foods is the nation's leading confectionery producer, with about a 35 percent share of the $11 billion U.S. candy market.

Through brand extension and a series of acquisitions, Hershey has assembled a long line of popular chocolate candies. Its top brands are Reese's, Kit Kat, Hershey's chocolate bar, and Hershey's Kisses. Other popular brands include Milk Duds, Peter Paul Almond Joy, Mounds Bars, Caramello, Cadbury's chocolate bars and Creme Eggs, Hershey's Big Block, Special Dark, Golden Almond, Golden Almond Nuggets, Krackel, and Rolo caramels.

Hershey is also the maker of Skor, Mr. Goodbar, Reese's Pieces, 5th Avenue, Bar None, York peppermint pattie, Whoppers, Whatchamacallit, Reese's NutRageous, ReeseSticks, and Symphony.

The company also produces a wide selection of nonchocolate candies, such as PayDay, Twizzlers, Jolly Ranchers, Good & Plenty, Good & Fruity, Amazin' Fruit gummy bears, Chuckles, Heide jujubes, Hershey's caramels and jelly beans, Sour Dudes, Nibs, Rain-Blo gumballs, Wunderbeans, and Zagnut and Zero candy bars. The company also produces Luden's cough drops.

In addition to its candies, Hershey offers a line of chocolate mixes, including Hershey's cocoa, chocolate milk mix, baking chocolate, chocolate syrup, fudge topping, chocolate chips and premium chunks, and chocolate flavor puddings. It also makes Reese's baking chips, Reese's peanut butter, and Mounds coconut flakes.

Hershey sold its pasta division in 1999, including Ronzoni, American Beauty, San Giorgio, Light 'n Fluffy, and Skinner brands.

Hershey products are sold in more than 90 countries worldwide, although its international operations account for slightly less than 10 percent of its $4.4 billion in annual revenue.

The company has about 15,000 employees and 44,000 shareholders. Hershey has a market capitalization of about $8 billion.

EARNINGS PER SHARE GROWTH ★

Past five years: 64 percent (10 percent per year)
Past ten years: 186 percent (11 percent per year)

STOCK GROWTH ★ ★

Past ten years: 251 percent (13.5 percent per year)
Dollar growth: $10,000 over ten years (including reinvested dividends) would have grown to $42,000.
Average annual compounded rate of return (including reinvested dividends): 15.5 percent

DIVIDEND ★★

Dividend yield: 1.4 percent
Increased dividend: 24 consecutive years
Past five-year increase: 61 percent (10 percent per year)

CONSISTENCY ★★★★

Increased earnings per share: ten consecutive years
Increased sales: ten consecutive years

SHAREHOLDER PERKS ★★

Direct stock purchase plan allows new investors to buy shares with a minimum $500 investment. Dividend reinvestment and stock purchase plan allows voluntary contributions of $100 to $20,000 per year.

Shareholders attending the annual meeting may be treated to a free packet of Hershey's new products samples as well as a gift certificate offering discounts on a variety of food and gift items.

HERSHEY FOODS AT A GLANCE

Fiscal year ended: Dec. 31
Revenue and net income in $ millions

	1993	1994	1995	1996	1997	1998	5-Year Growth Avg. Annual (%)	Total (%)
Revenue ($)	3,488	3,606	3,691	3,989	4,302	4,436	5	27
Net income ($)	257	264	280	309	337	341	6	33
Earnings/share ($)	1.43	1.52	1.69	2.00	2.23	2.34	10	64
Dividends/share ($)	0.57	0.63	0.69	0.76	0.84	0.92	10	61
Dividend yield (%)	2.3	2.7	2.4	1.9	1.6	1.4	—	—
PE ratio range	13–17	19–25	14–20	18–29	19–28	25–32	—	—

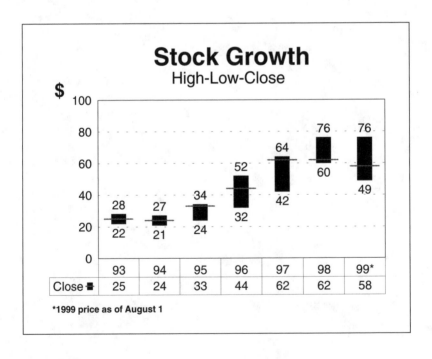

Stock Growth
High-Low-Close

	93	94	95	96	97	98	99*
Close	25	24	33	44	62	62	58

*1999 price as of August 1

83

Campbell Soup Company

Campbell Soup Company	

Campbell Place
Camden, NJ 08103
609-342-4800
www.campbellsoup.com

President and CEO: Dale Morrison
Chairman: David Johnson

Earnings Growth	★
Stock Growth	★ ★
Dividend	★ ★ ★
Consistency	★ ★ ★
Shareholder Perks	★ ★
NYSE: CPB	**11 points**

Campbell Soup Company has been trying to heat things up after seeing cooler growth in its earnings and revenue in recent years. The company has been upgrading its offerings—with more products available in microwavable packages—and marketing its soups more aggressively in foreign countries.

Campbell's holds a dominant position in the U.S. soup market—cans of Campbell's are found in more than 90 percent of American households—but until recently, sales have been scant outside the U.S. market.

The Camden, New Jersey operation has been buying its way into the international market. In 1998, Campbell acquired Liebig, the leading wet soup brand in France. Prior to that, it acquired Arnotts Limited, a leading soup maker in Australia, and Erasco, which is Germany's leading soup company. It also has entered joint ventures to market soup in several Asian countries.

International sales account for about 28 percent of the company's $6.7 billion in annual revenue. In all, the company has about 100 facilities in more than 20 countries, with sales on six continents.

In the U.S. market, the company continues to introduce a barrage of new soups and other products, sometimes ladling up as many as 20 new flavors a year. Its three biggest sellers, Chicken Noodle, Cream of Mushroom, and Tomato continue to generate increasing sales. Americans consume about two billion bowls per year of those three soups.

Many of Campbell's other products are leaders in their categories, including V8 vegetable juice, Vlasic pickles, Pace Mexican sauces, Swanson canned poultry, Franco-American gravy, Pepperidge Farm premium biscuits and crackers, and Godiva super premium chocolates.

The company is also a producer of specialty products for the food services industry. For instance, Campbell's food services division produces soups for Sysco (the nation's largest food service distributor), chicken pot pies for KFC, and soup for McDonald's.

Soups and sauces account for 66 percent of Campbell's annual revenue; biscuits and confectionery products make up 22 percent; food service sales, 6 percent; and other products, 4 percent of sales.

Campbell's condensed soups were first introduced a century ago in 1897. The first year, the company sold only about ten cans per week of the new soups. But by 1905, the company was selling 40,000 cases per week, and Campbell's was on its way to becoming an American staple.

The Campbell Soup Company has 24,000 employees and 51,000 shareholders. It has a market capitalization of $17.7 billion.

EARNINGS PER SHARE GROWTH   ★

Past five years: 71 percent (11 percent per year)
Past ten years: 304 percent (15 percent per year)

STOCK GROWTH

Past ten years: 264 percent (13.5 percent per year)
Dollar growth: $10,000 over ten years (including reinvested dividends) would have grown to $42,000.
Average annual compounded rate of return (including reinvested dividends): 15.5 percent

DIVIDEND

Dividend yield: 2.3 percent
Increased dividend: 24 consecutive years
Past five-year increase: 78 percent (12 percent per year)

CONSISTENCY

Increased earnings per share: nine consecutive years
Increased sales: eight of the past ten years

SHAREHOLDER PERKS

Direct purchase plan allows new investors to buy shares from the company with an initial minimum investment of $500. Dividend reinvestment and stock purchase plan allows voluntary contributions of $50 to $25,000 per year.

The company often hands out a bag of freebies at the annual meeting, including a variety of soups and other Campbell's products.

CAMPBELL SOUP AT A GLANCE

Fiscal year ended: July 31
Revenue and net income in $ millions

	1993	1994	1995	1996	1997	1998	5-Year Growth Avg. Annual (%)	Total (%)
Revenue ($)	6,586	6,690	7,278	7,678	7,964	6,696	—	2
Net income ($)	557	630	698	802	873	874	9	57
Earnings/share ($)	1.11	1.26	1.40	1.61	1.85	1.90	11	71
Dividends/share ($)	0.46	0.55	0.61	0.67	0.75	0.82	12	78
Dividend yield (%)	2.2	2.8	2.7	2.3	1.7	1.5	—	—
PE ratio range	35–44	14–18	15–22	19–29	29–44	31–41	—	—

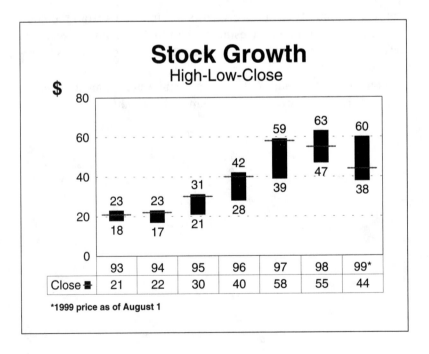

Stock Growth
High-Low-Close

Close ■	93	94	95	96	97	98	99*
	21	22	30	40	58	55	44

*1999 price as of August 1

Safeway, Inc.

5918 Stonerdge Mall Road
Pleasanton, CA 94588
925-467-3000
www.safeway.com

Chairman, President, and CEO:
Steven A. Burd

Earnings Growth	★ ★ ★ ★
Stock Growth	★ ★ ★ ★
Dividend	
Consistency	★ ★
Shareholder Perks	
NYSE: SWY	**10 points**

With 1,500 stores in 18 states and four Canadian provinces, Safeway is not only one of North America's biggest grocery store chains, it is also one of the nation's most dramatic turnaround success stories.

Safeway Stores was initially acquired by the investment firm of Kolberg Kravis Roberts and Company (KKR) in 1986 in a leveraged buyout of its stock. In 1990, KKR brought the company public again with an initial stock offering. But after three years of disappointing financial results, the old management was swept out of power and a new management team was hired to revive the company and bolster its sagging returns. To say the least, the operation was an unmitigated success.

From 1992 to 1998, earnings grew from 21¢ a share to $1.59—a 657 percent increase—and the stock price climbed from a low of $2.40 (split-adjusted) to $61—a 2,400 percent gain. In real dollar terms, a $10,000 investment in the stock at its 1992 low would have grown to about $250,000 by the close of 1998.

Most of Safeway's 1,500 stores (including 324 Vons stores and 114 Dominick's stores) are in the western United States and the western provinces of Canada. It also has stores in Alaska, Hawaii, Illinois, Indiana, Maryland, and Virginia.

Saveway operates 43 manufacturing and processing facilities, including 11 milk plants, eight bread plants, seven ice cream plants, three cheese and meat packaging plants, four soft drink bottling plants, five fruit and vegetable processing plants, one pet food plant, and four other food processing facilities.

The newer Safeway stores are fairly large supermarkets of about 55,000 square feet. They carry a wide selection of both food and general merchandise. About 90 percent of Safeway stores have specialty bakeries, delis, and floral centers. About 60 percent of its stores have pharmacies. Most of its older stores range in size from 30,000 to 50,000 square feet, although about 350 stores range in size from 5,000 to 29,000 square feet. The smaller stores are usually located in smaller communities or in areas with space limitations or community restrictions.

Safeway has about 170,000 employees. The company has a market capitalization of about $23 billion.

EARNINGS PER SHARE GROWTH   ★ ★ ★ ★

Past five years: 512 percent (43 percent per year)
Past ten years: 893 percent (26 percent per year)

STOCK GROWTH   ★ ★ ★ ★

Past nine years: 1,518 percent (36 percent per year)
Dollar growth: $10,000 over nine years would have grown to $160,000.
Average annual compounded rate of return: 36 percent

DIVIDEND

Safeway pays no dividends.

CONSISTENCY

Increased earnings per share: eight of the past ten years
Increased sales: ten consecutive years

SHAREHOLDER PERKS

The company does not offer a dividend reinvestment and stock purchase plan, nor does it offer other shareholder perks.

SAFEWAY AT A GLANCE

Fiscal year ended: Dec. 31
Revenue and net income in $ millions

	1993	1994	1995	1996	1997	1998	5-Year Growth Avg. Annual (%)	Total (%)
Revenue ($)	15,215	15,627	16,398	17,269	22,484	24,484	10	61
Net income ($)	123	250	326	461	622	807	46	556
Earnings/share ($)	0.26	0.51	0.68	0.97	1.25	1.59	43	512
Dividends/share ($)	—	—	—	—	—	—	—	—
Dividend yield (%)	—	—	—	—	—	—	—	—
PE ratio range	11–22	9–16	10–17	11–21	16–24	18–37	—	—

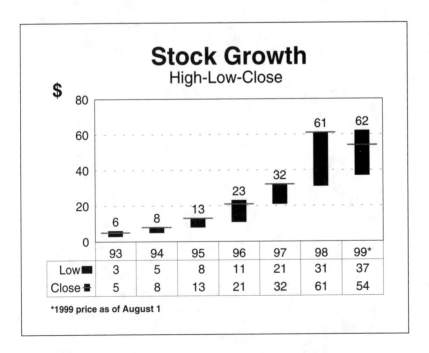

Stock Growth
High-Low-Close

	93	94	95	96	97	98	99*
Low	3	5	8	11	21	31	37
Close	5	8	13	21	32	61	54

*1999 price as of August 1

85

Danaher Corporation

1250 24th Street NW, Suite 800
Washington, DC 20037
202-828-0850
www.danaher.com

Chairman: Steven M. Rales
President and CEO: George M. Sherman

Earnings Growth	★ ★ ★ ★
Stock Growth	★ ★ ★ ★
Dividend	
Consistency	★ ★
Shareholder Perks	
NYSE: DHR	**10 points**

Originally established as a Massachusetts real estate investment trust in 1969, Danaher has strayed far from its corporate roots. The company is now a manufacturer of hand tools and other equipment that it distributes throughout the United States, Europe, Asia, and South America.

The company's best-known product line is its Craftsman hand tools, which it manufactures for Sears, Roebuck and Company. Danaher is also a primary supplier of specialized automotive service tools and general purpose mechanics' hand tools for the 6,500 NAPA auto parts stores.

The company's automotive service tools also are sold under the K-D Tools brand, and its industrial tools and products are sold under the Armstrong and Allen brand names. It also makes the Holo-Krome fastener tools and manufactures tools under a number of other brand names, including Matco Tools, Jacobs Chuck, Iseli, Delta, and Hennessy.

Danaher's tools and components division also makes toolboxes and storage devices, diesel engine retarders, wheel service equipment, drill chucks, hardware, and components for the power generation and transmission industries. Tools and components account for about 45 percent of the company's $2.9 billion in annual sales.

The company's other product segment, process and environmental controls, accounts for 55 percent of revenue. Danaher makes a broad range of monitoring, sensing, controlling, measuring, counting, and electrical power quality products, systems, and components. It also makes electronic test tools, underground storage tank leak detection systems, and motion, position, speed, temperature, level, and position instruments and sensing devices.

Danaher recently made three key acquisitions for its process and environmental controls division: Fluke Corp., Pacific Scientific Company, and Dr. Bruno Lange GmbH.

The District of Columbia–based manufacturer has operations in about 20 countries. Foreign sales account for about 20 percent of total revenue.

Danaher has about 11,600 employees and 5,000 shareholders. The company has a market capitalization of $8.7 billion.

EARNINGS PER SHARE GROWTH ★ ★ ★ ★

Past five years: 226 percent (27 percent per year)
Past ten years: 264 percent (14 percent per year)

STOCK GROWTH ★ ★ ★ ★

Past ten years: 1,618 percent (33 percent per year)
Dollar growth: $10,000 over ten years (including reinvested dividends) would have grown to $142,000.
Average annual compounded rate of return (including reinvested dividends): 33 percent

DIVIDEND

Dividend yield: 0.1 percent
Increased dividend: no increase the past three years
Past five-year increase: 67 percent (11 percent per year)

CONSISTENCY

Increased earnings per share: eight of the past ten years
Increased sales: nine of the past ten years

SHAREHOLDER PERKS

The company offers no dividend reinvestment and stock purchase plan.

DANAHER AT A GLANCE

Fiscal year ended: Dec. 31
Revenue and net income in $ millions

	1993	1994	1995	1996	1997	1998	5-Year Growth Avg. Annual (%)	Total (%)
Revenue ($)	1,076	1,289	1,487	1,812	2,051	2,910	22	170
Net income ($)	54	82	106	128	155	183	28	239
Earnings/share ($)	0.47	0.70	0.89	1.07	1.29	1.53	27	226
Dividends/share ($)	0.03	0.03	0.04	0.04	0.05	0.05	11	67
Dividend yield (%)	0.4	0.3	0.3	0.2	0.2	0.1	—	—
PE ratio range	15–24	15–21	13–19	13–20	15–24	21–41	—	—

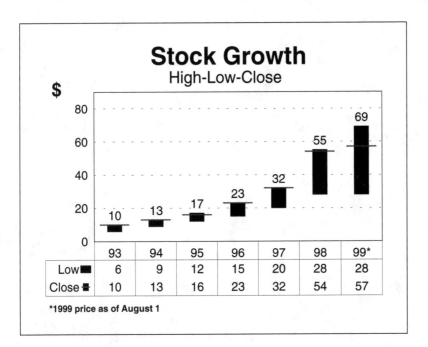

Stock Growth
High-Low-Close

	93	94	95	96	97	98	99*
Low	6	9	12	15	20	28	28
Close	10	13	16	23	32	54	57

*1999 price as of August 1

Biomet, Inc.

Airport Industrial Park
P.O. Box 587
Warsaw, IN 46581
219-267-6639
www.biomet.com

Chairman: Niles L. Noblitt
President and CEO: Dane A. Miller, Ph.D.

Earnings Growth	★ ★
Stock Growth	★ ★ ★ ★
Dividend	
Consistency	★ ★ ★ ★
Shareholder Perks	
Nasdaq: BMET	**10 points**

Biomet would give an arm and a leg to earn your business. Or, more accurately, a knee, an elbow, a shoulder, or a hip. The company specializes in reconstructive devices used to replace joints that have degenerated due to arthritis, osteoporosis, or injury.

About 60 percent of Biomet's $651 million in annual sales comes from its reconstructive devices segment. The company has developed— or in some cases acquired—several models of knee replacement devices that can be surgically implanted. It also manufactures several hip and shoulder replacement systems and has recently developed replacement products for elbows and ankles.

The Warsaw, Indiana operation also does a substantial business in the manufacturing and marketing of special screws, nuts, nails, plates, pins, wires, and other "fixation" products used by surgeons to set and stabilize fractures. It also makes drills and saws used for cranial and small bone surgery. Biomet has developed electrical stimulation devices used for the treatment of recalcitrant bone fractures that have not healed through conventional surgical and nonsurgical methods. Fixation and related products account for about 22 percent of the company's total revenue.

Biomet's other primary segment is its spinal products division, which accounts for 6 percent of revenue. The company makes a spinal fusion stimulation system used in conjunction with bone grafting to increase the probability of successful fusion. It also makes spinal fixation systems, including a modular titanium link and a polydirectional screw that enable the surgeon to tailor the spinal segmental construction to the patient's anatomy.

Biomet also manufactures operating room supplies, such as filters, glove liners and drapes, casting materials and splints, arthroscopy products, and orthopedic support devices such as braces, knee immobilizers, and elbow, wrist, abdominal, thigh, and ankle supports. Those products, which Biomet classifies as "other products," account for about 12 percent of total revenue.

The company spends about $36 million each year in research and development.

Biomet has manufacturing or office facilities in more than 25 locations worldwide. Its products are sold in more than 100 countries. Foreign sales account for about 29 percent of total revenue.

Incorporated in 1977, Biomet has about 2,400 employees and 9,000 shareholders. It has a market capitalization of about $4.6 billion.

EARNINGS PER SHARE GROWTH   ★ ★

Past five years: 98 percent (15 percent per year)
Past ten years: 825 percent (25 percent per year)

STOCK GROWTH ★ ★ ★ ★

Past ten years: 664 percent (22.5 percent per year)
Dollar growth: $10,000 over ten years (including reinvested dividends) would have grown to $75,000.
Average annual compounded rate of return (including reinvested dividends): 22.5 percent

DIVIDEND

Dividend yield: 0.3 percent
Increased dividend: two consecutive years
Past one-year increase: 10 percent

CONSISTENCY ★ ★ ★ ★

Increased earnings per share: 21 consecutive years
Increased sales: 21 consecutive years

SHAREHOLDER PERKS

The company does not offer a dividend reinvestment and stock purchase plan, nor does it provide other shareholder perks.

BIOMET AT A GLANCE

Fiscal year ended: May 31
Revenue and net income in $ millions

	1993	1994	1995	1996	1997	1998	5-Year Growth Avg. Annual (%)	Total (%)
Revenue ($)	335	373	452	535	580	651	14	94
Net income ($)	64	70	79	94	107	125	14	95
Earnings/share ($)	0.56	0.61	0.69	0.82	0.94	1.11	15	98
Dividends/share ($)	—	—	—	—	0.10	0.11	—	10
Dividend yield (%)	—	—	—	—	0.6	0.4	—	—
PE ratio range	14–27	13–21	16–24	13–22	13–24	22–32	—	—

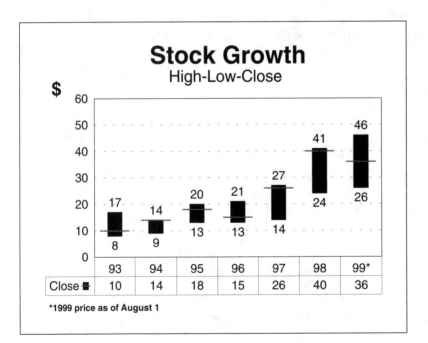

Stock Growth
High-Low-Close

	93	94	95	96	97	98	99*
Close	10	14	18	15	26	40	36

*1999 price as of August 1

G&K Services, Inc.

5995 Opus Parkway, Suite 500
Minnetonka, MN 55343
612-912-5500
www.gkservices.com

Chairman: Richard M. Fink
President and CEO: Thomas Moberly

Earnings Growth	★ ★ ★ ★
Stock Growth	★ ★ ★
Dividend	
Consistency	★ ★ ★
Shareholder Perks	
Nasdaq: GKSRA	**10 points**

G&K Services dresses more than a million people a day. The company is the nation's third largest uniform supplier. It manufactures, sells, and rents work uniforms and related products.

The Minneapolis operation has 125 locations, with more than 100,000 client companies in 36 states and Canada. In all, it provides the uniforms for more than 1.4 million workers each day.

Customers include divisions of more than half of the Fortune 100 companies, although most of its 100,000 client companies are small to midsize operations. Customers include auto dealerships, schools, delivery services, service stations, restaurants, delivery services, pharmacies, and a wide range of other organizations. The company also has begun manufacturing special uniforms for sterile environments and laboratories at electronics and pharmaceutical manufacturing facilities.

G&K manufactures the uniforms that it rents and provides laundry services and pickup and delivery for its customers. The company rents about 95 percent of the uniforms it manufactures and sells the rest. Uniform sales, rental, and service account for about 65 percent of the company's $500 million in annual revenue.

G&K's other major business is leasing and sales of related items, such as floor mats, dust mops, dust cloths, wiping towels, aprons, and linens. The firm also offers a service filling soap dispensers, replacing cloth towels in the pull-down towel racks, and selling waterless hand cleaner, moisturizing soaps, and air fresheners. G&K's mat, mop, towel, and cleaner service accounts for about a third of its total revenue.

The company has been very profitable in recent years, posting increased earnings per share 14 of the past 15 years. It has tried to maintain its profitability by setting up an advanced support system using computerized systems to identify and track garments and an automated garment sorting system and washer-dryer system to service its rental uniforms.

Founded in 1902, G&K has about 7,800 employees and 7,000 shareholders. The company has a market capitalization of about $850 million.

EARNINGS PER SHARE GROWTH   ★ ★ ★ ★

Past five years: 214 percent (25 percent per year)
Past ten years: 324 percent (15.5 percent per year)

STOCK GROWTH   ★ ★ ★

Past ten years: 475 percent (19 percent per year)
Dollar growth: $10,000 over ten years (including reinvested dividends) would have grown to $58,000.
Average annual compounded rate of return (including reinvested dividends): 19.5 percent

DIVIDEND

Dividend yield: 0.2 percent
Increased dividend: no increases in recent years
Past five-year increase: no increase

CONSISTENCY

Increased earnings per share: nine of the past ten years
Increased sales: ten consecutive years

SHAREHOLDER PERKS

The company does not offer a dividend reinvestment and stock purchase plan, nor does it offer other shareholder perks.

G&K SERVICES AT A GLANCE

Fiscal year ended: June 30
Revenue and net income in $ millions

	1993	1994	1995	1996	1997	1998	5-Year Growth Avg. Annual (%)	5-Year Growth Total (%)
Revenue ($)	208	225	263	305	351	503	19	142
Net income ($)	10	15	18	23	29	32	26	220
Earnings/share ($)	0.50	0.73	0.90	1.11	1.42	1.57	25	214
Dividends/share ($)	0.07	0.07	0.07	0.07	0.07	0.07	0	0
Dividend yield (%)	0.6	0.5	0.4	0.3	0.2	0.2	—	—
PE ratio range	20–29	17–24	17–29	20–34	20–30	22–35	—	—

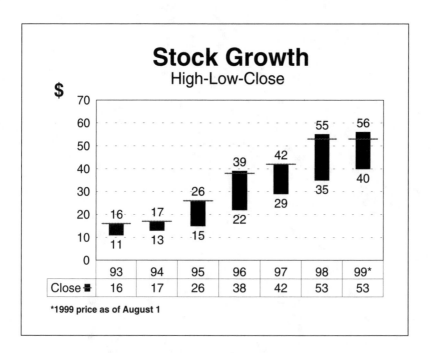

Stock Growth
High-Low-Close

	93	94	95	96	97	98	99*
Close	16	17	26	38	42	53	53

*1999 price as of August 1

H. J. Heinz Company

600 Grant Street
Pittsburgh, PA 15219
412-456-5700
www.heinz.com

Chairman: Anthony J. F. O'Reilly
President and CEO: William R. Johnson

Earnings Growth	★
Stock Growth	★
Dividend	★ ★ ★ ★
Consistency	★ ★
Shareholder Perks	★ ★
NYSE: HNZ	**10 points**

Morris the Cat meet Charlie the Tuna, but watch out for the ketchup. It's one big, happy family at H. J. Heinz, maker of Star-Kist Tuna, 9-Lives cat food, and enough ketchup to sink the Titanic.

Heinz is the world's leading ketchup maker, selling about $1 billion worth a year. The Pittsburg-based operation accounts for about half of all ketchup sold in the United States and 70 percent in Canada. It also sells ketchup in about 100 other countries.

Ketchup, sauces, and other condiments account for 19 percent of the company's $9.4 billion in annual revenue.

Tuna and other seafood products account for about 12 percent of total revenue, led by its Star-Kist brand. Heinz accounts for about 20 percent of all branded tuna sales in the world and 50 percent in the U.S. market. It's the world's largest purchaser of tuna.

Heinz is also a major player in the pet food market, which accounts for 14 percent of its total revenue. In addition to its 9-Lives brand, the company's leading pet food products include Vet's Choice, Reward, Cycle, Kibbles 'n Bits, Gravy Train, Ken-L Ration, Meaty Bone, Jerky Treats, and Snausages. Heinz controls 20 percent of U.S. cat food sales, 15 percent of dog food sales, and 29 percent of pet treat sales.

The company's other products account for 55 percent of sales. Its food service business is among the nation's leading suppliers of prepared food to the restaurant and food service market. It specializes in ketchup, single-serve condiments, frozen soups, sauces, baked goods, and tomato products. It sells about 11 billion ketchup packets a year to food service operations throughout the United States.

The firm's Ore-Ida potato brand accounts for about 55 percent of all processed potato sales worldwide.

The company's other major segment is weight control products. Its Weight Watchers brand has annual food and service revenues of about $1 billion worldwide. Weight Watchers operates in more than 20 countries and is by far the world's number-one weight control brand. Heinz has been in the process of selling the Weight Watchers programs but will probably continue to produce Weight Watchers foods.

Heinz has operations worldwide. It does a strong infant foods business outside the United States, where it makes about 90 percent of its sales. In all, foreign sales account for about 47 percent of the company's total revenue.

Heinz was founded in 1869 by Henry J. Heinz and was first incorporated in 1900. Heinz has about 41,000 employees and 68,000 shareholders. The company has a market capitalization of about $18 billion.

EARNINGS PER SHARE GROWTH   ★

Past five years: 70 percent (11 percent per year)
Past ten years: 116 percent (8 percent per year)

STOCK GROWTH

Past ten years: 158 percent (10 percent per year)
Dollar growth: $10,000 over ten years (including reinvested dividends)
would have grown to $34,000.
Average annual compounded rate of return (including reinvested dividends): 13 percent

DIVIDEND

Dividend yield: 2.8 percent
Increased dividend: every year since 1967
Past five-year increase: 56 percent (9 percent per year)

CONSISTENCY

Increased earnings per share: eight of the past ten years
Increased sales: seven of the past ten years

SHAREHOLDER PERKS ★ ★

Good dividend reinvestment and stock purchase plan; voluntary stock
purchase plan allows contributions of $25 to $5,000 per month.

Shareholders who attend the annual meeting receive a gift package of
some of the company's newer products.

H. J. HEINZ AT A GLANCE

Fiscal year ended: April 30
Revenue and net income in $ millions

	1993	1994	1995	1996	1997	1998	5-Year Growth Avg. Annual (%)	5-Year Growth Total (%)
Revenue ($)	7,047	8,087	9,112	9,357	9,209	9,375	6	33
Net income ($)	541	591	659	658	802	886	10	64
Earnings/share ($)	1.41	1.59	1.75	1.76	2.15	2.40	11	70
Dividends/share ($)	0.86	0.94	1.04	1.14	1.24	1.34	9	56
Dividend yield (%)	3.6	3.8	3.3	3.1	2.5	2.5	—	—
PE ratio range	15–19	13–16	14–20	36–47	16–26	18–53	—	—

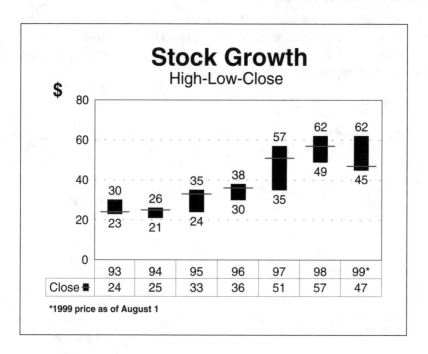

Stock Growth
High-Low-Close

Close ■	93	94	95	96	97	98	99*
	24	25	33	36	51	57	47

*1999 price as of August 1

89
Bestfoods

BESTFOODS

700 Sylvan Avenue
International Plaza
Englewood Cliffs, NJ 07632
201-894-4000
www.bestfoods.com

Chairman, President, and CEO:
Charles Shoemate

Earnings Growth	★	
Stock Growth	★ ★	
Dividend	★ ★	
Consistency	★ ★ ★	
Shareholder Perks	★ ★	
NYSE: BFO	**10 points**	

Formerly known as CPC International, Bestfoods has shed its name but not its international trademark. The company has operations in 60 countries and sales in 110 countries. About 60 percent of its $8.4 billion in annual revenue comes from outside the United States.

Bestfoods is the maker of Skippy peanut butter, Hellmann's mayonnaise, Henri's salad dressings, Mueller's macaroni, Karo corn syrup, Mazola oil, and other food products.

The Englewood Cliffs, New Jersey operation also makes the Knorr line of soups and other foods, which is sold in more than 60 countries and is the leading soup brand in more than 30 countries. Knorr products account for about 24 percent of the company's total sales.

In addition to its Knorr group, Bestfoods divides its operations into several key segments, including:

- **Dressings** (23 percent of revenue). The division includes Hellmann's products, salad dressings, and Mazola oil. Hellmann's is the world's leading brand of mayonnaise.
- **Baking** (20 percent of revenue). The company produces a broad range of premium baked goods such as breads, rolls, cookies, cakes, and pastries. Brands include Entenmann's desserts and Arnold and Brownberry breads. It is the nation's leading fresh premium baker.
- **Starches** (6 percent of revenue). The company's Maizena starch is the number-one brand in Latin America. The company also makes cereals, syrups, and a soy-based beverage.
- **Bread spreads** (4 percent of revenue). In addition to its Skippy peanut butter, the company sells other brands of peanut butter, jams, and other spreads in Europe and Asia.
- **Desserts** (3 percent of revenue). Bestfoods sells a variety of dessert products in the United Kingdom and other parts of Europe and Latin America.

All other sales, including its international food service division, account for about 6 percent of total revenue.

About 41 percent of the company's revenue comes from its European operations, 3 percent comes from Asia, and 13 percent comes from Latin America.

Bestfoods, which was founded in 1896 as the American Cotton Oil Company, has about 42,000 employees and 25,000 shareholders. The company has a market capitalization of about $15 billion.

EARNINGS PER SHARE GROWTH   ★

Past five years: 50 percent (8.5 percent per year)
Past ten years: 141 percent (9 percent per year)

STOCK GROWTH   ★ ★

Past ten years: 253 percent (13.5 percent per year)
Dollar growth: $10,000 over ten years (including reinvested dividends) would have grown to about $44,000.
Average annual compounded rate of return (including reinvested dividends): 16 percent

DIVIDEND

Dividend yield: 2.0 percent
Increased dividend: 13 consecutive years
Past five-year increase: 47 percent (8 percent per year)

CONSISTENCY   ★ ★ ★

Increased earnings per share: nine of the past ten years
Increased sales: eight of the past ten years

SHAREHOLDER PERKS   ★ ★

Good dividend reinvestment and stock purchase plan; voluntary stock purchase plan allows contributions of a minimum of $25 per month and a maximum of $25,000 per year.

BESTFOODS AT A GLANCE

Fiscal year ended: Dec. 31
Revenue and net income in $ millions

	1993	1994	1995	1996	1997	1998	5-Year Growth Avg. Annual (%)	Total (%)
Revenue ($)	6,738	7,425	8,432	9,844	8,400	8,374	4	24
Net income ($)	455	482	549	580	585	662	8	45
Earnings/share ($)	1.48	1.58	1.84	1.97	1.95	2.22	9	50
Dividends/share ($)	0.64	0.69	0.74	0.79	0.86	0.94	8	47
Dividend yield (%)	2.9	2.8	2.4	2.2	1.9	1.7	—	—
PE ratio range	14–17	20–25	21–30	17–22	26–37	14–34	—	—

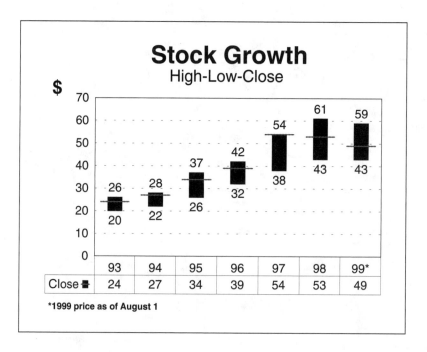

Stock Growth
High-Low-Close

$	93	94	95	96	97	98	99*
Close	24	27	34	39	54	53	49

*1999 price as of August 1

Equifax, Inc.

1600 Peachtree Street, NW
Atlanta, GA 30302
404-885-8000
www.equifax.com

Chairman, President, and CEO:
Thomas F. Chapman

Earnings Growth	★ ★
Stock Growth	★ ★
Dividend	★
Consistency	★ ★ ★
Shareholder Perks	★ ★
NYSE: EFX	**10 points**

Whether you're spending, saving, borrowing, or charging, Equifax is always watching. The Atlanta-based business is the nation's largest credit reporting operation. It provides consumer credit reports for banks, retailers, financial institutions, utilities, oil companies, credit card companies, auto finance and leasing firms, and mortgage lenders.

The company also provides related services such as collection services, fraud detection and prevention, credit card marketing, database marketing and database management systems, mortgage loan origination information, mapping tools, and modeling and analytical services. Equifax also provides commercial credit reporting and check guarantee services in Canada. North American information services account for about 48 percent of the firm's $1.6 billion in annual revenue.

Equifax also operates three other key business segments:

1. **Payment services** (33 percent of revenue). Equifax provides online verification of checks written at the point of sale, credit card processing, and related services for banks and financial institutions.
2. **Equifax Europe** (13 percent of revenue). The firm provides consumer and commercial credit information and marketing services, credit scoring and modeling services, check guarantee services, and auto lien information in Europe.
3. **Equifax Latin America** (6 percent of revenue). Equifax offers consumer and commercial credit information and other financial, consumer, and commercial information in several Latin American markets.

Equifax was founded in 1899 as a credit reporting agency under the name Retail Credit Company. It changed its name to Equifax in 1975.

The company has about 14,000 employees and 7,000 shareholders. It has a market capitalization of $5.3 billion.

EARNINGS PER SHARE GROWTH   ★ ★

Past five years: 113 percent (16 percent per year)
Past ten years: 244 percent (13 percent per year)

STOCK GROWTH   ★ ★

Past ten years: 324 percent (15 percent per year)
Dollar growth: $10,000 over ten years (including reinvested dividends) would have grown to $50,000.
Average annual compounded rate of return (including reinvested dividends): 17.5 percent

DIVIDEND   ★

Dividend yield: 1.1 percent
Increased dividend: eight of the past ten years
Past five-year increase: 25 percent (4 percent per year)

CONSISTENCY

Increased earnings per share: nine of the past ten years
Increased sales: nine of the past ten years

SHAREHOLDER PERKS

Direct purchase plan allows new investors to buy stock directly from the company with a minimum $500 investment. Existing shareholders may make stock purchases of $50 to $10,000 per month and can have dividends automatically reinvested in additional shares.

EQUIFAX AT A GLANCE

Fiscal year ended: Dec. 31
Revenue and net income in $ millions

	1993	1994	1995	1996	1997	1998	5-Year Growth Avg. Annual (%)	5-Year Growth Total (%)
Revenue ($)	1,217	1,422	1,623	1,811	1,366	1,621	6	33
Net income ($)	95	120	148	178	186	193	15	103
Earnings/share ($)	0.63	0.81	0.98	1.22	1.26	1.34	16	113
Dividends/share ($)	0.28	0.31	0.32	0.33	0.35	0.35	4	25
Dividend yield (%)	2.5	2.2	1.8	1.3	1.1	0.9	—	—
PE ratio range	21–32	14–19	14–25	17–33	21–29	22–33	—	—

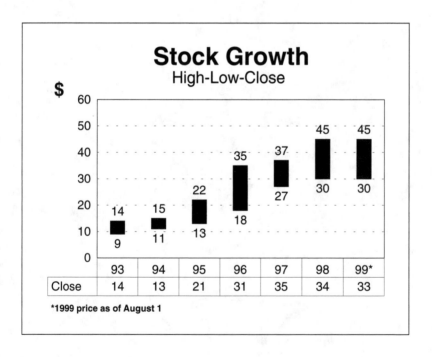

Stock Growth
High-Low-Close

	93	94	95	96	97	98	99*
Close	14	13	21	31	35	34	33

*1999 price as of August 1

Tellabs, Inc.

4951 Indiana Avenue
Lisle, IL 60532
630-378-8800
www.tellabs.com

President and CEO: Michael J. Birck

Earnings Growth	★ ★ ★ ★
Stock Growth	★ ★ ★ ★
Dividend	
Consistency	★
Shareholder Perks	
Nasdaq: TLAB	**9 points**

Tellabs moves voices and data across the country and around the world. The company manufactures voice and data transport equipment and network access systems used worldwide by phone companies, cellular and other wireless service providers, cable operators, government agencies, utilities, and businesses.

Founded in 1975 by current President and CEO Michael J. Birck, Tellabs has grown quickly by expanding into several key areas of the rapidly expanding telecommunications industry. It manufactures digital cross-connect systems, managed digital networks, network access products, and fiber-optic systems. Tellabs has posted more than 30 consecutive quarters of increased earnings.

The company's line of advanced digital cross-connect systems are used by telecommunications managers for centralized and remote testing of transmission facilities; grooming of voice, data, and video signals; automated installation of new services; and restoration of failed facilities.

Its managed digital networks are used by telecommunications services to provide businesses with high-speed data access, frame relay, and voice telephony. The company's MatrisDXX system acts as the transport infrastructure for mobile networks such as digital and analog cellular paging, trunked mobile radio, and mobile data.

Tellabs's network access products are used in a variety of areas, including echo cancellation, or removing feedback from one's own voice on many long distance connections and many wireless connections, and voice compression, which multiplies the capacity of digital transmission facilities used for voice and data services.

The Chicago-area manufacturer markets its products through its own direct sales force and through selected distributors. Regional Bell operating companies account for about 31 percent of the company's $1.66 billion in annual revenue. Independent phone companies account for about 3 percent; interexchange carriers make up 12 percent; and other companies, utilities, and agencies account for 22 percent. Tellabs has strong international sales, which account for about 32 percent of total revenue.

Tellabs went public with its initial stock offering in 1980. The company has 5,000 employees and 4,500 shareholders. It has a market capitalization of $23 billion.

EARNINGS PER SHARE GROWTH ★ ★ ★ ★

Past five years: 1,047 percent (63 percent per year)
Past ten years: 2,067 percent (35 percent per year)

STOCK GROWTH ★ ★ ★ ★

Past ten years: 12,500 percent (62 percent per year)
Dollar growth: $10,000 over ten years would have grown to $1,250,000.
Average annual compounded rate of return: 62 percent

DIVIDEND

Tellabs pays no dividends.

CONSISTENCY ★

Increased earnings per share: seven consecutive years
Increased sales: 15 consecutive years

SHAREHOLDER PERKS

Tellabs does not offer a dividend reinvestment and stock purchase plan, nor does it offer other shareholder perks.

TELLABS AT A GLANCE

Fiscal year ended: Dec. 31
Revenue and net income in $ millions

	1993	1994	1995	1996	1997	1998	5-Year Growth Avg. Annual (%)	Total (%)
Revenue ($)	321	494	635	869	1,204	1,660	38	417
Net income ($)	31	72	116	172	250	374	64	1,106
Earnings/share ($)	0.17	0.40	0.63	0.93	1.35	1.95	63	1,047
Dividends/share ($)	—	—	—	—	—	—	—	—
Dividend yield (%)	—	—	—	—	—	—	—	—
PE ratio range	9–39	14–35	18–40	23–71	22–45	15–44	—	—

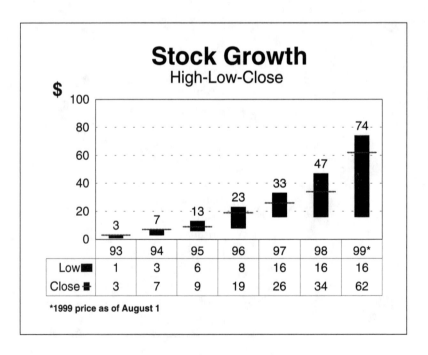

Stock Growth
High-Low-Close

	93	94	95	96	97	98	99*
Low	1	3	6	8	16	16	16
Close	3	7	9	19	26	34	62

*1999 price as of August 1

92

MCI WorldCom, Inc.

515 East Amite Street
Jackson, MS 39201
601-460-5600
www.wcom.com

Chairman: Bert Roberts, Jr.
President and CEO: Bernard J. Ebbers

Earnings Growth	★ ★ ★ ★
Stock Growth	★ ★ ★ ★
Dividend	
Consistency	★
Shareholder Perks	
Nasdaq: WCOM	**9 points**

MCI WorldCom was formed in 1998 through the merger of two of the nation's largest telecommunications companies. Technically, WorldCom acquired MCI Communications at a cost of about $40 billion.

The combined operation is the nation's second-largest long distance carrier behind AT&T. The company serves customers in all 50 states and parts of more than 200 countries worldwide.

The Jackson, Mississippi operation provides a wide range of communications-related services, including local, long distance, and Internet service for consumers, businesses, and government agencies through its networks of fiber-optic cables, digital microwave, and fixed and transportable satellite earth stations.

About 94 percent of its $30.4 billion in annual revenue comes from its communications services. In addition to local and long distance phone service, the company provides dedicated and dial-up Internet access, wireless services, 800 services, calling cards, private lines, broadband data services, debit cards, conference calling, messaging and mobility services, and advanced billing systems.

The company also offers enhanced fax and data connections, high speed data communications, facilities management, Web server hosting and integration services, and dial-up and interconnection networking services.

Outside the United States, MCI WorldCom has more than 200 operating agreements with foreign carriers to provide switched voice and private line service, which has helped make the company a leading provider of international long distance service.

In addition to its telecommunications services, MCI WorldCom also provides a wide range of information technology services to corporations and organizations. The company offers outsourcing, information technology consulting, systems integration, private network management, and applications and systems deployment. Its information technology segment accounts for about 6 percent of total revenue.

Organized in 1983, MCI WorldCom has 75,000 employees and 66,000 shareholders. The company has a market capitalization of about $165 billion.

EARNINGS PER SHARE GROWTH ★ ★ ★ ★

Past five years: 88 percent (13 percent per year)
Past ten years: 3,950 percent (44 percent per year)

STOCK GROWTH ★ ★ ★ ★

Past ten years: 6,746 percent (52 percent per year)
Dollar growth: $10,000 over ten years would have grown to $675,000.
Average annual compounded rate of return: 52 percent

DIVIDEND

The company pays no dividends.

CONSISTENCY ★

Increased earnings per share: three consecutive years
Increased sales: 12 consecutive years

SHAREHOLDER PERKS

The company does not offer a dividend reinvestment and stock purchase plan, nor does it offer other shareholder perks.

MCI WORLDCOM AT A GLANCE

Fiscal year ended: Dec. 31
Revenue and net income in $ millions

	1993	1994	1995	1996	1997	1998	5-Year Growth Avg. Annual (%)	5-Year Growth Total (%)
Revenue ($)	1,145	2,221	3,640	4,485	7,351	17,678	73	1,444
Net income ($)	104	20	268	440	384	1,059	59	918
Earnings/share ($)	0.43	-0.02	0.65	1.01	0.40	0.81	13	88
Dividends/share ($)	—	—	—	—	—	—	—	—
Dividend yield (%)	—	—	—	—	—	—	—	—
PE ratio range	17–31	—	14–27	15–40	93–174	—	—	—

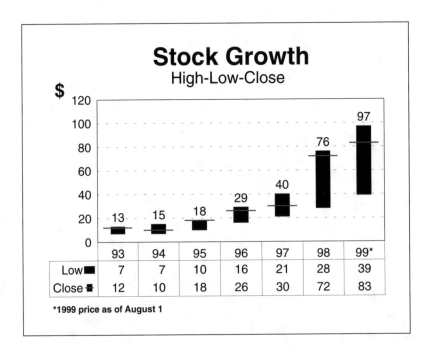

Stock Growth
High-Low-Close

	93	94	95	96	97	98	99*
Low	7	7	10	16	21	28	39
Close	12	10	18	26	30	72	83

*1999 price as of August 1

Anheuser-Busch Companies

One Busch Place
St. Louis, MO 63118
314-577-2000
www.anheuser-busch.com

Chairman and President:
August A. Busch III

Earnings Growth	
Stock Growth	★ ★
Dividend	★ ★
Consistency	★ ★ ★
Shareholder Perks	★ ★
NYSE: BUD	**9 points**

In the ever-brewing beer wars, Anheuser-Busch continues to pad its market share. Over the past 25 years, the company has doubled its share of the domestic beer market, from about 23 percent in the late 1970s to 46 percent in 1998. Its two closest rivals combined (Miller and Coors) fall far short of Anheuser's market dominance. Miller commands about 21 percent of the domestic beer market, and Coors controls about 10 percent.

Anheuser-Busch sells about 93 million barrels of beer a year in the United States. It is the world's largest brewer, boasting the top-selling regular beer (Budweiser) and the top-selling light beer (Bud Light).

The company also is expanding its international sales, particularly in Europe. In all, Anheuser-Busch sells about 7 million barrels of beer outside the United States. The company sells its products in more than 80 countries.

Beer sales account for about 95 percent of the St. Louis–based brewing company's $11.2 billion in annual revenue.

Among the company's other leading brands are Busch, Natural Light, O'Doul's (nonalcoholic), Elk Mountain Amber Ale, Red Wolf Lager, Hurricane Malt Liquor, Tequiza, Safari Lager, and Natural Pilsner. Its Michelob brand includes several varieties, including Michelob, Michelob Golden Draft, Light, Dry, Classic Dark, Malt, Amber Bock, Pale Ale, Honey Lager, Porter, and Hefe-Weizen.

Busch's brewing business is fully integrated. It operates 13 breweries in the United States and owns a beverage can manufacturer, a barley processing plant, a label printing operation, and a refrigerated rail car transportation subsidiary. It is the nation's second largest manufacturer of aluminum beverage containers, and the world's largest recycler of aluminum beverage cans. Not so coincidentally, it also has interests in malt production, rice milling, and transportation services. It markets its beer through 700 independent wholesalers.

The firm also owns and operates nine theme parks, including two Busch Gardens parks (in Tampa, Florida and Williamsburg, Virginia), Adventure Island in Tampa, Sesame Place in Pennsylvania, four Sea World parks, and Water Country USA in Williamsburg. The company also operates the Baseball City Sports Complex near Orlando.

Anheuser-Busch traces its roots to a small St. Louis brewery started in 1852. After a few years of lackluster results, the original owner, George Schneider, sold out the struggling operation to an investment group headed by St. Louis soap tycoon Eberhard Anheuser. Anheuser ultimately turned the business over to his son-in-law, a portly, gregarious man by the name of Adolphus Busch.

Mr. Busch, who converted the small brewery into a national force, is generally recognized as the founder of Anheuser-Busch. Budweiser, which Mr. Busch helped develop in 1876, was one of the first beers to achieve widespread distribution. Michelob, the company's premium beer, was first brought to market in 1896. When Adolphus Busch died in 1913, his son August A. Busch assumed control of the business. The reins have since been passed through two more generations of the Busch family. August A. Busch III, 61, now directs the company as its chairman of the board and president.

Anheuser-Busch has 24,000 employees and 65,000 shareholders. The company has a market capitalization of $33.8 billion.

EARNINGS PER SHARE GROWTH

Past five years: 42 percent (7 percent per year)
Past ten years: 106 percent (15.5 percent per year)

STOCK GROWTH

Past ten years: 335 percent (16 percent per year)
Dollar growth: $10,000 over ten years (including reinvested dividends) would have grown to $54,000.
Average annual compounded rate of return (including reinvested dividends): 18.5 percent

DIVIDEND

Dividend yield: 1.6 percent
Increased dividend: 26 consecutive years
Past five-year increase: 59 percent (9.5 percent per year)

CONSISTENCY ★ ★ ★

Increased earnings per share: nine of the past ten years
Increased sales: nine of the past ten years

SHAREHOLDER PERKS ★ ★

Good dividend reinvestment and stock purchase plan: voluntary stock purchase plan allows contributions of $25 to $5,000 per month.

New shareholders of record are sent a letter of welcome, a fact book on the company, and a pamphlet on its dividend reinvestment plan.

The company makes a point of moving its annual meetings around the country. In recent years, meetings have been staged in Tampa and Orlando, Florida; Williamsburg, Virginia; and Fort Collins, Colorado. Those who attend get a chance to sample all of the company's brews.

Shareholders also are entitled to a discount on admission to the company's amusement parks.

ANHEUSER-BUSCH AT A GLANCE

Fiscal year ended: Dec. 31
Revenue and net income in $ millions

	1993	1994	1995	1996	1997	1998	5-Year Growth Avg. Annual (%)	5-Year Growth Total (%)
Revenue ($)	11,505	12,054	10,341	10,884	11,066	11,246	0	−2
Net income ($)	981	1032	986	1,123	1,179	1,233	4	26
Earnings/share ($)	1.78	1.94	1.90	2.21	2.36	2.53	7	42
Dividends/share ($)	0.68	0.76	0.84	0.92	1.00	1.08	10	59
Dividend yield (%)	2.7	3.0	2.8	2.5	2.3	1.6	—	—
PE ratio range	18–25	12–14	15–20	14–19	16–20	17–27	—	—

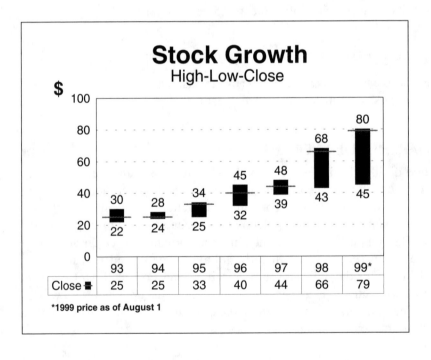

Stock Growth
High-Low-Close

	93	94	95	96	97	98	99*
Close	25	25	33	40	44	66	79

*1999 price as of August 1

Bristol-Myers Squibb

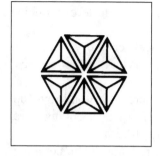

345 Park Avenue
New York, NY 10154
212-546-4000
www.bristolmyers.com

Chairman, President, and CEO:
Charles A. Heimbold, Jr.

Earnings Growth	
Stock Growth	★ ★ ★
Dividend	★ ★
Consistency	★ ★
Shareholder Perks	★ ★
NYSE: BMY	**9 points**

Bristol-Myers Squibb attacks death and disease on many fronts. It produces medications for a wide range of ailments, including cardiovascular problems, metabolic and infectious disease, central nervous system and dermatological disorders, and cancer.

The company is also a leader in the areas of beauty care and nutritional products, as well as consumer medicines, such as Excedrin, Bufferin, Comtrex, and Nuprin. Bristol-Myers also designs and manufactures orthopedic devices, such as artificial knee and hip replacements.

In all, Bristol-Myers invests more than $1.5 billion a year in new product research and development.

Pharmaceuticals are the leading source of revenue for Bristol-Myers, accounting for 68 percent of the company's $18.3 billion in annual revenue. Its leading pharmaceuticals segment is cardiovascular medications, including inhibitors such as Pravachol, Capoten, Monpril, and Plavix, as well as beta blockers Sotacor and Corgard and the cholesterol-reducing drug Questran.

The company's second leading pharmaceuticals category is anticancer agents, followed by anti-infectives, central nervous system medications, and analgesics.

Beauty care products account for about 13 percent of total revenue. Leading products include Nice 'N Easy, Clairol, Hydrience, Loving Care, Herbal Essence, Sea Breeze, Vital Nutrients, and Ultress.

Nutritionals makes up about 10 percent of revenues. The company produces Enfamil, Prosobee, Nutramigen, and Lactofree infant formula products; Isocal, Nutrament, Boost, Choco Milk, and Sustagen nutritional supplements; and Pusssz, Poly-Vi-Sol, and Natalins vitamins.

Medical devices account for about 9 percent of sales, including knee and hip replacement systems, ostomy care products, and wound care products.

Bristol-Myers does a strong international business, with sales in more than 100 countries. Foreign sales account for about 31 percent of the company's total revenue.

Bristol-Myers merged with Squibb in 1989, making it one of the world's leading pharmaceuticals manufacturers. The company has about 55,000 employees and 135,000 shareholders. It has a market capitalization of about $145 billion.

EARNINGS PER SHARE GROWTH

Past five years: 41 percent (7 percent per year)
Past ten years: 115 percent (8 percent per year)

STOCK GROWTH   ★ ★ ★

Past ten years: 449 percent (19 percent per year)
Dollar growth: $10,000 over ten years (including reinvested dividends) would have grown to $75,000.
Average annual compounded rate of return (including reinvested dividends): 22.5 percent

DIVIDEND

Dividend yield: 1.3
Increased dividend: 26 consecutive years
Past five-year increase: 11 percent (2 percent per year)

CONSISTENCY ★ ★

Increased earnings per share: eight of the past ten years
Increased sales: nine of the past ten years

SHAREHOLDER PERKS ★ ★

Good dividend reinvestment and stock purchase plan; voluntary stock purchase plan allows contributions of $100 per week up to $10,025 per month for those holding 50 shares or more.

BRISTOL-MYERS SQUIBB AT A GLANCE

Fiscal year ended: Dec. 31
Revenue and net income in $ millions

	1993	1994	1995	1996	1997	1998	5-Year Growth Avg. Annual (%)	5-Year Growth Total (%)
Revenue ($)	11,400	12,000	13,800	15,100	16,700	18,300	10	61
Net income ($)	2,269	2,330	2,600	2,850	3,205	3,141	7	38
Earnings/share ($)	1.10	1.15	1.28	1.42	1.61	1.55	7	41
Dividends/share ($)	0.72	0.73	0.74	0.75	0.76	0.78	2	11
Dividend yield (%)	4.9	5.2	4.3	3.3	2.0	1.4	—	—
PE ratio range	13–18	14–17	16–24	14–20	16–30	28–43	—	—

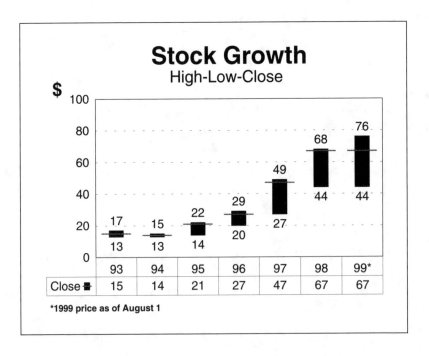

Stock Growth
High-Low-Close

	93	94	95	96	97	98	99*
Close ■	15	14	21	27	47	67	67

*1999 price as of August 1

Molex, Inc.

2222 Wellington Court
Lisle, IL 60532
630-969-4550
www.molex.com

Chairman and CEO: Frederick A. Krehbiel
President: John H. Krehbiel

Earnings Growth	★ ★ ★
Stock Growth	★ ★
Dividend	★
Consistency	★ ★ ★
Shareholder Perks	
Nasdaq: MOLX	**9 points**

The high-tech revolution is strung together by thousands of miles of wires, cables, plugs, switches, and fiber-optic connections. Molex has helped construct that high-wire, high-tech network as the world's second largest manufacturer of electronic, electrical, and fiber-optic interconnection products and switches.

Molex markets its wires and connectors to a variety of manufacturers, including the automotive, computer, computer peripheral, business equipment, telecommunications, consumer products, and building wiring industries.

The Chicago-based operation is global in scope, with 49 plants in 21 countries and sales in more than 50 countries around the world. Foreign sales account for about 66 percent of the company's $1.6 billion in annual revenue.

Molex was founded in 1938 in Brookfield, Illinois, as a manufacturer of a plastic molding material developed by company founder, Frederick Krehbiel. Trademarked Molex, the material was used for a variety of products, including toy guns and clock castings.

A few years later, the company discovered that its Molex plastic had excellent electrical insulating properties and began using it for a variety of electrical connection applications. Today, Molex offers more than 100,000 products, including electric terminals, connectors, planer cables, cable assemblies, backplanes, and mechanical and electric switches. The firm also manufactures crimping machines and terminal inserting equipment.

Molex sells its goods almost entirely to original manufacturers for use in other products rather than to consumers or retailers. Sales to computer, telecommunications, and business equipment manufacturers account for 52 percent of the company's revenue; consumer product manufacturers, 22 percent; and automotive, 16 percent. Other industries such as medical equipment, electronic products, vending machines, and security equipment account for the other 10 percent.

Molex has about 12,500 employees and 11,000 shareholders. It has a market capitalization of $4.9 billion.

EARNINGS PER SHARE GROWTH ★ ★ ★

Past five years: 135 percent (19 percent per year)
Past ten years: 188 percent (11.5 percent per year)

STOCK GROWTH ★ ★

Past ten years: 370 percent (16.5 percent per year)
Dollar growth: $10,000 over ten years (including reinvested dividends) would have grown to $48,000.
Average annual compounded rate of return (including reinvested dividends): 16.6 percent

DIVIDEND ★

Dividend yield: 0.3 percent
Increased dividend: 19 consecutive years
Past five-year increase: 500 percent (43 percent per year)

CONSISTENCY ★ ★ ★

Increased earnings per share: nine of the past ten years
Increased sales: ten consecutive years

SHAREHOLDER PERKS

The company offers no dividend reinvestment or stock purchase plan.

MOLEX AT A GLANCE

Fiscal year ended: June 30
Revenue and net income in $ millions

	1993	1994	1995	1996	1997	1998	5-Year Growth Avg. Annual (%)	Total (%)
Revenue ($)	859	964	1,198	1,383	1,540	1,623	14	89
Net income ($)	75	95	124	146	167	182	20	143
Earnings/share ($)	0.49	0.61	0.79	0.93	1.06	1.15	19	135
Dividends/share ($)	0.01	0.02	0.02	0.04	0.05	0.06	43	500
Dividend yield (%)	0.1	0.1	0.1	0.2	0.2	0.2	—	—
PE ratio range	22–32	20–30	20–30	19–28	20–36	20–34	—	—

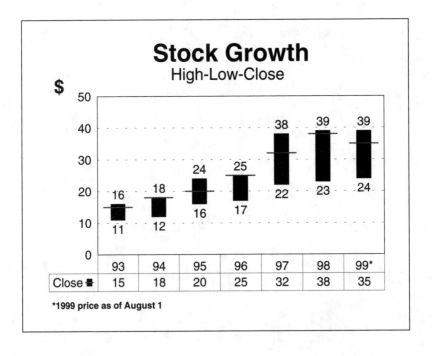

Stock Growth
High-Low-Close

	93	94	95	96	97	98	99*
Close	15	18	20	25	32	38	35

*1999 price as of August 1

Genuine Parts Company

2999 Circle 75 Parkway
Atlanta, GA 30339
770-953-1700
www.genpt.com

Chairman and CEO: Larry L. Prince
President: Thomas Gallagher

Earnings Growth	
Stock Growth	
Dividend	★ ★ ★
Consistency	★ ★ ★ ★
Shareholder Perks	★ ★
NYSE: GPC	**9 points**

It's no Indy race car, but the Genuine Parts Company continues to motor steadily forward, posting increased sales for 49 consecutive years and increased net earnings for 38 consecutive years. The company has raised its shareholder dividend for 42 straight years.

Genuine Parts is a distributor of automotive parts for nearly 6,000 NAPA auto parts stores, including about 750 company-owned stores. In all, the company carries more than 200,000 different replacement parts and accessory items.

The Atlanta-based operation is the market leader in the auto parts industry, with annual revenue of $6.6 billion. The firm's auto parts division accounts for 49 percent of its total revenue. In addition to its broad line of auto parts, the company handles parts for trucks, buses, motorcycles, water craft, recreational vehicles, farm equipment, small engines, and heavy duty equipment.

In Canada, Genuine Parts owns a 49 percent interest in UAP/NAPA, which operates 16 automotive parts distribution centers and 250 auto parts stores. UAP also serves as a distributor for about 400 other auto parts dealers.

Genuine Parts does no manufacturing itself but serves strictly as a wholesale distributor. It buys parts from about 150 suppliers.

The company also operates in three other segments:

1. **Industrial parts** (30 percent of revenue). Through its Motion Industries subsidiary, the company is a distributor of industrial replacement parts, including bearings and fluid transmission equipment, hydraulic and pneumatic products, and agricultural and irrigation equipment. In all, the company serves about 165,000 customers in North America.
2. **Office products** (18 percent of revenue). The S.P. Richards Company subsidiary of Genuine Parts distributes a broad line of computer supplies, office furniture, office machines, and general office supplies. The company distributes more than 20,000 items to more than 6,000 office supply dealers in 31 states and western Canada.
- **Electrical and electronic materials** (3 percent of revenue). Formed in 1998 through the acquisition of EIS, Inc., this division distributes materials for the manufacture and repair of electrical and electronic apparatus. It has branches in 42 U.S. cities and Mexico and stocks more than 100,000 items, from insulating and conductive materials to assembly tools and test equipment.

Founded in 1928, Genuine Parts has about 24,000 employees and 7,000 shareholders. It has a market capitalization of about $6 billion.

EARNINGS PER SHARE GROWTH

Past five years: 42 percent (7 percent per year)
Past ten years: 90 percent (6.5 percent per year)

STOCK GROWTH

Past ten years: 95 percent (7 percent per year)
Dollar growth: $10,000 over ten years (including reinvested dividends) would have grown to $26,000.
Average annual compounded rate of return (including reinvested dividends): 10 percent

DIVIDEND

Dividend yield: 3.1 percent
Increased dividend: 42 consecutive years
Past five-year increase: 41 percent (7 percent per year)

CONSISTENCY ★ ★ ★ ★

Increased earnings per share: 38 consecutive years
Increased sales: 49 consecutive years

SHAREHOLDER PERKS

Good dividend reinvestment and stock purchase plan; voluntary stock purchase plan allows contributions of $10 to $3,000 per quarter.

GENUINE PARTS AT A GLANCE

Fiscal year ended: Dec. 31
Revenue and net income in $ millions

	1993	1994	1995	1996	1997	1998	5-Year Growth Avg. Annual (%)	5-Year Growth Total (%)
Revenue ($)	4,384	4,858	5,262	5,721	6,005	6,614	9	51
Net income ($)	259	289	309	330	342	356	6	37
Earnings/share ($)	1.39	1.55	1.68	1.82	1.90	1.98	7	42
Dividends/share ($)	0.70	0.77	0.84	0.89	0.96	0.99	7	41
Dividend yield (%)	2.9	3.2	3.2	3.0	3.0	2.9	—	—
PE ratio range	16–19	14–17	14–17	15–17	15–19	14–19	—	—

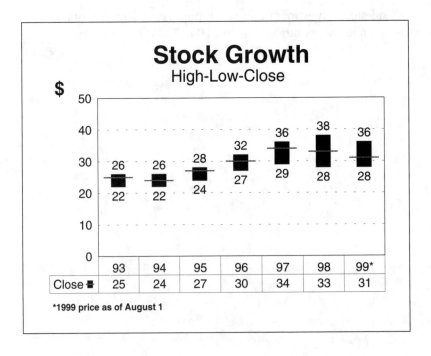

Stock Growth
High-Low-Close

	93	94	95	96	97	98	99*
Close	25	24	27	30	34	33	31

*1999 price as of August 1

Bank One Corporation

One First National Plaza
Chicago, IL 60670
312-732-4000
www.bankone.com

Chairman: Verne G. Istock
President and CEO: John B. McCoy

Earnings Growth	
Stock Growth	★ ★
Dividend	★ ★ ★
Consistency	★ ★
Shareholder Perks	★ ★
NYSE: ONE	**9 points**

Bank One has entered a new frontier in the banking business—the Internet. The Chicago-based institution has plunged headfirst into the online banking business through a series of innovations.

The nation's fourth largest bank holding company, Bank One already has more than 300,000 online customers. Through a new service offered by the company, its customers can receive and pay bills online as well as check account balances, monitor account activities, transfer money, apply for a credit card, and apply for loans.

The company also signed a five-year agreement with America Online in 1999 to market its credit cards online. Bank One also reached a deal with Internet provider Excite to market its retail banking products online.

Since its formation in 1968, Bank One has grown quickly through a very aggressive series of acquisitions. In all, the company has acquired more than 100 banking institutions. It has more than 2,000 branch offices in 34 states and the District of Columbia.

Bank One also has expanded overseas, offering commercial banking services in ten foreign countries, including Australia, China, Germany, Hong Kong, England, Mexico, South Korea, Singapore, Taiwan, Japan, and Canada.

In addition to its banking operations, the company also owns subsidiaries engaged in credit card and merchant processing, consumer finance, mortgage banking, insurance, trust and investment management, brokerage, investment and merchant banking, venture capital, equipment leasing, and data processing.

It is one of the nation's largest credit card lenders, the second-largest consumer and commercial finance company, and the third-largest bank lender to small businesses.

Bank One's loan portfolio breaks down this way: commercial loans, 27 percent; real estate, 35 percent; consumer loans, 25 percent; credit card and other loans, 13 percent.

The company has 91,000 employees and 106,000 shareholders. Bank One has a market capitalization of $69 billion.

EARNINGS PER SHARE GROWTH

Past five years: 40 percent (7 percent per year)
Past ten years: 162 percent (10 percent per year)

STOCK GROWTH ★ ★

Past ten years: 343 percent (16 percent per year)
Dollar growth: $10,000 over ten years (including reinvested dividends) would have grown to $59,000.
Average annual compounded rate of return (including reinvested dividends): 19.5 percent

DIVIDEND ★ ★ ★

Dividend yield: 3.0 percent
Increased dividend: 28 consecutive years
Past five-year increase: 73 percent (11.5 percent per year)

CONSISTENCY

Increased earnings per share: eight of the past ten years

SHAREHOLDER PERKS ★ ★

Good dividend reinvestment and stock purchase plan; voluntary stock purchase plan allows contributions of $25 to $5,000 per month.

BANK ONE AT A GLANCE

Fiscal year ended: Dec. 31
Total assets and net income in $ millions

	1993	1994	1995	1996	1997	1998	Avg. Annual (%)	Total (%)
							5-Year Growth	
Total assets ($)	79,919	88,923	90,454	101,848	115,901	261,496	27	227
Net income ($)	1,121	1,005	1,278	1,427	1,306	4,044	29	261
Earnings/share ($)	2.42	2.00	2.65	2.94	1.99	3.40	7	40
Dividends/share ($)	0.88	1.02	1.13	1.24	1.38	1.52	12	73
Dividend yield (%)	2.8	3.9	4.2	3.6	3.1	2.9	—	—
PE ratio range	8–11	8–13	8–12	9–15	13–20	14–25	—	—

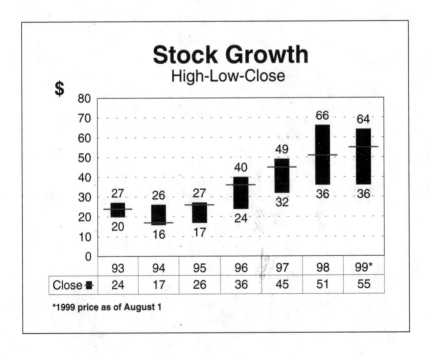

Stock Growth
High-Low-Close

Close ■	93	94	95	96	97	98	99*
	24	17	26	36	45	51	55

*1999 price as of August 1

PepsiCo, Inc.

700 Anderson Hill Road
Purchase, NY 10577
914-253-2000
www.pepsico.com

Chairman and CEO: Roger A. Enrico

Earnings Growth	
Stock Growth	★ ★
Dividend	★ ★
Consistency	★ ★
Shareholder Perks	★ ★
NYSE: PEP	**8 points**

PepsiCo is trying to regain some lost fizzle. After several years of flat earnings and revenue, the soft drink maker has redefined and repositioned itself to prepare for what management hopes will add some punch to its balance sheet.

PepsiCo spun off its massive chain of fast-food franchises—Taco Bell, Pizza Hut, and Kentucky Fried Chicken—in 1997 and announced plans to sell a majority stake of its Pepsi-Cola bottling subsidiary in 1999. It also bought Tropicana from Seagram in 1998.

What's left is a more streamlined company that is primarily in the business of selling soft drink concentrate and snack foods. The company's Frito-Lay division is the largest snack food producer in the world.

The Purchase, New York operation is the maker Pepsi, Pepsi One, Diet Pepsi, Mountain Dew, All Sport, Mug Root Beer, Tropicana, Slice, and 7Up (outside the U.S.).

PepsiCo has about a 31 percent share of the U.S. soft drink market, compared with a 44.5 percent share for Coca-Cola. The company's flagship Pepsi-Cola brand accounts for 46 percent of PepsiCo's beverage sales in North America, followed by Mountain Dew (21 percent), diet colas (19 percent), and Lipton teas (4 percent). Other carbonated drinks make up 5 percent, and other noncarbonated drinks account for the other 5 percent.

PepsiCo sells its products in about 200 countries around the world. About 55 percent of its revenues are generated in the United States, followed by 15 percent in Latin America, 11 percent each in Europe and Asia, and 8 percent in the Middle East and Africa.

Beverage sales account for about 50 percent of PepsiCo's $22.3 billion in annual revenue, while snack food sales make up the other 50 percent.

Frito-Lay is the maker of Lay's potato chips, Fritos, Doritos, Cheetos, Ruffles, Tostitos, Sun Chips, and other snack chips. The company recently acquired Cracker Jack. Frito-Lay products account for about 60 percent of all U.S. snack chip sales. Frito-Lay also has sales in 42 other countries (primarily in Europe and Asia). Frito-Lay brands are the market leader in more than half of those countries.

PepsiCo was founded in 1919. It has about 142,000 employees and 207,000 shareholders. The company has a market capitalization of $53.5 billion.

EARNINGS PER SHARE GROWTH

Past five years: 18 percent (3 percent per year)
Past ten years: 142 percent (9 percent per year)

STOCK GROWTH   ★ ★

Past ten years: 322 percent (15.5 percent per year)
Dollar growth: $10,000 over ten years (including reinvested dividends) would have grown to $48,000.
Average annual compounded rate of return (including reinvested dividends): 17 percent

DIVIDEND ★ ★

Dividend yield: 1.5 percent
Increased dividend: more than 26 consecutive years
Past five-year increase: 68 percent (11 percent per year).

CONSISTENCY ★ ★

Increased earnings per share: eight of the past ten years
Increased sales: more than 23 consecutive years

SHAREHOLDER PERKS ★ ★

Good dividend reinvestment and stock purchase plan; voluntary stock
purchase plan allows contributions of $25 to $5,000 per month.

PEPSICO AT A GLANCE

Fiscal year ended: Dec. 31
Revenue and net income in $ millions

	1993	1994	1995	1996	1997	1998	5-Year Growth Avg. Annual (%)	Total (%)
Revenue ($)	25,021	28,472	30,421	31,645	20,917	22,348	—	−11
Net income ($)	1,588	1,784	1,990	1,865	1,730	1,757	2	11
Earnings/share ($)	0.98	1.11	1.24	1.17	1.10	1.16	3	18
Dividends/share ($)	0.31	0.35	0.39	0.45	0.49	0.52	11	68
Dividend yield (%)	1.6	2.0	1.7	1.4	1.4	1.4	—	—
PE ratio range	18–22	13–19	17–33	45–60	29–42	20–33	—	—

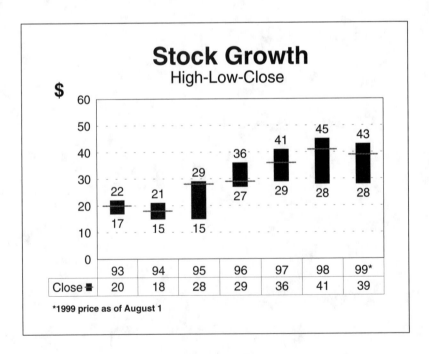

Stock Growth
High-Low-Close

	93	94	95	96	97	98	99*
Close ■	20	18	28	29	36	41	39

*1999 price as of August 1

The Walt Disney Company

500 South Buena Vista Street
Burbank, CA 91521
818-560-1000
www.disney.com

Chairman and CEO: Michael D. Eisner

Earnings Growth	★ ★ ★
Stock Growth	★ ★
Dividend	★ ★
Consistency	★
Shareholder Perks	
NYSE: DIS	**8 points**

It's been doom and gloom in the Magic Kingdom the past couple of years, but that's not unusual for The Walt Disney Company. This is a very cyclical operation.

As Disney President Michael Eisner recently put it in attempting to explain the company's stagnant earnings: "At Disney we live by a 60-month calendar. We set our goals over rolling five-year time lines. In this context, each year is more like a season. Some are sunny and some are overcast, but each is merely a period of passage and not a destination." There's been no sunshine in the Magic Kingdom recently—just a pouring rain.

But Disney is famous for happy endings, and its story is likely to perk up in due time. It should bounce back with its next solid round of block-buster movies—whenever that should occur. For company shareholders, the sooner the better. The company's movie segment has been holding steady at about $10 billion a year in revenues for the past few years.

Disney produces motion pictures under several studio names, including Walt Disney Pictures, Touchstone Pictures, Hollywood Pictures, Miramax Film, and Caravan Pictures. Disney also produces a wide range of home videos, including about 1,300 titles. It also produces several popular television programs, including *Home Improvement, Boy Meets World,* and *Unhappily Ever After.* Disney's "creative content" segment, which includes movies and television shows, accounts for about 44 percent of the company's $23 billion in annual revenue.

Disney's second largest segment is its broadcast division, which accounts for about 31 percent of revenue. The company acquired the ABC television network in 1996. ABC has 224 primary affiliated stations that reach 99.9 percent of the U.S. population. It also operates the ABC Radio Network, which reaches 144 million people through 4,400 stations.

Disney also operates a number of cable television stations, including the Disney Channel, ESPN, ESPN2, ESPN Classic, ESPN News, A&E, Lifetime Entertainment, and E! Entertainment.

The company's other segment, theme parks and resorts, accounts for about 24 percent of revenue. Disney operates a number of resorts, including Walt Disney World in Orlando, Florida, with three theme parks: The Magic Kingdom, Epcot, and the Disney-MGM Studios Theme Park. Other parks include Disneyland in Anaheim, California, and Tokyo Disneyland. The company is a 39 percent shareholder of Disneyland Paris in France.

Foreign sales account for about 22 percent of total revenue.

The Burbank, California operation has about 117,000 employees and 660,000 shareholders. Disney has a market capitalization of about $62 billion.

EARNINGS PER SHARE GROWTH   ★ ★ ★

Past five years: 67 percent (11 percent per year)
Past ten years: 181 percent (11 percent per year)

STOCK GROWTH

Past ten years: 257 percent (14 percent per year)
Dollar growth: $10,000 over ten years (including reinvested dividends) would have grown to $38,000.
Average annual compounded rate of return (including reinvested dividends): 14.5 percent

DIVIDEND

Dividend yield: 0.8 percent
Increased dividend: 11 consecutive years
Past five-year increase: 150 percent (20 percent per year)

CONSISTENCY

Increased earnings per share: seven of the past ten years
Increased sales: 16 consecutive years

SHAREHOLDER PERKS

The company does not offer a dividend reinvestment plan.

DISNEY AT A GLANCE

Fiscal year ended: Sept. 30
Revenue and net income in $ millions

	1993	1994	1995	1996	1997	1998	5-Year Growth Avg. Annual (%)	Total (%)
Revenue ($)	8,529	10,055	12,112	21,238	22,473	22,976	22	169
Net income ($)	889	1,110	1,344	1,533	1,890	1,871	16	110
Earnings/share ($)	0.54	0.68	0.84	0.74	0.92	0.90	11	67
Dividends/share ($)	0.08	0.10	0.12	0.14	0.17	0.20	20	150
Dividend yield (%)	0.6	0.7	0.7	0.7	0.7	0.6	—	—
PE ratio range	29–39	19–24	17–25	27–39	23–34	25–47	—	—

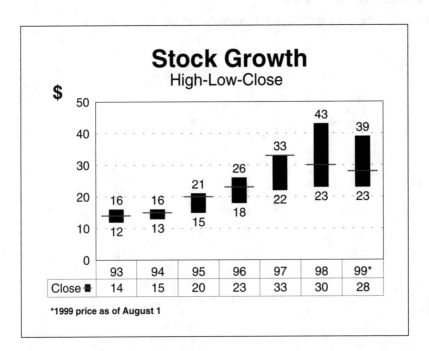

Stock Growth
High-Low-Close

$							
	93	94	95	96	97	98	99*
Close ■	14	15	20	23	33	30	28

*1999 price as of August 1

C&K Witco Corporation

One Station Place
Metro Center
Stamford, CT 06902
203-353-5400
www.crompton-knowles.com

Chairman: E. Gary Cook
President and CEO: Vincent A. Calarco

Earnings Growth	★
Stock Growth	★
Dividend	
Consistency	★ ★
Shareholder Perks	★ ★
NYSE: CNK	**6 points**

Formerly known as Crompton & Knowles, C&K Witco has grown quickly to become a world market leader in the production of additives, specialty chemicals, and polymers through a series of major acquisitions.

In 1996, the company nearly tripled its size when it acquired the Uniroyal Chemical Corp. In 1999, it doubled its size again with the acquisition of Witco Corp., a $2 billion a year (revenue) manufacturer of specialty chemicals and petroleum products. Along the way, the company has made a number of other smaller acquisitions.

Traditionally, C&K has focused on dyes for clothing, carpeting, fabrics, upholstery, leather, and paper products, and flavorings, fragrances, and coatings for beverages, prepared foods, pharmaceuticals, toiletries, perfumes, and other cosmetics. It also manufactures flavorings and color additives for the food processing, bakery, beverage, and pharmaceutical industries.

The addition of Uniroyal added a broad range of new products to the company's stable, including chemicals and polymers for automotive, industrial, and construction applications; crop protection chemicals such as miticides, seed treatments, growth regulants, and fungicides; and specialty products such as additives for plastics, petroleum, and petrochemical products.

With the Witco acquisition, the company added a long line of specialty chemicals for use in the manufacture of soaps, detergents, creams, and lotions; rubber, paper, asphalt, and textiles; plastics, furniture, textiles, personal care products, health care products, adhesives, sealants, automotive and construction products, carpeting, rubber products, fiberglass, electronics, antifreeze, coatings, agricultural products, and insulated appliances; and oils, lubricants, waxes, and greases.

Known originally as Crompton Loom Works, the company first opened for business in 1840. When Crompton joined with Knowles in 1898, the merged company became the world's largest manufacturer of fancy looms.

The company's loom business is long gone, but it has continued to expand its presence in the fabrics industry. C&K sells its products throughout the world with foreign sales accounting for about 25 percent of total revenue.

C&K Witco has about 10,000 employees and 8,000 shareholders. The company has a market capitalization of about $2 billion.

EARNINGS PER SHARE GROWTH ★

Past five years: 48 percent (8 percent per year)
Past ten years: 311 percent (15 percent per year)

STOCK GROWTH ★

Past ten years: 193 percent (11 percent per year)
Dollar growth: $10,000 over ten years (including reinvested dividends) would have grown to $35,000.
Average annual compounded rate of return (including reinvested dividends): 13 percent

DIVIDEND

Dividend yield: 0.3 percent
Increased dividend: The company cut its dividend in 1996 and 1997 and has not raised it since 1995.
Past five-year increase: dividend decreased

CONSISTENCY

Increased earnings per share: eight of the past ten years
Increased sales: nine of the past ten years

SHAREHOLDER PERKS   ★ ★

Good dividend reinvestment and stock purchase plan; voluntary stock purchase plan allows contributions of $30 to $3,000 per quarter.

C&K WITCO AT A GLANCE

Fiscal year ended: Dec. 31
Revenue and net income in $ millions

	1993	1994	1995	1996	1997	1998	5-Year Growth Avg. Annual (%)	Total (%)
Revenue ($)	558	590	665	1,804	1,851	1,796	26	222
Net income ($)	52	51	40	65	92	103	14	198
Earnings/share ($)	1.00	1.00	0.84	0.90	1.22	1.48	8	48
Dividends/share ($)	0.38	0.46	0.53	0.27	0.05	0.05	—	–99
Dividend yield (%)	1.7	2.5	3.4	1.7	0.2	0.2	—	—
PE ratio range	21–32	—	6–9	—	14–22	5–13	—	—

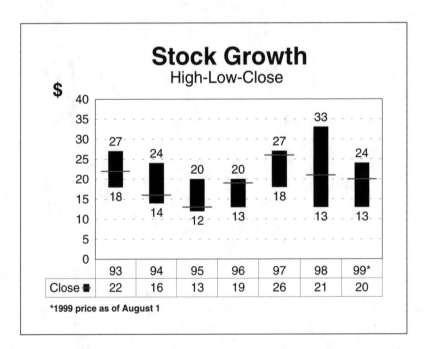

Stock Growth
High-Low-Close

$	93	94	95	96	97	98	99*
Close ■	22	16	13	19	26	21	20

*1999 price as of August 1

The 100 Best by Industry

Industry	Ranking
Computers and Office Equipment	
Cisco Systems, Inc.	42
Computer Associates International, Inc.	55
Dell Computer Corp.	67
Intel Corp.	48
Maxim Integrated Products	45
Microsoft Corp.	41
Oracle Corp.	70
Pitney Bowes, Inc.	57
Xerox Corp.	54
Consumer Products	
Clorox Company	56
Colgate-Palmolive Company	72
Gillette Company	20
Procter & Gamble Company	10
Corporate Services	
Automatic Data Processing, Inc.	53
Computer Sciences Corp.	74
Cintas Corp.	52
Equifax, Inc.	90
Fiserv, Inc.	47
G&K Services, Inc.	87
Interpublic Group of Companies, Inc.	23
Omnicom Group, Inc.	27
Paychex, Inc.	5
Electronics	
Emerson Electric Company	78
General Electric Company	8
Hubbell Incorporated	63
Molex, Inc.	95
Food and Beverage Production	
Bestfoods	89
Campbell Soup Company	83
Coca-Cola Company	59
ConAgra, Inc.	65

Industry	Ranking
Food and Beverage Production (continued)	
H. J. Heinz Company	88
Hershey Foods Corp.	82
PepsiCo, Inc.	98
Sara Lee Corp.	79
Sysco Corp.	62
William Wrigley, Jr. Company	37
Food and Drug Retail	
Albertson's, Inc.	31
McDonald's Corp.	76
Safeway, Inc.	84
Walgreen Company	28
Health Care and Medical	
Abbott Laboratories	34
American Home Products Corp.	33
Becton Dickinson and Company	36
Biomet, Inc.	86
Bristol-Myers Squibb	94
Cardinal Health, Inc.	44
Johnson & Johnson	14
Medtronic, Inc.	1
Merck and Company, Inc.	9
Pfizer, Inc.	17
Schering-Plough Corp.	6
Stryker Corp.	50
Warner-Lambert Company	19
Household and Commercial Furnishings	
Newell Rubbermaid, Inc.	81
Industrial Equipment	
Carlisle Companies, Inc.	58
Danaher Corp.	85
Dionex Corp.	73
Donaldson Company, Inc.	24
Illinois Tool Works, Inc.	25
Tyco International, Ltd.	51

The 100 Best by State

State	Ranking
Alabama	
Protective Life Corp. (Birmingham)	21
SouthTrust Corp. (Birmingham)	35
Arkansas	
Wal-Mart Stores, Inc. (Bentonville)	29
California	
Cisco Systems, Inc. (San Jose)	42
Clorox Co. (Oakland)	56
Computer Sciences Corp. (El Segundo)	74
Dionex Corp. (Sunnyvale)	73
Walt Disney Co. (Burbank)	99
Franklin Resources, Inc. (San Mateo)	13
The Gap, Inc. (San Francisco)	69
Intel Corp. (Santa Clara)	48
Maxim Integrated Products (Sunnyvale)	45
Oracle Corp. (Redwood Shores)	70
Safeway, Inc. (Pleasanton)	84
Charles Schwab Corp. (San Francisco)	46
Wells Fargo & Co. (San Francisco)	39
Connecticut	
C&K Witco Corp. (Stamford)	100
General Electric Co. (Fairfield)	8
Hubbell Inc. (Orange)	63
Pitney Bowes, Inc. (Stamford)	57
Xerox Corp. (Stamford)	54
District of Columbia	
Danaher Corp. (Washington)	85
Fannie Mae (Washington)	11

State	Ranking
Florida	
Carnival Corp. (Miami)	18
Georgia	
AFLAC, Inc. (Columbus)	32
Coca-Cola Co. (Atlanta)	56
Equifax, Inc. (Atlanta)	90
Genuine Parts Co. (Atlanta)	96
Home Depot, Inc. (Atlanta)	3
SunTrust Banks, Inc. (Atlanta)	75
Synovus Financial Corp. (Columbus)	15
Idaho	
Albertson's, Inc. (Boise)	31
Illinois	
Abbott Laboratories (Abbott Park)	34
Bank One Corp. (Chicago)	97
Illinois Tool Works, Inc. (Glenview)	25
McDonald's Corp. (Oak Brook)	76
Molex, Inc. (Lisle)	95
Newell Rubbermaid, Inc. (Freeport)	81
Sara Lee Corp. (Chicago)	79
Tellabs, Inc. (Lisle)	91
Walgreen Co. (Deerfield)	28
William Wrigley, Jr. (Chicago)	37
Indiana	
Biomet, Inc. (Warsaw)	86
Massachusetts	
Gillette Co. (Boston)	20
Staples, Inc. (Framingham)	43
State Street Corp. (Boston)	12
Michigan	
Stryker Corp. (Kalamazoo)	50

State	Ranking

Minnesota

Bemis Co., Inc. (Minneapolis)	66
Donaldson Co., Inc. (Minneapolis)	24
Ecolab, Inc. (St. Paul)	60
Fastenal Co. (Winona)	49
G&K Services, Inc. (Minnetonka)	87
Medtronic, Inc. (Minneapolis)	1
ReliaStar Financial Corp. (Minneapolis)	40
Valspar Corp. (Minneapolis)	61

Mississippi

MCI WorldCom, Inc. (Jackson)	92

Missouri

Anheuser-Busch Cos. (St. Louis)	93
Emerson Electric Co. (St. Louis)	78
May Department Stores Co. (St. Louis)	80

Nebraska

ConAgra, Inc. (Omaha)	65

New Hampshire

Tyco International, Ltd. (Exeter)	51

New Jersey

American Home Products Corp. (Madison)	33
Automatic Data Processing, Inc. (Roseland)	53
Becton Dickinson (Franklin Lakes)	36
Campbell Soup Co. (Camden)	83
Bestfoods (Englewood Cliffs)	89
Johnson & Johnson (New Brunswick)	14
Merck and Co., Inc. (Rahway)	9
Schering-Plough Corp. (Madison)	6
Warner-Lambert Co. (Morris Plains)	19

State	Ranking
New York	
Alliance Capital Management (New York)	4
American International Group, Inc. (New York)	71
Bristol-Myers Squibb (New York)	94
Carlisle Cos., Inc. (Syracuse)	58
Colgate-Palmolive Co. (New York)	72
Computer Associates International, Inc. (Islandia)	55
Interpublic Group of Cos., Inc. (New York)	23
M&T Bank Corp. (Buffalo)	22
Omnicom Group, Inc. (New York)	27
Paychex, Inc. (Rochester)	5
PepsiCo, Inc. (Purchase)	98
Pfizer, Inc. (New York)	17
North Carolina	
Jefferson Pilot Corp. (Greensboro)	38
Ohio	
Cardinal Health, Inc. (Dublin)	44
Cintas Corp. (Cincinnati)	52
Fifth Third Bancorp (Cincinnati)	7
Procter & Gamble Co. (Cincinnati)	10
RPM, Inc. (Medina)	77
Sherwin-Williams Co. (Cleveland)	64
Pennsylvania	
H. J. Heinz Co. (Pittsburgh)	88
Hershey Foods Corp. (Hershey)	82
Tennessee	
Dollar General Corp. (Nashville)	26
Texas	
Dell Computer Corp. (Round Rock)	67
Sysco Corp. (Houston)	62

State	Ranking
Virginia	
Freddie Mac (McLean)	30
Washington	
Microsoft Corp. (Redmond)	41
Wisconsin	
Firstar Corp. (Milwaukee)	2
Fiserv, Inc. (Brookfield)	47
Harley-Davidson, Inc. (Milwaukee)	16
Kohl's Corp. (Menomonee Falls)	68

Index